Frederick (Rick) Funston, Jon Lukomnik
Adapt or Fail!

The Alexandra Lajoux Corporate Governance Series

Edited by
Alexandra Reed Lajoux

Frederick (Rick) Funston, Jon Lukomnik

Adapt or Fail!

A 5x5 Governance Framework for Boards of Directors

DE GRUYTER

ISBN 978-3-11-134397-6
e-ISBN (PDF) 978-3-11-134402-7
e-ISBN (EPUB) 978-3-11-134404-1
ISSN 2629-8155

Library of Congress Control Number: 2024950699

Bibliographic information published by the Deutsche Nationalbibliothek
The Deutsche Nationalbibliothek lists this publication in the Deutsche Nationalbibliografie;
detailed bibliographic data are available on the internet at http://dnb.dnb.de.

www.degruyter.com
Questions about General Product Safety Regulation:
productsafety@degruyterbrill.com

Advance Praise for *Adapt or Fail!*

Funston and Lukomnik have seen enough to know that boards can checklist themselves to oblivion. That's why, in this groundbreaking book, the two take readers below the superficial to the life force of corporate vitality, offering fresh insights on how directors can harness success.

–**Stephen Davis**, Senior Fellow,
Harvard Law School Program on Corporate Governance

There has never been a time where the role of the corporate director has been under more scrutiny or when directors have faced more pressure. Directors have little time to make big decisions and their actions, or lack thereof, can have significant ramifications for all shareholders. In their book, *Adapt or Fail!*, Rick Funston and Jon Lukomnik have provided a new template for decision making in the board room. Their adaptive Governance Framework provides directors with an easy to follow guideline for assessing both threats and opportunities – in five clearly defined steps. As an experienced corporate director, I was immediately drawn to their logical and clear approach and look forward to introducing these disciplines to the boards I sit on. I predict *Adapt or Fail!* will become an essential tool for any board striving for excellence in today's fast paced, high stakes environment.

–**Nancy Lockhart**, Corporate Director

As Funston and Lukomnik point out, corporate executives and boards and their investors have seen massive change: Cultural, legislative, technological, demographic, geopolitical. The challenges boards face can seem overwhelming. This book is a most welcome, and above all, practical guide for board members that will make it easier for them to perform their most essential tasks of risk management, from CEO compensation and succession to asset allocation, shareholder engagement, and knowing what the right questions are and what to do if they don't get good answers. It is an indispensable resource.

–**Nell Minow**, Vice Chair, ValueEdge Advisors

Both Bart Madden's *Value Creation Principles* and my book *Governance Reimagined* provide systems-based frameworks for the continuous innovation necessary for organizations to thrive in the long run. The board of directors establishes the conditions for these frameworks to succeed. Rick Funston and Jon Lukomnik have taken their immense experience and insights in this same spirit and focused it specifically on the work that happens in the boardroom. This laser focus fills a critical gap. Where most governance writers focus on tick-the-box elements of board governance, Funston and Lukomnik get to the life of the board's work,

https://doi.org/10.1515/9783111344027-202

which ultimately gives permission to the organization to thrive. Their work is important reading!

–**David R. Koenig**, President and Chief Executive Officer,
The DCRO Risk Governance Institute, Author,
*Governance Reimagined: Organizational Design, Risk,
and Value Creation* and *The Board Member's Guide to Risk*

Few business experts have the depth of knowledge and insight that comes from decades of board service, institutional investing, and ground-breaking research as Rick Funston and Jon Lukomnik. Their book provides corporate boards a clear framework designed to maximize the chances of making business decisions that succeed – the purpose of corporate governance – in an environment where there are more decisions to be made, increasing amounts of data with which to make them, and a diverse set of stakeholders who are harder to satisfy than ever before. The title of their book says it all: *Adapt or Fail!*

–**Douglas K. Chia**, President of Soundboard Governance
and Senior Fellow at Rutgers Center for Corporate Law and Governance

This is a terrific book for corporate directors. It is clever and thoughtful. And best of all, the stories recounted therein are worth the recall and provide superb insights into contemporary business culture.

–**Charles Elson**, Edgar Woolard Chair in Corporate Governance (ret.) and
Founding Director, Weinberg Center for Corporate Governance,
University of Delaware

For Irina, Nina, Sara, Michelle, Rachel, David, Shayna, Rachel S., and Joseph
For Lynn, Julia, and Aidan

Acknowledgments

We deeply thank editor Alexandra Lajoux and Jaya Dalal of De Gruyter publishing for their invaluable assistance in bringing this project to life. Your guidance, expertise, and unwavering support have been instrumental in shaping the final product.

We also owe a debt of gratitude to Sara Lussow for her help with the initial research and to the following for their assistance in reviewing portions of the manuscript and providing expertise: Robert Cubbins, Nancy Lockhart, Ralf Hess, Doug Chia, and Keith Johnson. Your thoughtful insights and constructive critiques have greatly enhanced the quality of this work.

Frederick (Rick) Funston and Jon Lukomnik
August 2024

https://doi.org/10.1515/9783111344027-203

Contents

Preface

Life short, art long, opportunity fleeting, experience misleading, judgment difficult.
Hippocrates, 400 BCE

In 2400 years nothing has changed in human nature, but everything else has. The first quarter of the 21st century has witnessed colliding waves of change from every direction – social, political, economic, technological, demographic, legal, environmental. The momentum of change, its mass and velocity, is accelerating exponentially. We are in an era of extreme uncertainty, complexity, and instability.

One result of all this change is that corporate life is getting much shorter. Since 1957, the average life expectancy of an S&P 500 company has declined by more than 70 percent, and it is still falling.[1] Today's organizations may have shorter life spans because conventional collective decision-making processes cannot keep pace with the external rate of change.

This manifests itself in several ways. There are numerous examples of boards (and their executives) who did not recognize and seize upon existential external opportunities, which later became existential threats. Others recognized the need for change but failed to execute the needed changes. Others failed to detect internal control weaknesses and fraud. For example, between 1999 and 2010, chief executive officers (CEOs) or chief financial officers (CFOs) were involved in 89 percent of U.S. Securities and Exchange Commission (SEC)-prosecuted fraud cases.[2]

This is despite numerous governance reforms over the past 50 years that have focused mainly on board structural issues, such as independence, composition, and director tenure. Those reforms, while necessary, were not sufficient, as they tended to prioritize form over substance in collective decision-making processes. The board's function is to make effective decisions. Form should follow function, not the reverse.

Conventional governance has tended to approach decision-making in isolation rather than as a system. Currently, there is no comprehensive framework for adaptive governance to enable and accelerate the board's collective decision-making functions and powers. There is no coherent and practical way of better organizing the board's most valuable and irreplaceable resource: its own time.

The nature of business and the "rules" are changing. What worked in the past may not work today and in the future. Judgment is indeed difficult. Creative destruction is alive and well. Organizations succeed by creating, delivering, capturing, and protecting value. When they cease to do so, they fail. The overarching duty of every board is to enable its organization's success despite uncertainty, complexity, and inevitable adversity.

If longevity is the measure of adaptation, many boards have failed and will likely continue to fail despite their best efforts. Directors are spending more and more time on board matters and are being inundated with more and more data. It is unlikely to help and may even exacerbate the situation.

https://doi.org/10.1515/9783111344027-205

Boards, by their nature, must make decisions collectively. Assuming the directors of failed companies were smart and well-intentioned, what went wrong? If whether to adapt or fail is the overarching governance question, then how best to adapt?

People and organizations are not perfect and cannot be perfected. Sooner or later, all will succumb. But can this be forestalled? Can more value be created, delivered, captured, and protected? Can corporate longevity be increased? What lessons can be learned from the successes and failures of others?

Will your organization adapt or fail? That is the existential governance question.

Our motivation for writing the book. While complex systems tend to fail in complex ways, a practical framework for adaptive governance to enable a board's collective decision-making need not and must not be complex itself.

This book is aimed at directors of boards of organizations large and small, complex and simple, for-profit and not-for-profit. The focus is on the board's powers and role and only indirectly on the executives' and third parties' roles. For example, when we discuss the key decisions that require board approvals, we discuss the board's role in seeing its due diligence requirements are met but not the roles of executives and others in performing such due diligence.

The book is also aimed at executives, corporate secretaries, internal auditors, and others who frequently work with the board to help improve their ability to support and enable achieving a common and synergistic understanding of reciprocal roles and expectations.

The 21st-century acceleration of change poses both greater threats and greater opportunities. Rapid adaptative choices demand situational awareness and decision discipline. Once the opportunity to adapt has passed, good choices were either made or not. Only time will tell. That is why we wrote this book.

The structure of the book. We know directors' and executives' time is extremely limited. We have tried to structure the book to make it easier for you to skim and then dive in where you are interested. Each chapter begins with a summary of Lessons Worth Learning.

Chapter 1 describes why boards and their organizations must adapt or fail and why a framework for adaptive governance is needed.

Chapter 2 ("A Framework for Practical Adaptive Governance") describes five essential powers common to every board and a practical process and principles for Adaptive Governance.

We describe five steps in systematic and deliberate adaptation:
1. Detect signals (external/internal)
2. Interpret (as threats or opportunities)
3. Respond (experiment/innovate)
4. Learn about the effectiveness of the response (better/same/worse)
5. Adapt as necessary

We then dedicate a chapter to each of the five essential powers common to all boards:
1. Conduct the business of the board.
2. Set direction and policy.
3. Approve key decisions, then prudently delegate.
4. Oversee the execution of direction within policy.
5. Verify the reliability of advice and information before trusting.

While the book proceeds linearly, all the powers are interdependent and interactive. There are feedback loops. Each power requires input and feedback from every other power and decision discipline.

Other than the conclusion, each chapter begins with a high-level summary of lessons worth learning that allows you to pinpoint your areas of greatest interest. It asks critical questions that every board should always ask of itself and others in exercising each power. The questions are intended as examples to frame the discussion and are not intended to be exhaustive. In answer to those questions, each chapter presents case examples and lessons worth learning from the successes and failures of others and practical tools for use by boards and executives.

Our goals are to help make your job easier, help you and your board become more effective, and make the highest and best use of your limited and valuable time. We offer our opinions based on our research but particularly with regard to our experience as board members, consultants, academics, and authors studying organizational governance. Our recommendations are, of course, subject to our own unavoidable biases. We don't expect anyone to adopt everything we recommend. Take what you will.

One size fits one! We believe that, if acted upon, a more disciplined exercise of a board's five essential powers combined with a systematic and deliberate process for adaptation can help drive sustainable value creation. Since we're dealing with the real world, we rarely can isolate a result and trace it back to a single factor. Instead, we suggest a hybrid approach of symmetric and asymmetric strategies to improve the chances of successful adaptation.

We provide a framework for improving collective decision-making in extreme instability. In today's highly volatile environment, how do people of good intent, with a common purpose, more quickly agree on how to make decisions collectively and then develop the discipline to carry them out in the face of inevitable adversity? Adaptive boards agree on how collective decisions will be made, stick to it, and improve it. How well does your board perform? We have provided a short Self-Assessment at the end of the book.

Of course, no one joins a board to fail. Most directors come to boards with a track record of success and no doubt wish this to continue. But success requires knowing how to learn, change, and adapt to changing conditions to drive sustainable value. If that is your goal, then this book is for you.

Extinction is the rule. Survival is the exception.
Carl Sagan, American Astronomer and Planetary Scientist

Chapter 1
Adapt or fail!

Adapt or Fail! Summary Lessons Worth Learning
– Shifts happen fast!
– The momentum of change is accelerating exponentially.
– Extreme uncertainty and instability will continue for the foreseeable future.
– Conventional risk assessment doesn't apply in extreme uncertainty and instability.
– Resilience improves value, including shareholder returns.
– Agile organizations adapt to the market faster.
– Faster rises, faster falls. Life at the top is getting a lot shorter.
– Failure to adapt is a failure of governance.
– Where was the board? What questions should they have asked?
– Dinosaurs, Unicorns, Unicorpses, and Zombies – no one is immune.
– Luck plays a role, but don't count on it.
– Recognizing the need to change is not new. But neither is failure to change.
– Despite major structural reforms in governance over the past 50 years, the decline in corporate longevity continues.
– The board's collective decision-making processes need to be more adaptive.

Introduction

> According to Darwin's *Origin of Species*, it is not the most intellectual of the species that survives; it is not the strongest that survives; but the species that survives is the one that is able best to adapt and adjust to the changing environment in which it finds itself.[3]
>
> *Leon C. Megginson, Professor*

The more finely adapted an organism or species is to a specific set of conditions, the more likely it is to succeed ... provided those conditions remain relatively stable. If conditions become unstable, then the most finely adapted are more likely to fail, independent of their intelligence, size, or experience.[4]

Given that 99.9 percent of all species that have ever lived on the planet are now extinct, it seems clear that most species have found it hard to adapt to adverse change, especially if it happens quickly.[5] They must at least keep pace with the external rate of change or die. They didn't have a choice. Either they were suited to changes in their environment or not. More coarsely adapted species have better chances of survival, but they still have no choice.[6]

https://doi.org/10.1515/9783111344027-001

The same challenge applies to boards and their corporations, except they have a choice: whether to adapt or fail, and, if so, how? No board chooses to fail. So why do so many organizations succumb?

The board has a critical role in enabling their organization's success. Good governance is about making better choices. It means being better prepared for inevitable adversity, having viable options in place before they are needed, recognizing and seizing on existential opportunities before they become existential threats, developing and maintaining decision discipline, and exercising the five essential powers of the board.

Lesson Worth Learning: Shifts happen fast!

True shifts result in more than incremental change. They represent a sea change. They transform the environment. For example, WeWork, a coworking real estate company, was valued at $47 billion in 2019 (Figure 1.1).[7] It was optimized for an economy that assumed white-collar workers and a low-interest rate environment. By 2023, neither of those assumptions were valid. COVID had created legions of former office workers who now worked remotely, and interest rates were heading higher. By November of that same year, the company had filed for bankruptcy.[8] WeWork was too finely adapted to a specific set of circumstances.

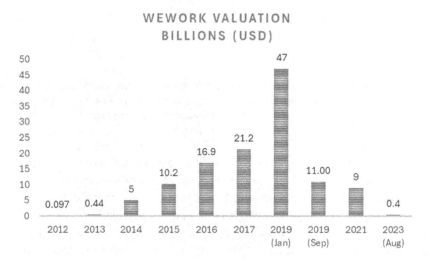

Figure 1.1: WeWork Valuation.

Lesson Worth Learning: The momentum of change is accelerating exponentially

> Said the Queen 'Now, here, you see, it takes all the running you can do, to keep in the same place. If you want to get somewhere else, you must run at least twice as fast as that!'
> *Red Queen in Lewis Carroll's* Through the Looking-Glass

The Red Queen. According to the Red Queen effect, constant adaptation and evolution are needed just to stand still and maintain one's relative position. Unfortunately, standing still has proven to be a recipe for disaster for any organization over the long term. A willingness to fail and to take intelligent and necessary risks must be embraced to innovate, adapt to changing circumstances, and achieve the mission. Of course, unnecessary risks need to be avoided or mitigated.

This is why situational awareness (for early warning) and strategy (to take the necessary risks intelligently and avoid being buffeted by unanticipated risks) work synergistically. It is far preferable in extreme uncertainty to have a range of options. It is also why developing a range of realistic options (from the least to the most that could be done) is so valuable.

The momentum of external change (its mass and velocity) continues to accelerate exponentially. Every day inevitably propels us toward more unforeseen crises. Shifts interact virally, potentiating one another.

The result is a wave train of different tsunamis of change: technical shifts, scientific breakthroughs, medical advances, multiomics, cyber-security threats, environmental changes and demands, workforce expectations, demographic changes, rapid regulatory changes, artificial intelligence (AI) and generative AI, social media, and instantaneous reputational risk. The list is virtually endless, with unknowable causes and effects that every organization must navigate to adapt successfully.

Lesson Worth Learning: Extreme uncertainty and instability will continue for the foreseeable future

> Doubt is not a pleasant condition, but certainty is an absurd one.
> *Voltaire, French Philosopher*

Current and foreseeable conditions are extraordinary. WeWork ran into two "once in a lifetime" crises almost back-to-back. But in the 21st century, that's not unusual; there seems to be a new "once-in-a-lifetime" crisis every couple of months. The global financial crisis. Drought. Deluge. Pandemics. Market events. Wars. And, of course, competition (both symmetric and asymmetric).

Lesson Worth Learning: Conventional risk assessment (impact and likelihood) doesn't apply in extreme uncertainty

> It is not just that we do not know what will happen. We often do not even know the kinds of things that might happen . . . This is a world of uncertain futures and unpredictable consequences, about which there is necessary speculation and inevitable disagreement – disagreement which often will never be resolved. And it is that world which we mostly encounter.[9]
> *Sir John Kay, British Economist*

Economists John Kay and Mervyn King explore the concept of decision-making in radical uncertainty and challenge the conventional approach. The authors distinguish between "risk" and "radical uncertainty." In the authors' terms, risk refers to situations with enough historical information to assign probabilities to potential outcomes, allowing for mathematical analysis. Uncertainty, by contrast, implies an unknowable future and builds on the work of legendary economist Frank Knight almost 100 years before.[10]

Quantitative analysis – the assumption of a knowable risk probability – underpins actuarial and insurance models of risk. Most quantitative conventional risk assessment models are based on established historical cause–effect relationships using large data sets. This has led to guidance on risk assessment for purposes of internal control and enterprise risk management from, for example, COSO, the Committee of Sponsoring Organizations of the Treadway Commission.[11]

Unfortunately, COSO's guidance, among others, encourages subjective probabilistic estimates, which are inevitably biased. Such estimates are seriously flawed but are still the norm despite having been identified as biased for almost 50 years.[12]

As the failure rates clearly illustrate, conventional risk assessment and decision-making models are inadequate in the face of radical uncertainty. In radical uncertainty, probabilities cannot be assigned. There are no relevant precedents or large bodies of data with established cause–effect relationships that can be used to establish risk experience and premia.

While we agree with Kay and King on uncertainty, we see risk differently. Risk is the potential for an unwanted difference between actual and expected performance regardless of cause. Clearly, there is risk with uncertainty, just as there is in situations with probabilistic precedents.

The ultimate expression of uncertainty is chaos. Chaos is the absence of cause and effect. It is a state of utter confusion. It is the antithesis of probability. In chaos, decision-makers must focus on building resilience and agility into their strategies rather than trying to predict specific outcomes with finely tuned plans. Resilience and agility involve designing systems and strategies that can adapt to a range of unknowable possible future developments.

Resilience is the ability of an organization to absorb shocks, recover quickly from disruptions, and maintain or even improve its essential functions. This includes recovering from known risks and being prepared for unexpected "black swan" events, especially since these seem to be occurring with increasing frequency.[13]

Lesson Worth Learning: Resilience protects value, including shareholder returns

> One of my great advantages is that I have very low expectations. People with very high expectations have very low resilience. And unfortunately, resilience matters in success . . . To this day, I use the phrase 'pain and suffering' inside our company with great glee . . . You want to refine the character of your company. You want greatness out of them, and greatness is not intelligence. Greatness comes from character and character is formed out of smart people who suffered.
>
> *Jen-Hsun "Jensen" Huang, CEO, Nvidia*

One key component of adaptation is resilience during and after adversity. Research by BCG Henderson Institute highlights that, although crises occur in only about 10 percent of calendar quarters, relative total shareholder return (TSR) during these times accounts for approximately 30 percent of a company's long-run relative TSR.[14] This means that performance during crisis periods has almost three times the impact of performance during more stable periods.

The research by BCG Henderson Institute shows that two-thirds of companies that outperformed their industries over the past 25 years were outperformers during crises. During crises, the gap between top and bottom performers widens significantly. For example, in the 18 months following the COVID-19 shock, the gap in total shareholder returns between the 25th and 75th percentile performers across industries increased to 105 percentage points, compared to just 18 percentage points in the 18 months before the crisis.[15]

Resilience creates benefits across multiple timescales of a crisis:
- absorbing the immediate impact
- recovering faster than peers
- thriving in the new circumstances after a crisis

Research by McKinsey[16] and others emphasizes that building resilience should be an ongoing priority, not just a response to immediate crises.[17] Companies that systematically embed resilience thinking into organizational systems and behaviors are better positioned to thrive despite potential disruptions.[18]

Lesson Worth Learning: Agile organizations adapt to the market faster

> Intelligence is the ability to adapt to change.
> *Stephen Hawking, Theoretical Physicist*

Agility reflects an organization's ability to quickly and effectively respond to environmental changes and opportunities. It requires excellent situational awareness through improved signal detection, pattern recognition, and interpretation, escalation of policy implications, a range of response options, learning and adjustment, and adaptation. That, in turn, enables organizations to identify shifts in markets, technology, or other factors and adapt their strategies and operations accordingly.

Organizational agility involves flexibility, quick decision-making, and a proactive approach to innovation. Agile organizations can more quickly recognize and respond to existential opportunities, market trends, and changes, giving them a competitive edge.

Agility promotes an environment where innovation thrives, enabling companies to experiment and implement new ideas faster and more efficiently. Being agile allows organizations to capitalize on new opportunities faster than competitors, driving growth and market expansion.

Agile companies can better manage risks by continuously monitoring the environment and adjusting strategies as needed. Flexibility in processes and structures helps organizations withstand and recover from disruptions more effectively.

As the following five companies demonstrate, organizational agility is vital for identifying and seizing opportunities in a rapidly changing business environment.

Amazon has transitioned from an online bookstore to a global e-commerce giant and then to a leader in cloud computing (Amazon Web Services (AWS)). AWS was initially developed to support Amazon's e-commerce operations but was later offered as a commercial service, seizing the burgeoning cloud computing market.

Netflix originally started as a DVD rental service but quickly adapted to the rising trend of online streaming. By investing in streaming technology and original content, Netflix transformed itself into a leading global entertainment provider.

Under CEO Satya Nadella, Microsoft shifted its focus from traditional software to cloud computing. This strategic pivot has driven significant growth and positioned Microsoft as a key player in the cloud industry.

Spotify continuously adapts to changing market dynamics and consumer preferences. It has expanded from music streaming to podcasts and live audio, ensuring its relevance in the competitive audio-streaming market.

Zara's agility in fashion retail allows it to quickly design, produce, and distribute new clothing lines based on current fashion trends. This rapid turnaround model ensures that Zara stays ahead of fashion cycles and consumer demand.

As these five examples show, building a culture of flexibility, continuous learning, and quick decision-making allows organizations to navigate uncertainties more effectively and capitalize on emerging opportunities.

Resilience and agility are essential in today's extremely uncertain and unstable conditions. They complement each other: Resilience provides a foundation for an organization to withstand shocks, while agility enables it to seize opportunities and navigate change proactively. However, as experience clearly demonstrates, change is much more easily said than done.

Lesson Worth Learning: Faster rises, faster falls. Life at the top is getting a lot shorter

> The best measure of adaptation to unanticipated risks in the biological setting is the length of time a species has survived.[19]
> *Richard Bookstaber, Author*

Using that measure, corporate survival rates have plummeted as the momentum of change has accelerated, as has the volatility of both growth and decline. We can see this by looking at changes in the S&P Index, which is based on factors such as market capitalization, liquidity, public float, and governance.

Start-ups are making meteoric rises to the top of the S&P, knocking out century-old blue chips that have suffered declining market values. The average lifespan of a company on the S&P index has dropped from 61 years in 1957 to just about 18 years today – a decline of more than 70 percent in almost as many years.[20]

Some are forecasting it will be as low as 12 years by the end of this decade (Figure 1.2).[21] As of 2021, on average, an S&P company was being replaced every two weeks. It is estimated that 75 percent of the 2019 S&P 500 firms will be replaced by 2027.[22] U.S. companies are not alone. Of the 100 companies in the FTSE 100 in 1984, only 24 were still listed in 2012.[23]

The landscape constantly shifts – quickly. Disruptive events can emerge at any time. Businesses (large or small) may fail if they cannot keep up with or respond effectively to new entrants, industry shifts, or market demands. Established companies that become too complacent or are too finely adapted to specific circumstances are especially vulnerable to disruptive forces. Existential opportunities may be missed and become existential threats.

Big businesses often have more resources to weather some of these challenges but still succumb if issues are not addressed promptly and effectively. Staying agile, adaptable, and forward-thinking is crucial for the long-term success of any business, regardless of its size.

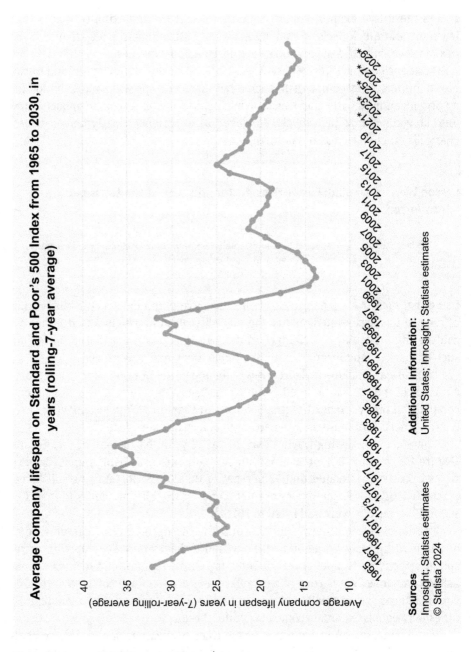

Figure 1.2: Average S&P 500 company lifespan.[i]

---

i The composition of the S&P 500 Index changes over time due to various factors such as mergers, bankruptcies, and changes in market capitalization. While acquisitions or mergers may have been the plan for some, for others, entire industries have been displaced, not just companies.

Lesson Worth Learning: Failure to adapt is a failure of governance

Table 1.1 provides a list of examples of companies removed from the S&P 500 from 2000 to 2024 for reasons other than mergers or acquisitions, such as financial difficulties, decreased market capitalization, and/or bankruptcy or conservatorship. (In some cases, these companies did merge into acquirers, but these mergers and acquisitions (M&A) transactions were often precipitated by their distressed conditions.) Many of these companies were "household names." Presumably, there were a lot of smart people on these boards. Where did they go wrong? What questions should they have been asking?

Table 1.1: Examples of Delisted S&P 500 companies 2000–2024[ii].

Owens Corning	Bethlehem Steel	Pacific Gas and Electric
Polaroid	Enron	Fruit of the Loom
Kmart	Winn-Dixie	Lucent Technologies
Gateway Inc.	Global Crossing	WorldCom
Delta Air Lines	Maytag Corporation	ConAgra Foods
Dana Corporation	Eastman Kodak	El Paso Corp
Fannie Mae	Calpine Corporation	D.R. Horton
Washington Mutual	Freddie Mac	Lehman Brothers
Bank of America	General Motors	Citigroup
Office Depot	New York Times Co.	Eastman Kodak
RadioShack	Dynegy Inc.	Qwest Communications
JCPenney	Supervalu	Advanced Micro Devices
Abercrombie & Fitch	Tenet Healthcare	Apollo Group
Peabody Energy	Allegheny Technologies	Pitney Bowes
Windstream Holdings	SunEdison	Alpha Natural Resources
Yahoo! Inc.	Frontier Communications	Chipotle Mexican Grill
Transocean Ltd.	Mattel, Inc.	Urban Outfitters
SCANA Corporation	Foot Locker, Inc.	Helmerich & Payne, Inc.
Whirlpool Corporation	TripAdvisor	Macy's
Xerox Holdings Corp.	SL Green Realty Corp.	Flowserve Corporation
Meta Platforms Inc.	Match Group Inc.	AT&T Inc.
Align Technology	DISH Network Corp.	SVB Financial Group
Navient Corp.	Robert Half International	Macerich Co.

No company, no matter how established or venerated, is immune to governance failure, which can lead, in turn, to business failure. Table 1.2 describes some of the possible causes of these failures. These causes are not mutually exclusive, and they interact. Have a look at this list and see how many of these warning signs are evident in your organization.

---

ii NOTE: Some have re-entered later.

Table 1.2: Possible Causes of Governance Failures.

Possible Causes of Governance Failures	Warning Signs
Conflicts of interest/Ethical failures	Financial mismanagement, fraud, or self-dealing.
Lack of agreement on essentials	Widely differing interpretations of mission, vision, purpose, functions, incentives/ disincentives.
Single fixed plan with no Plan B	Assume nothing major would change. Too unified view, singular focus, continuous improvement only, disincentives to cannibalize existing order.
Lack of collaboration and stakeholder engagement	Fail to collaborate with diverse stakeholders, including community members, experts, government agencies, and organizations. Lack of stakeholder engagement in decision-making processes, leading to delayed and/or ineffective solutions.
Lack of adaptive leadership	They are not open to change, incapable of navigating uncertainty, or unwilling to challenge existing paradigms, and they actively discourage innovation and learning within their organizations.
Lack of situational awareness	Fail to recognize signals – sometimes the signal is weak, and, in others, it is flashing neon but still ignored. Fail to recognize emerging patterns – didn't see the writing on the wall due to culture, lack of learning and feedback, hubris, and cognitive biases.
Lack of learning and experimentation	Fail to recognize uncertainty and the need for real options. Discourage ongoing learning through experimentation, monitoring, and feedback. Don't allow their organizations to adjust their strategies as new information becomes available.
Lack of resilience and failure to anticipate	Hope for the best, but don't plan for the worst.
Lack of flexibility and insufficient delegation of authority	Decision-making authority was not distributed to lower levels of an organization or to local communities. Centralization did not allow for more flexible and context-specific responses.
Lack of resources/external constraints	Fail to manage or lack financial, technological, or human resources to respond effectively to changing circumstances, such as regulatory constraints, market dynamics, or geopolitical events.
Lack of monitoring and evaluation	Lack of regular monitoring and evaluation of strategies and needed adjustments results in an inability to adapt. Without such processes to help track progress, unable to quickly identify successes and failures and make informed adjustments.

Table 1.2 (continued)

Possible Causes of Governance Failures	Warning Signs
Lack of feedback on actual performance	The lack of feedback on the effectiveness of decisions and policies prevents real-time adjustments and fine-tuning based on outcomes.
Failure to verify/Ineffective systems of internal control	It was too good to be true, but no one checked to be sure. Lack of checks and balances.
Suspending ethics rules	It erodes trust, increases the risk of corruption and fraud, has legal and regulatory consequences, negatively impacts organizational culture, causes long-term damage rather than short-term gains, and obviously undermines ethical standards.
Frequent related-party transactions	Frequent dealings between the organization and its affiliates, such as executives, board members, or family members, can be a significant warning sign in financial analysis for several reasons: potential conflicts of interest, risk of misrepresentation, increased risk of fraud, lack of transparency, and regulatory and compliance risks.

Lesson Worth Learning: Where was the board? What questions should they have asked?

When things go wrong, one of the first questions is, "Where was the board?" and one of the first answers is, "They weren't asking the right questions."

When Albert Einstein was a professor at Princeton, he was told he needed to change the questions he asked on the final exam. Apparently, students had discovered that Einstein kept asking the same questions, so they passed them around. He refused to change the questions. When asked, "Why?" he replied, "Because the answers keep changing."

What critical questions should boards always ask of themselves and others?
- What's essential?
- What are the most important things a board can do to enable rapid adaptation?
- How can a board make the highest and best use of organizational resources, including everyone's time?

Lesson Worth Learning: Dinosaurs, Unicorns, Unicorpses, and Zombies – no one is immune

Dinosaurs. "Dinosaurs" are companies that fail to adapt to changing market dynamics, technologies, or consumer preferences, resulting in outdated business models. These companies can become obsolete and lose market relevance quite quickly. Blockbuster, Kodak, BlackBerry, and, more recently, Bed Bath & Beyond failed to adapt to technological advancements and/or shifting consumer behavior.

BlackBerry introduced its first pager in 1999. The company's smartphones were so popular that they were called "crackberries" because users seemed addicted to them. Then, in 2007, Apple introduced the iPhone. By December 1, 2012, the company had only 79 million BlackBerry users worldwide, with only 9 million in the United States. Five years later, they had zero.[24]

BlackBerry's failure to innovate and adapt to changing consumer preferences and technological trends was a major factor in its decline. While competitors like Apple and Android introduced touch-screen smartphones with advanced operating systems, BlackBerry continued to rely on its traditional physical keyboard and proprietary operating system.

Blackberry also lacked an app ecosystem, making it less attractive to users and developers. As employees increasingly began using their personal smartphones for work purposes, a trend known as Bring Your Own Device (BYOD) eroded BlackBerry's dominance in the enterprise market. Employees preferred using consumer-focused smartphones with more features and apps.

BlackBerry's reputation for security and reliability initially attracted corporate and government clients. However, as other platforms improved their security features and offered more attractive devices, BlackBerry lost many of these lucrative contracts. Its security features also resulted in perceptions of a lack of user-friendliness. It was also slow to respond to the changing market landscape. Even when it introduced touch-screen devices, they failed to gain traction due to hardware and software issues. Leadership changes and management issues, including internal conflicts and a lack of strategic direction, hindered BlackBerry's ability to make timely decisions and execute effective turnaround strategies.

However, ultimately, BlackBerry's inability to adapt to the changing smartphone landscape, coupled with missteps in product development and marketing, led to its decline. While the company continues to exist and has shifted its focus to software and cyber-security services, it is no longer a player in the smartphone market.

Unicorns. "Unicorns" are companies valued at $1 billion or more without being publicly listed. These startups are known for rapid growth and innovation. Unicorns often disrupt traditional industries. Examples include Airbnb, Uber, Stripe, SpaceX, and DoorDash.

Founded in 2008, Airbnb has transformed how people find and book accommodations and changed the dynamics of the short-stay market. In December 2020, Airbnb went public through an initial public offering (IPO). It has a market capitalization of almost $94 billion as of this writing.[25] That is almost twice the market capitalization of Hilton, a traditional hotel company with a hundred-plus-year history.[26]

Airbnb tapped into the sharing economy concept, allowing individuals to rent out their homes, apartments, or spare rooms to travelers. This created an alternative to traditional hotels: A vast and diverse inventory of accommodations that catered to various tastes and budgets. Travelers could stay in local neighborhoods and live like residents, which resonated with those seeking authenticity in their travels.

Airbnb transformed the way people think about accommodations and travel. By disrupting the traditional hospitality sector and providing travelers with more options and hosts with income opportunities, Airbnb has created a nearly $100 billion business.

Unicorpses. Unicorns are not immune to situational blindness and inability to adapt. Unicorns can quickly become "unicorpses." Unicorpses boasted high valuations at some point but then struggled to sustain their growth and experienced rapid declines in their market capitalization. Examples include WeWork, 23andMe, and Peloton.

Peloton Interactive, Inc. is an American company specializing in exercise equipment and media, including stationary bicycles, treadmills, and indoor rowers, all equipped with internet-connected touch screens.

Peloton experienced a surge in demand for its products and services during the COVID-19 pandemic as people sought home fitness solutions. Its stock price peaked in December 2020, reaching a valuation of almost $50 billion. However, the company faced challenges in sustaining that growth rate as pandemic-related restrictions eased and competition in the home fitness industry intensified.

Like many companies, Peloton grappled with supply chain disruptions caused by the pandemic. These disruptions led to delays in product deliveries and frustrated customers. Peloton also faced safety-related incidents involving its Tread and Tread+ treadmill products.

Reports of accidents, injuries, and even the death of a child were associated with these products. Peloton had to recall two treadmill models, leading to financial losses and reputational damage. As the company navigated these challenges, Peloton also experienced changes in its executive leadership, including the departure of its CEO, John Foley.[27] Its share price has since fallen by 80 percent,[28] and its market capitalization is now just $1.5 billion.[29]

Zombies. "Zombies" are businesses that continue to operate despite being unable to cover their operating costs, including debt servicing expenses, with their current revenues. These companies may be unprofitable, highly leveraged, and even insolvent. They often rely on external support or lenient creditors to stay afloat. Some eventually go out of business, but they can stay zombies for years. Examples of zombie companies included, at various times, Sears, RadioShack, Toys "R" Us, and Hertz.

Hertz, the car rental company, filed for bankruptcy in 2020, citing the impact of the COVID-19 pandemic on its business. Despite its bankruptcy status, it continues to operate and has attempted to raise capital through stock offerings. It made a huge investment in electric vehicles, but, in January 2024, Hertz announced it planned to sell a third of its U.S. electric vehicle fleet (20,000 vehicles). It said it would reinvest in gas-powered cars due to weak demand and high repair costs for its battery-powered Teslas.[30]

Not only are there zombie businesses, but there are also zombie industries.

At times, the airline industry has been a zombie industry with most airlines experiencing ongoing losses, heavy debt burdens, and reliance on external support to stay afloat. Since 2000, in the United States alone, 72 airlines have sought some form of bankruptcy protection through Chapter 7 (liquidation) or Chapter 11 (debt restructuring).[31]

Due to their need for liquidity, those challenged carriers often reduced fares to attract flyers, thereby putting margin pressure on their competitors, some of whom filed for bankruptcy. In effect, like a bad movie, the zombies infected the healthier companies.

Clearly, life at the top can be very short indeed. Where some companies may thrive and innovate (unicorns), others fail to adapt and become obsolete (dinosaurs), some struggle to maintain their valuation (unicorpses), and others persist despite financial challenges (zombies). Adverse regulatory change, competition, change in the competitive environment, or failure to stay abreast of technology, consumer trends, or business context can quickly impair an organization. The ability to adapt, innovate, and overcome inertia is crucial for companies to remain competitive in such an extraordinarily volatile and uncertain business environment.

Lesson Worth Learning: Luck plays a role, but don't count on it

> Things worthwhile generally don't just happen. Luck is a fact but should not be a factor.
> Good luck is what is left over after intelligence and effort have combined at their best.
> Negligence or indifference are usually reviewed from an unlucky seat. The law of cause
> and effect and causality both work the same with inexorable exactitudes.
> Luck is the residue of design.
> *Branch Rickey, Baseball Executive who signed Jackie Robinson to play for the Brooklyn Dodgers*[32]

Nvidia. In the 1990s, Nvidia was on the brink of collapse due to setbacks with its initial chip designs. The company's future was uncertain, and bankruptcy loomed. At this critical juncture, Nvidia's CEO, Jen-Hsun "Jensen" Huang, sought a $5 million lifeline to keep the company afloat. Shoichiro Irimajiri, a prominent executive from Sega, stepped in with an act of kindness that would change the course of Nvidia's history. Irimajiri, recognizing the potential in Huang's vision, provided the much-needed funds without any obligation to do so.

This timely and fortunate investment not only saved Nvidia from imminent failure but also enabled the company to develop a breakthrough graphics processing unit (GPU) for Sega's Dreamcast console. Despite initial setbacks, Irimajiri's unwavering support and belief in Nvidia's capabilities were crucial. This investment and support paved the way for Nvidia's eventual success, including its public offering in 1999. Today, Nvidia is the leading player in the tech industry, with a market valuation of more than $2 trillion.[33]

Netflix. In the late 1990s, Netflix co-founders Reed Hastings and Marc Randolph conceived the idea of a mail-order DVD rental service. They sent a DVD to themselves to test the feasibility of the idea. They didn't know it then, but they used one of the few remaining post offices that still sorted mail manually.

This manual sorting was more gentle and less likely to damage the DVD, which "proved" that DVDs could indeed be sent safely through the mail, thus validating the business concept. Had they known it was just by chance, it would have changed everything because they incorrectly assumed it would work in every post office.[34]

This "successful" test led to the launch of Netflix in 1997, which initially operated as a subscription-based DVD rental service. The innovative model allowed customers to rent DVDs without late fees, fundamentally changing the home video rental market and setting the stage for Netflix's later transition to a streaming giant. Today, Netflix moves data via networks rather than DVDs via mail, but the concept is the same. Netflix started with a good idea and adapted it to shape our times.

Oaktree Capital Management. In 1969, Howard Marks, co-founder and chairman of Oaktree Capital Management, armed with degrees from Wharton and the University of Chicago Booth School of Business, was searching for his first job. He wanted one job more than any other. He didn't get it; it went to his roommate instead.

Thirty years later, Marks learned the reason from the recruiter who had interviewed him. The recruiter revealed that the partner in charge had come in hungover on the day of the decision and called the wrong candidate. Reflecting on this twist of fate, Marks humorously noted that, had he gotten that job, he might have spent 30 years at Lehman Brothers, which infamously collapsed in 2008.[35]

FedEx. In the early 1970s, FedEx was facing severe financial difficulties. The company had run out of money, with only $5,000 left in its account, while it needed $24,000 to pay a critical fuel bill. Traditional funding options were exhausted, and the company's future was in jeopardy.

In a desperate bid to save FedEx, CEO Fred Smith took the remaining $5,000 and flew to Las Vegas. Using his skills as a card counter, he played blackjack and turned the $5,000 into $27,000. This unexpected windfall allowed FedEx to pay the fuel bill and keep its operations running for another week.

This gamble provided immediate relief and symbolized a turning point for the company. It boosted morale and demonstrated Smith's commitment to saving the company. Following this, Smith secured an additional $11 million in funding, stabilizing FedEx's finances and allowing it to continue growing. By 1976, FedEx had made its first profit, and, by 1983, it had reported $1 billion in revenue.[36]

Don't count on it. Luck or chance plays a significant yet often underestimated role in business success. However, resilience and adaptability create success from a chance occurrence. If Smith hadn't been a card counter, if Marks had sulked after chance denied him his dream job, they still wouldn't have succeeded even if the lucky break had happened exactly as it did.

Viewed through that lens, it's easy to imagine a counterfactual world in which they failed and what is now considered their lucky break is considered bad luck.

Once you think of it that way, it's intuitive that "luck" – if not acted upon with skill – evens itself out, resulting in a sort of regression to the mean. And, indeed, that seems to be the case. Chengwei Liu, an associate professor of strategy and behavioral science, researched the 50 companies featured in Jim Collins' three books: *In Search of Excellence, Good to Great*, and *Built to Last*. He found that 16 failed within five years after the books were published, and 23 became mediocre as they underperformed the S&P 500 Index.[37]

Only 5 of the remaining 11 firms maintained a similar level of excellence. He concludes, "What happened after becoming great is clearly not enduring greatness but strong regression to mediocrity." Therefore, in the words of Rickey, "Luck is a fact, but should not be a factor." You can't count on luck if you and your board want to control your organization's future. You – and your board – need to understand how the world and your organization's place in it are changing and control how you adapt to those changes.

Lesson Worth Learning: Recognizing the need to change is not new. But neither is failure to change

> The only thing we learn from history is that we learn nothing from history.
> *Georg W. F. Hegel, German Philosopher*

Has the need for change become a cliché? One might think so. It's not like companies haven't tried to change or people are just waking up to the need for change. American futurists Alvin Toffler, John Naisbitt, and others have issued warnings for decades.[38] Although many boards and their CEOs have long recognized the need for change, McKinsey reports that 70 percent of such efforts fail.[39] According to a 2021 Gartner study of data optimization initiatives, only 42 percent reported they were on track.[40]

Despite efforts to enact changes, whether in strategic direction or governance, increasing corporate mortality rates indicate that these initiatives have not been particularly effective if the ultimate objective was to ensure survival. In other words, while the operation may have been deemed successful, the patient – the corporation – did not survive. The cause of death was the failure to adapt – or, put another way, an inability to overcome inertia.[41]

Once in motion, inertia is the tendency to keep moving in the same direction until external forces intervene, as they inevitably will. Organizational inertia (momentum) is sustained by past success and factors such as continuous improvement, current customer demands, and disincentives to cannibalize existing profit centers.[42] Like a rock rolling downhill, momentum can come to a sudden stop at the bottom of the hill.

While the old proverb is that nothing succeeds like success, the unfortunate reality is that success often breeds failure, as the conditions that enabled success change around it, but the organization does not. This is what business consultant Clayton Christensen called the "Innovator's Dilemma."[43] And it's why "success is a poor teacher."[44]

Successful adaption demands that the internal rate of change at least keep pace with or (better yet) get ahead of the external rate of change.[45] Discontinuous improvement, also known as breakthrough improvement or radical innovation, is needed to create new sources of momentum to escape inertia. It is a significant and transformative change in processes, systems, products, or services that results in substantial gains in performance, efficiency, or effectiveness.

Unlike incremental or continuous improvements, which involve small, incremental changes over time, discontinuous improvement involves revolutionary shifts or breakthroughs that fundamentally alter how things are done or perceived.

Lesson Worth Learning: Despite major structural reforms in governance over the past 50 years, the decline in corporate longevity continues to accelerate

Not only has the external environment shifted, but so has governance. Over the past 50 years, there have been major structural changes in corporate governance driven by shifts in economic conditions, shareholder expectations, and regulatory reforms. These include, for example:
- increased board independence
- enhanced board diversity

- new requirements for committee independence and charters
- strengthened audit and risk oversight
- enhanced transparency and disclosure
- executive compensation reform
- director compensation reform
- improved shareholder rights
- internal controls and whistleblower protection
- global standards and codes of practice
- rise of corporate governance ratings/assessments

These structural governance reforms aimed to enhance transparency, account-ability, alignment, and shareholder protection. Ultimately, the goal was to con-tribute to more sustainable and responsible businesses.

Such structural changes may have been necessary. After all, who knows what might have happened without them? But are they sufficient? Arguably not. Shifts happen, and the world has changed and continues to change at a pace that was inconceivable just a few decades ago. So, although salutary, these governance re-forms did not provide practical advances in collective decision-making practices or change management for boards.

Given the accelerating corporate mortality rate, what's missing? Why are the success rates not higher? Perhaps conventional governance/decision-making pro-cesses are better suited to relatively stable conditions, and it's time to rethink their use. Or, at least, to complement decision-making reforms rather than add more structural ones.

Lesson Worth Learning: Collective decision-making processes at the board need to be more adaptive

Insufficient attention has been paid to change management within the board it-self. How does the board enable or inhibit adaptation? How does it spend its valu-able time? The board cannot delegate its responsibility or its requirements for de-cision-making to the organization. There are always decisions that must be made by the board alone – and the board must do so collectively.

A board typically must approve large-scale change initiatives. Yet the board's role in change management has been undervalued and underexamined. Early signal detection, pattern recognition, and timely interpretation are critical. Boards need bet-ter, faster escalation of policy implications to keep pace with and even get ahead of the external rate of change. Delays in the board's process can impair response times.

Board reports are like most conventional board processes. They were for a time when boards had less on their plates, when the outside (and inside) context of their organizations changed at a much slower pace and less substantively, and when the chief executive or executive director was, at many organizations, an overwhelming center of gravity and power and the board just an afterthought. Most board processes were developed at a time when, as Harvard Professor Myles Mace put it, directors were "ornaments on a corporate Christmas tree."[46]

Conventional decision discipline was more about structure and rules of order and less about enabling collective decision-making. Change management was focused on executive leadership and organization. We believe more attention needs to be paid to the board's role as a necessary precursor and contributor to major internal change and overcoming inertia.

Can conventional board decision-making processes adapt rapidly? Do they enhance insight? Do they keep the focus on the essentials? Do they help transform the dialogue? Many directors would argue that these processes could be improved because they were designed for a different era. This may be one of the reasons why companies are experiencing diminishing lifespans. The way boards govern is too often excluded from discussions on how organizations can build resilience and adaptability, which are now more critical than ever for business sustainability.

Structural governance reforms have failed under conditions of extreme instability. A system of governance better suited to adapting to extreme instability is required.

Critical questions. The board is ultimately responsible for the success or failure of the organization. Below is a list of critical questions, organized by the five powers of the board, that a board should ask itself regarding its five essential powers. These are not exhaustive but are illustrative.

Conduct the Business of the Board
1. Do we have a high-performing culture that promotes value creation, ethical behavior, transparency, and accountability?
2. Do our board dynamics enable consensus building and make the highest and best use of everyone's time?
3. Do our committee assignments and board members' expertise effectively address the organization's specific issues and challenges?
4. Do we effectively plan director succession, including the nomination and compensation processes?
5. Do we do a good job of selecting, evaluating, compensating, and planning for the succession of the chief executive officer?

Set Direction and Policy
1. Is the board clear about its role in setting direction and policy?
2. Is there alignment on the mission and values?
3. Is the strategic plan truly strategic?

4. Have critical issues been identified?
5. What are the existential opportunities and threats?
6. What are our strategic options?
7. Have strategic options been systematically evaluated?
8. Have strategic goals and metrics been agreed upon?
9. Is the organization aligned with the strategy?
10. Are we on track?

Approve Key Decisions, then Prudently Delegate
1. Has the board clearly identified the key decisions requiring board approval?
2. Does the board have a disciplined decision process?
3. Does the board require that appropriate due diligence be performed before a request for board approval?
4. Have appropriate accountability, authority, and resources been prudently delegated?
5. How can we improve the board's approval process and track record of success?

Oversee the Execution of Direction within Policy
1. How should we exercise oversight?
2. How can we prevent oversight failures?
3. How do we know if vital performance is under control?
4. How do we get reliable, timely intelligence and policy insights for direction setting?
5. How should we respond?
6. What did we learn?
7. How do we adapt?

Verify before Trusting
1. What is our role in obtaining reasonable assurance?
2. Why and how should we verify before trusting?
3. Why and how can we obtain independent reassurance that information, advice, and reports are reliable?
4. How can we be reassured that the system of internal control is effective?

Conclusion

> There is no such thing as bad weather. Only unsuitable clothing.
> *Alfred Wainwright, Author of British guidebooks*

Board work today is dangerous. The world is changing. Boards are usually composed of accomplished people. They are well-intentioned but too often ill-equipped. But like experienced explorers in uncharted territory who encounter severe storms, extreme heat or cold, parched deserts, or raging rivers, boards today should not expect to proceed in a straight line if they want to reach their objective.

Explorers need situational awareness of the challenges and opportunities nature throws at them, and boards need high situational awareness to meet the challenges and opportunities a rapidly changing world puts in their way.

Explorers constantly evaluate whether their chosen path is safe and efficient. They do the same for the stages ahead. If they find that their current approach isn't working, they adapt by altering their route, equipment, transportation mode, and clothing.

Similarly, boards must continuously assess whether their organization effectively creates, captures, delivers, and protects value. Will it continue to do so in an unpredictable future? If the answer is no, boards can leverage their powers to change strategies, reallocate resources, and make other necessary adjustments – essentially, to "re-dress" the organization in a better direction and with more suitable "clothing" to ensure its ongoing success.

The balance of this book examines the lessons worth learning from the successes and failures in exercising each of the board's five essential powers. But, first, we examine the process and principles of a framework for practical adaptive governance.

Success is not final; failure is not fatal:
It is the courage to continue that counts.
Sir Winston Churchill, twice former Prime Minister of Great Britain

Chapter 2
A practical framework for adaptive governance

Practical Adaptive Governance: Lessons Worth Learning
– Make sure the organization's purpose is clear.
– Boards, by their nature, must make decisions collectively.
– A board cannot delegate responsibility, only authority and resources.
– Ceaselessly optimize value.
– Delivering, capturing, and protecting value are as important as creating it.
– Build consensus.
– Use majority rule only as the last resort.
– Don't wait for a crisis to develop decision discipline.
– Adopt a disciplined adaptive governance process.
– Building consensus can take time, but sudden shifts and crises provide little time for deliberation.
– Focus relentlessly on the essentials.
– Challenge constructively, not destructively.
– Build constructive challenge into board and organizational processes.
– Develop constructive critical questions the board should always ask of itself and others.
– Decide iteratively in extreme uncertainty.
– Take intelligent, necessary risks while minimizing or avoiding unnecessary risks.
– Not taking calculated risks is very risky.
– "One size fits one!"
– Stakeholder relationships are essential.
– Fiduciary duties are full-time responsibilities even though directors are part-time.
– Exercise the board's five essential powers to enable organizational success.

Introduction

What is governance? Fundamentally, it means choosing, directing, overseeing, and controlling – something other species lack. Certainly, there is a vast and kaleidoscopic literature on the various elements of governance. Unfortunately, there is no practical organizing framework for board governance. If you search for systems of governance, you get answers like socialism, communism, and democracy.

Boards must make decisions collectively. How well and quickly they choose has major consequences for the organization's adaptive ability. Let's look at how the Lilly board made some informed choices.

https://doi.org/10.1515/9783111344027-002

Eli Lilly. Lilly (LLY) is an example of an adaptive board that saw the signals and acted to speed up processes to match the rate of change and successfully adapt. It demanded an overhaul of the company's product development processes before it was too late.

Historically, Lilly used multiple committees to review its new product pipeline. Members of these committees were often business unit heads who tried to protect the sales of existing products and, therefore, turned down otherwise promising developments that would have cannibalized those sales. There was little sense of urgency and strong incentives to delay, dither, or deny.

In 2015, after losing out on several major opportunities, the board decided that transformational change was needed. The board asked Dr. Daniel Skovronsky, Lilly's chief scientific and medical officer, to review major failures over the past decade and recommend how to accelerate the product development process. Lilly has since successfully introduced a significant number of blockbuster products, and product development time has been cut from eleven years to six with the goal of further acceleration.[47]

"Every program we do, we look at what our competitors have done, who's done it the fastest, and then we set a goal to go even faster," said Dr. Skovronsky. "Speed becomes our No. 1 incentive, which is hard because it's a cultural change."[48]

As of June 28, 2024, Lilly had gone from leader to laggard back to the leader and has become the most valuable pharmaceutical company in the world with a market capitalization of \$815 billion[49] and annual revenues of more than \$30 billion.[50] Its share price has grown from \$86.20 in December 2015 to \$909 by June 27, 2024, an increase of more than 950 percent. Its market capitalization has doubled in the past year alone.[51] The Lilly board played a crucial role in mandating the transformation by challenging conventional product development times and processes. Others have been much less prescient.

Clearly, the way you choose to govern can make a difference or not. But even Lilly's board may have been slow to respond. As early as 2009, John Lechleiter, then Lilly's chief executive, realized that things needed to change. Why did it take the board until 2015 to mandate a change? Were they not informed? Or did it just take a long time to get the board on board? Could it have been done sooner?

Throughout this book, we will discuss the lessons worth learning from the successes and failures of boards that were able to adapt and those that weren't. Let's dig a little deeper into practical adaptive governance and some lessons learned.

Lesson Worth Learning: Make sure the organization's purpose is clear

Lilly's mission is to "unite caring with discovery to create medicines that make life better for people around the world." Launched in 2022, Lilly's Mounjaro™ has become one of the best-selling pharmaceuticals ever. Despite this success, and perhaps because of it, the current CEO, Dave Ricks, is pushing his scientists to find an even more potent anti-obesity treatment. "Lilly's got a lead, and we plan to exploit that lead." One of his top priorities is speed. "We want to be first and best. Our saying is, 'The patient is waiting.'"[52]

Mounjaro is an extraordinary example of the successful overhaul of the product pipeline initiated by Lilly's board. Ricks brought it to market two years ahead of schedule.

Purpose of the organization. Adaptive governance begins with a clear and shared understanding of the organization's mission and its vital functions. Whatever the organization (public company, startup, or not-for-profit) is it must be able to continue to sustainably create, deliver, capture, and protect value, or it risks failure. An adaptive organization fulfills its purpose despite inevitable uncertainty, risk, and adversity.

Purpose is paramount. Organizations' purposes vary, so being clear about them is paramount. A well-defined purpose serves as a guiding light for the organization. It provides clarity on why the organization exists and where it is headed. It sets clear goals and objectives. When the purpose is clear, it becomes easier to align the efforts of all stakeholders, including employees, management, and investors. Everyone understands the common goal and works toward it.

Purpose guides decision-making at all levels of the organization. It is the organizational North Star. When faced with choices, purpose can act as a filter, helping to make decisions that align with the organization's mission. A clear purpose is a powerful communication tool. It helps convey the organization's values and mission to external stakeholders such as customers, partners, and the community.

Organizations with a well-defined purpose tend to have a longer-term perspective. They are more likely to adapt and evolve while staying true to their core mission. A strong sense of purpose can provide resilience during challenging times or crises. It gives the organization and its members a reason to persevere and overcome obstacles.

A unique and well-communicated purpose can set an organization apart from competitors. It helps build a distinct brand identity and attract like-minded employees, customers, and partners. A clear sense of purpose is the foundation upon which an organization's strategy, culture, and actions are built. It provides direction, alignment, and motivation, ultimately contributing to the organization's success and long-term sustainability.

Lesson Worth Learning: Boards, by their nature, must make decisions collectively

Boards of directors are the stewards of any organization, be it a for-profit company, charity, public purpose entity, association, or anything else. Today, boards are expected to handle a broad and ever-growing range of highly interactive issues, from overseeing vital functions to determining whether to make public statements about the issues of the day.

A board's effectiveness and efficiency are determined by how well it collectively exercises its key powers and makes decisions. Boards must act collectively; any one director, or even a group of directors, cannot exercise the board's powers.[iii]

The need for boards to act collaboratively is both a strength and a weakness. Ineffective or delayed collective decision-making can impede rapid adaptation, particularly when there is a short response window to a threat or opportunity.

Lesson Worth Learning: A board cannot delegate responsibility, only authority and resources

A board can and should delegate executive authority and resources to enable rapid adaptation and achieve the organization's mission. Delegation to a chief executive creates a single point of accountability for accomplishing the mission despite extreme uncertainty and inevitable adversity. However, the board cannot delegate its responsibility or collective decision-making authority.

The Lilly board did this in an exemplary manner. They assigned a senior executive with the objective of transforming the product development process. The Lilly board agreed this was a top priority and then made sure it was carried out.

Lesson Worth Learning: Ceaselessly optimize value

> I very frequently get the question: 'What's going to change in the next 10 years?' And that is a very interesting question; it's a very common one. I almost never get the question: 'What's not going to change in the next 10 years?' And I submit to you that that second question is actually the more important of the two – because you can build a business strategy around the things that are stable in time.
>
> *Jeff Bezos, Founder, Executive Chairman, and former President and CEO of Amazon*

---

iii Boards can, of course, delegate certain functions to a single director or a group of directors. But their power is limited to the board's designation.

The board's role is to enable the success of their organization despite the rapid change and extreme uncertainty that are the hallmarks of the 21st century. The organization's success depends on its ability to sustainably create, deliver, capture, and protect value. That immediately begs two overarching questions.

What is value? Why do organizations need to sustainably create, deliver, capture, and protect it? Since at least 1970, the dominant school of thought about business value has been the doctrine of the economist Milton Friedman. "There is one and only one social responsibility of business – to use its resources and engage in activities designed to increase its profits so long as it stays within the rules of the game."[53] In other words, in for-profit companies, maximizing enterprise profit was the singular goal.

Maximizing aims to achieve the greatest possible result in a specific situation in the shortest possible time without constraints, limitations, or regard for the impacts of that maximization. Governments and markets made rules for the game, and companies (including not-for-profits) played within them.

Things have changed a lot since Friedman wrote those words. In investment terms, there have been shifts from individual to institutional investors and from focusing on individual stocks to diversified portfolios. Today, about 90 percent of the market is institutional, and virtually all investments are diversified (mutual funds, exchange-traded funds (ETFs), index funds, etc.). This means investors typically care more about their overall portfolio value than any one company.

Another widely understood change is that traditional financial statements (and, therefore, Friedman's profits) do not account for an organization's total external impact. Moreover, those externalities, both good and bad, matter more to today's investors. While investors care about profits, they also care about how that company affects the market, the general economy, and the social, environmental, and financial systems on which they rely.

Yet another change is that the relative power of business and government has evolved. Friedman was writing at the height of the post-World War II activist government consensus. Since then, who makes rules and how they are made have changed. As Chris Pinney, CEO of High Meadows Institute, notes,

> Today, thanks to globalization and the international economy, we live in a world in which the neat dividing line between business and governments in terms of their role and responsibilities for society is blurring rapidly . . . over half the world's top economies are global firms with an influence and impact on society exceeding that of many countries. Not surprisingly, in this environment, society is looking to businesses to take greater responsibility for their impact.[54]

Where does that leave boards of directors? The 21st-century reality is that business value is multidimensional, not monolithic. There is economic, ethical, moral, cultural, and social value. Like beauty, value is in the eye of the beholder: customers and stakeholders. As their views change and evolve, so does the concept of value. Anyone who has tried attracting skilled young workers knows they value different things than their generational predecessors.

Good situational awareness helps boards and board members understand that values are dynamic, not static. With the passage of time, that is obvious. In the early 19th century, American slaves were used as collateral for bank loans.[55] In the 20th century, U.S. regulations changed as society did to reflect different views on child labor, forced labor, health and safety issues, and workplace discrimination.

Already, in the 21st century, we have seen changes in what is expected behavior regarding sexual harassment and abuse and the environment. Boards are increasingly asked to engage in a much broader range of topics, such as gender diversity, social media, data privacy, and the environment, and they are praised or excoriated for doing so.

As a result of those and other changes, boards at all types of organizations are confronted with managing the impact on their organizations of an extraordinarily challenging environment and their organizations' impact on the world today and in the future. It means thinking about the long-term consequences.

Boards need to be aware of these and other changes and challenges and determine what their organization considers "valuable" – its constraints and enablers. What values should be enduring? What will be considered valuable 5, 10, or 20 years from now?

Optimizing, rather than maximizing, involves finding the best possible balance of solutions given a set of constraints and criteria across a broad range of situations. In uncertainty, optimizing under constraints means having greater flexibility and is more likely to be sustainable over the longer term.

In optimizing, voluntary constraints are what the organization considers enduringly valuable, i.e., its values. The optimizing organization achieves its vision and mission within certain constraints, e.g., operating ethically and environmentally responsibly and acting according to certain expectations as defined by the board.

We believe boards should seek to optimize, not maximize, value as a more sustainable (adaptive) and, thus, longer-lived strategy. Ultimately, each board must decide for itself what it considers valuable and what constraints it will impose on its organization's behavior.

If taken seriously, determining the organization's values is more than an abstract and esoteric exercise in "doing good and avoiding evil." It establishes the guideposts for future decision-making and organizational behavior. A keen understanding and situational awareness of the contextual dynamics surrounding the organization should be embedded into its values, strategies, and policies (see "Set Direction and Policy").

**Lesson Worth Learning: Delivering, capturing, and protecting value
are as important as creating it**

**Why is there a need to sustainably create, deliver, capture, and protect
value?** Because each element is necessary but not sufficient. They all need to
work synergistically.

Xerox PARC is an example of an organization that created enormous value,
including the graphical user interface (GUI), the computer mouse, ethernet networking, laser printing, and object-oriented programming. Yet, it was unable to
commercialize it.

Napster pioneered the peer-to-peer (P2P) file-sharing service. It created and
delivered value by enabling users to share and download music files for free. It
revolutionized the music industry by providing easy and widespread access to a
vast library of songs. However, it could not capture value because of copyright
and regulatory issues and the lack of a sustainable business model to compensate
artists and monetize its service. It provided immense value to users but did not
generate significant revenue to sustain its operations.

BlackBerry created, delivered, and captured value but could not protect it. Recall from Chapter 1, Blackberry was a pioneer in the smartphone market and became a dominant player in the early 2000s. At its peak, it held a significant market share in the smartphone industry and was considered a leader in mobile
communication technology.

BlackBerry's story is a cautionary tale of how a company can create, deliver,
and capture significant value but still fail to protect it due to complacency, slow
innovation, and misjudgment of market dynamics. To sustain long-term success,
companies must remain agile, continuously innovate, and be situationally aware
of market changes and competitive pressures to sustainably create, deliver, capture, and protect value.

Lesson Worth Learning: Build consensus

Consensus is a process that optimizes diverse opinions. It ensures all opinions
are heard, resulting in the best decision under the circumstances. The result is a
decision that everyone can live with, i.e., no one says, "Not over my dead body."
Unfortunately, achieving consensus usually takes time, skill, and patience.

In 2008, Starbucks faced significant challenges due to the economic down-
turn, including declining sales and store closures. During this period, the board of
directors had to develop a consensus on a strategic plan to revive the company.

The Starbucks board engaged in facilitated discussions to gather insights
from all members. These discussions included external stakeholders such as environmental experts and supply chain partners. Through open dialogue, the board

recognized a shared commitment to sustainability and corporate responsibility, aligning with Starbucks' core values.

Board members identified common ground in improving the company's environmental footprint and enhancing community relations as key drivers of long-term growth. The board collaboratively explored various sustainability initiatives, such as ethical sourcing, reducing waste, and investing in renewable energy. They balanced these with financial considerations to ensure viability.

Through iterative discussions and adjustments, the board reached a consensus on a comprehensive sustainability strategy. This strategy included goals like 100 percent ethically sourced coffee and reducing carbon emissions.[56] Starbucks' consensus approach worked for 16 years.

Not bad, but nothing is forever. In April 2024, Starbucks reported a drop in same-store sales for the first time in nearly three years and lower-than-expected profits, leading to a cut in its annual sales forecast.[57] The company has been grappling with weaker demand in its two largest markets, the United States and China.

Former CEO Howard Schultz, who remains one of Starbucks' biggest investors, publicly called for an overhaul of the company's U.S. operations.[58] Activist investor Elliott Investment Management had built a sizable position in Starbucks and had been holding private discussions with Starbucks' management to explore ways to improve the company's stock performance.[59]

The board calmly evaluated the company's position and took quick, decisive action. Within two months it had recruited its targeted CEO directly, without the use of an executive search firm. By August 13, 2024, CEO Laxman Narasimhan was out, and Brian Niccol from Chipotle was in.[60] Time will tell whether the change works as the board expects, but the board quickly reached a definitive consensus and acted decisively to address the situation.

Lesson Worth Learning: Use majority rule only as the last resort

If consensus can't be reached quickly, some boards will resort to majority rule. It may be necessary in some circumstances, but continuing split decisions reflect underlying issues and can result in divisions. Yes, it takes time to build consensus, and yet crises, by their nature, afford little or no time.

The longer a board takes to get up to speed, understand the critical issues, and set direction and policy, the longer it takes to begin executing those initiatives. Advance preparation and decision discipline can help forge consensus quickly when it's most necessary.

An adaptive board should focus on consensus building rather than procedural orthodoxy, which may lead to divisive majority voting. This is especially true with narrow margins; nowhere is this more evident than in the U.S. Supreme Court.

Split decisions on the Supreme Court, typically those decided by a narrow 5–4 margin, often have profound and divisive effects on American society. Split decisions can create contentious legal precedents that reflect deep ideological divides within the Court. For instance, the decision in *Citizens United v. FEC* (2010) allowed unlimited corporate spending in elections, fundamentally altering campaign finance laws and sparking ongoing debate about the influence of money in politics.[61]

Such decisions can lead to inconsistent interpretations of the law, especially when future cases revisit the issues decided by a divided Court. This can create legal uncertainty and instability as different courts and jurisdictions interpret the precedents differently.[62]

Narrowly decided cases often reveal and amplify ideological splits within the Court, leading to perceptions of partisanship. This can erode public trust in the judiciary as an impartial arbiter of the law. For example, the 2024 decision on presidential immunity was seen by many as politically motivated and damaged the Court's reputation for impartiality.[63]

Split decisions in the place of consensus can lead to legislative gridlock, as they often settle contentious issues in a way that one side finds unacceptable. This can make it difficult for Congress to pass laws addressing these issues, especially in a highly polarized political environment.

Narrow decisions often become focal points for future legal challenges and can lead to shifts in legal interpretations as the composition of the Court changes. For instance, the ongoing debates over abortion rights illustrate how narrowly decided cases can be revisited and potentially overturned as new justices bring different perspectives to the bench.

Now imagine that dynamic in a board room that has functioned on majority rule and tolerated multiple split decisions rather than seeking consensus. A new board member is elected. That new board member now has the power to revisit decisions previously made. Nothing is unified. Factions talk to the executive, either reinforcing the current policy or telling it that the policy will be reversed. While there may be matters on which board members feel a need to dissent as a matter of principle, defaulting to such factionalization as a modus operandi rather than seeking consensus is not just sub-optimal but damaging.

The destructive effects of split decisions can be profound and long-lasting. Majority rule should only be considered as a last respite, as continued split decisions can result in factions.

By contrast, an adaptive board should make its best efforts to achieve consensus. Directors can help build consensus by actively listening to the viewpoints of all stakeholders involved in the decision-making process and by paying attention to their concerns, interests, and perspectives without interruption. Consensus is a process that ensures all opinions are heard, resulting in the best decision under the circumstances. Consensus optimizes diverse opinions. (For more on consensus, see Chapter 3, "Conduct the Business of the Board.")

Except for ethical and legal issues, directors should be willing to compromise and be flexible in their approach to finding common ground. After all, no one is 100 percent correct all the time. Each director should be willing to consider alternative solutions that address the needs and interests of the organization as a whole.

Lesson Worth Learning: Don't wait for a crisis to develop decision discipline

> Be quick, not hasty. When crisis strikes, response times are paramount, but a rushed reply can make matters worse. Preparation beforehand will help your team know how to respond with consideration and get ahead of the situation without looking frazzled or fractured.
> *Cyndee Harrison, Principal, Synaptic*

Better and faster direction setting is essential. Disciplined decision-making is a skill that can be practiced, so it becomes second nature. That is a useful ability in a crisis.

It's sort of like an athlete's muscle memory. Batters don't "think" during the 400 milliseconds it takes for a major league fastball to travel from the mound to home plate. During that time, a batter must see the ball coming out of the pitcher's hand, analyze the spin and release point to figure out if it's a fastball or curveball and where the pitch is likely to be as it crosses the plate, and, if the batter chooses, start to swing.[64] That's why athletes rely on training and repetition; if they had to think about the mechanics of pitch recognition and swinging a bat every time, they'd strike out every time.

Thankfully, boards have more time than a batter to make a disciplined decision. Installing a process to make decisions in a disciplined manner, then repeating, refining, and repeating, gives an adaptive board a type of institutional knowledge about what works for it, akin to the muscle memory that a hall-of-fame baseball player develops to hit a fastball. The board needs to agree to institute and practice a disciplined process for exercising its powers and maintain that discipline, especially when time constrained.

Lesson Worth Learning: Adopt a disciplined adaptive governance process

To adapt, these pillars must be interwoven with a disciplined process of constantly improving governance to enable faster organizational adaptation and better decisions. No one thread is sufficient alone. All are needed to weave together adaptive governance.

Successful adaptation to an ever-changing environment depends on the ability to quickly identify important changes in the environment, interpret them, choose how to respond, assess the effects, learn from them, and then continuously adapt.

Accordingly, we have described an adaptive governance process (AGP) that applies to each of a board's five essential powers. It is an evolution of the OODA loop (observe, orient, decide, and act) developed by Air Force Colonel John Boyd for military use.[65] The AGP enables the board to be adaptive. It can and should be continually refined. It is how an adaptive board conducts its business – systematically and with decision discipline.

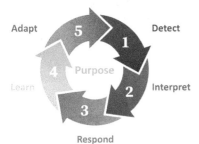

Figure 2.1: Adaptive governance process (AGP).

Figure 2.1 describes an adaptive governance process (AGP) as a cycle. A disciplined approach can help the board fulfill its duty to enable successful adaptation. It enables the board to exercise its governance powers, learn from the results, and then adapt by maintaining, adjusting, or changing the current course to achieve the organizational purpose. It applies to the board's direction and policy setting, approval, oversight, and verification powers.

1. **Detect signals.** Be situationally aware. What's vital, such as customers, competition, economics, social, environmental, financial, regulatory, geopolitical, and technological? What's changing? How fast? What is not changing? Can you detect a weak signal amidst a lot of background noise and data overload? Do you know what to look for? Are you set up to detect asymmetric signals?[iv]

2. **Interpret the signal.** What do they mean for strategic direction, finances, risk, operations, stakeholders, legal/regulatory, and other matters? How quickly can you recognize patterns? Is it a threat, an opportunity, or an unknown? How capable are you of recognizing an asymmetric opportunity or threat? What are the policy implications?

---

iv Symmetric signals are consistent with conventional approaches, i.e., business as usual. An asymmetric signal could be an anomalous or unusual activity or a unique value proposition that attacks a conventional business model from an unknown vector, such as streaming attacking cable television that had previously attacked by over-the-air television.

3. **Respond.** What are your options? What's the least you could do? What's the most? How well prepared are you? In extreme uncertainty, it is far preferable to have a range of response options and the ability to act incrementally because you don't know what will happen.[66] The last thing you want to do is find yourself with few or no viable options.

    Most species have just three response options: flight, fight, or freeze. Unlike other species, people and organizations have choices regarding how they will adapt.

    Whether you have options depends on how well you have prepared and how prepared you can afford to be. What's the least you can do? What's the most you can do? What are the pros and cons? Who decides? Can they decide fast enough? By their nature, boards must decide collectively. That requires time and patience. Conventionally, collective decision-making takes longer. Delaying, dithering, or denying certainly doesn't help. You need to prepare in advance.

4. **Learn.** Assess the effectiveness of your response. How does actual performance compare to expectations? Did it work? Is it too soon to tell? What are the direction and policy implications? Are further changes/refinements required?

5. **Adapt.** Should you stay the course, adjust the course, or change the course?

Rinse, repeat, and continuously improve the adaptive governance process. Remember that "one size fits one!" The exercise of these powers – and how they interact – will vary by organizational purpose, circumstances, and jurisdiction. The rest of this book is about the five essential powers and a disciplined process of adaptive governance.

Lesson Worth Learning: Building consensus can take time, but sudden shifts and crises provide little time for deliberation

Achieving consensus within a board setting is challenging yet essential. Consensus decisions are not about unanimous agreement or majority preference but instead involve building a common understanding, acceptance, and commitment while eliciting and respecting diverse opinions to reach the best possible solution under the circumstances.

Disciplined decision-making is crucial for timely and effective decisions in both crisis and routine situations. Consensus building engenders cooperation, understanding, and positive outcomes in decision-making and problem-solving, particularly when time is limited.

Rapid adaptation relies on the board's commitment to constructive challenge and engagement, open communication, and collaboration to find mutually agreeable solutions. A key role of the chair is to help determine the board's will and maintain decision discipline. In return, a key role of the board is to support the chair in maintaining discipline and supporting the consensus.

> Even when big decisions require us to be quick to avoid being left behind, it's critical that we still have discipline to give our businesses the best chances for success. It's fairly common to make a decision and then wonder how that conclusion was reached. That's a scenario we want to avoid as much as possible.
> *Allan Gray, Director of Purdue University's Center for Food and Agricultural Business*[67]

Discipline in decision-making takes the necessary time to clarify the decision's true objective, consider the options to achieve it, and analyze each alternative thoroughly, especially in time-constrained situations.

The more you do it, the easier it gets. The sooner you start, the better prepared you will be. A disciplined decision process, including the presentation of data and analysis, constructive challenges, policy insights, and consensus-building, may seem deliberate and, therefore, slow. Still, it ultimately saves time and enhances decision effectiveness. Moreover, once such a process becomes the norm and internalized, it remains deliberate, but the time needed to decide speeds up. The result is a robust process that is more effective and faster than an ad hoc one.

Lesson Worth Learning: Focus relentlessly on the essentials

When Steve Jobs returned to Apple in 1997, he dramatically shifted the company's product strategy. He streamlined Apple's product lineup significantly, reducing it from a staggering 350 products to 10 key products within two years. This strategic move allowed Jobs to allocate Apple's resources and talent to what he called the "A-Team," ensuring that the company could dedicate its best people and efforts to each product.[68,69]

In a rapidly changing environment, focusing on essentials enables quicker adaptation to new challenges and opportunities. Directing energy and resources toward the most important issues increases the likelihood of achieving desired outcomes. An unrelenting focus on the essentials requires identifying and prioritizing the most critical elements. It involves recognizing what truly matters and concentrating resources, time, and effort on those key areas. It requires a commitment to eliminating or minimizing distractions and non-essential activities that can divert attention and resources away from the core goals.

It allows organizations to stay agile and responsive. Prioritizing the essentials helps individuals and organizations maintain a clear sense of purpose and direction. It ensures that resources, time, and energy are directed toward what truly matters, preventing distractions and diluting efforts.

By eliminating non-essential tasks or activities, people can accomplish more with less effort and resources, leading to better results. Limited resources – and time, money, and personnel are always limited – can be allocated more effectively when concentrated on essential tasks and goals. Devoting attention to the essentials enables higher quality and excellence.

There is more refinement and improvement when efforts are concentrated on core activities or products. Focusing on the essentials simplifies complex processes or strategies, making them easier to understand and execute, thereby reducing unnecessary complications and potential errors.

Lesson Worth Learning: Challenge constructively, not destructively

> Fix the problem, not the blame.
> *Japanese proverb*

History is littered with the wreckage of organizations whose boards fail to challenge one another and management. Theranos, FTX, WorldCom, HealthSouth, Silicon Valley Bank, Volkswagen, and Wells Fargo, to name just a few.

Adaptive boards constructively challenge underlying assumptions and then welcome solutions. They don't raise objections just to be difficult, nor do they remain passive and silent, sitting there like potted plants.

There are fundamentally two ways to challenge: constructively and destructively. Some directors feel that if they are to fulfill their duties, then they are obliged to confront, criticize, denigrate, and micro-manage. While that may work in rare cases, being disagreeable while disagreeing is generally more of a problem than a solution. The key is to challenge constructively.

Table 2.1 shows some differences in style between constructive vs. destructive challenge.

Table 2.1: Constructive vs. Destructive Challenge.

Challenge	Constructive – Helpful	Destructive – "Gotcha"
Focus	Mission/Values	Personal agendas/factions
Intent	Solution-oriented/Improvement	Problem-oriented
Attitude	Positive	Negative

Table 2.1 (continued)

Challenge	Constructive – Helpful	Destructive – "Gotcha"
Communication	Respectful/Professional/ Impersonal	Disrespectful/Bullying/Adversarial/Personalized attacks
Rationale	Evidence-based/Logical	Personal opinion
Openness	Open-minded/Open questions/Skeptical	Close-minded/Closed questions/Form over substance/ Excessive formality
Approval	Informed consent	Rubber stamping/Go along to get along/Passive or passive aggressive
Situation	Situational	One style fits all
Diversity	Diverse perspectives	Singular/Entrenched/Groupthink
Preparedness	Prepared to discuss	Disorderly/Unprepared/Micro-manage

Passive acceptance is the opposite of constructive challenge. Boards that refuse to challenge one another confuse passive acceptance with collegiality and respect at their own risk. It is always easier to go along rather than to challenge constructively.

Passive acceptance is not appropriate simply because the directors don't know the questions to ask if the issue is a major initiative with significant implications or if they are simply "going along to get along." Collegiality should be an enabler for constructive challenge, not an excuse not to engage.

Passive acceptance as the "modus operandi" can lead to groupthink and the board simply "rubber-stamping" management's recommendations. This can be a particular challenge for organizations with charismatic or controlling chief executives. Passive acceptance can also undermine stakeholder confidence in the board, leading to accusations that management was "managing the board," thereby usurping its role and increasing its liability.

Let's be clear: It is not dysfunctional to have constructive tension and challenge. It is, in fact, essential that it be encouraged. Constructive challenge is the pursuit of clarity and common understanding through respectful and insightful questions. Constructive challenge may be one of the hardest things to do for some boards. Yet adaptive boards are characterized by it.

> In exceptional boardrooms, the intellectual rigor generated by a challenging question is both an accepted norm and a precursor to reaching informed decisions. This is the crucial edge that sets apart boards that lead from boards that follow. Exceptional boards embrace creative tension fully and ensure its presence continually in engaging the management teams they govern.[70]
> *Punit Renjen, former Chairman of the board of Deloitte LLP*

Constructive challenge is an essential component of effective decision-making and corporate governance. It involves questioning, critical thinking, and offering alternative viewpoints to enhance the quality of decisions.

Another reason for constructive challenge, beyond forging a common understanding, is that it helps form the legal and logical basis for the board to prudently and reasonably rely on management's representations and information. Prudence is demonstrated by due diligence and process. In the end, a lack of constructive challenge and professional skepticism hurts everyone.

Caveat: **Clearly, personal style is important.** Personalities are important. Some people are extroverted, others introverted. Some people are better at some things than others. Some may play "gotcha" with their questions; they just can't help themselves. We have all seen examples of both constructive and destructive challenges and differences in personal styles.

In theory, asking board members to stop speaking or behaving in destructive ways should lead them to change. In reality, some people have difficulty disagreeing respectfully. Unfortunately, relying on board members to be constructive simply when asked, regardless of the issue, is unrealistic.

Lesson Worth Learning: Build constructive challenge into board and organizational processes

Processes for constructive challenge should be built into board meetings. Constructive challenge should not depend primarily on the chair, the personalities of directors, and everyone's willingness and ability to challenge one another and convention constructively. Unless the entire board embraces constructive challenge, there is the risk that those who challenge convention can be seen as disruptors and dissidents and may be ostracized and ignored, thus decreasing the board's effectiveness.

Without a systematic, "built-in" process of constructive challenge, it may be very difficult, if not impossible, for individual directors to challenge conventional wisdom. Without challenge, inertia and ensuing decline may be inevitable.

Consider the following ways of building constructive challenge into processes rather than just bolting them on:

- Require planning assumptions to be made explicit.
- Require stage-gate processes (milestones combined with go/no go/modify decisions) in requests for board approval that require critical evaluation before progressing.
- Require the use of critical issue options summaries (discussed in "Set Policy and Direction").
- Require that pros and cons be identified when policy options are considered.

Lesson Worth Learning: Develop constructive critical questions the board should always ask of itself and others

Constructive challenge begins with knowing what questions to ask and how best to ask them. The board and each of its committees should develop a set of questions to provide constructive challenge specific to the circumstances and not just a "check the box" approach. Knowing what questions to ask is a distinguishing characteristic of expertise. Leading governance consultancies (whether law firms, accounting firms, or specialty consultants) frequently publish publications with titles like "20 Questions Boards Should Ask About . . ." They are questions, not answers.

Absent a constructive challenge, a board may miss changes. Staying static in a dynamic world is not usually a winning formula.

The questions are a starting point, not a conclusive list. Look at them critically and then use your judgment to constructively challenge them. Are they appropriate to your situation? How would you change them? Is further information needed before you can ask them?

Constructive challenge is a much-needed tool for deeply understanding issues, sorting out strategic alternatives, and helping boards forge consensus. Much as a Damascus steel sword forged out of many layers is often stronger and more flexible than one crafted from mono-steel, so too is a board decision that results from bringing together diverse opinions. Those opinions are the different layers of steel, and constructive challenge is the forge that aligns them to work together.

Lesson Worth Learning: Decide iteratively in extreme uncertainty

> Test, fail, fix, fly.
> *SpaceX motto*

Miguel de Cervantes wrote, "Don't put all your eggs in one basket," back in 1605[71]. It was good advice then because Don Quixote was facing a changing world. So it's even better now. Don't rely on a single, fixed plan. Instead, make incremental decisions and continuously assess outcomes and options as the situation becomes clearer.

This allows organizations to adjust strategies as needed over time to adapt. Incremental decision-making requires timely, intelligent feedback on essential performance to aid continuous learning and experimentation. It also requires flexibility in delegating authority and resources and quick directional changes. It is a practical approach to "practice makes perfect."

Iterate. Iterate. Iterate. The iterative approach is like real options theory, a framework that allows organizations to make small, incremental decisions. This approach preserves the right to take a set of specific actions in the future but doesn't obligate the company to do so. Meanwhile, the organization gains insight into the potential outcomes, skills, and resources needed to optimize a future course of action.

During the development of SpaceX's reusable Falcon 1 rocket, iterative decision-making in the face of extreme uncertainty played a crucial role.[72] SpaceX faced numerous technical challenges and uncertainties in developing the Falcon 1, their first orbital launch vehicle. The company had to design and test new propulsion systems, control systems, and rocket structures, all while facing intense competition and financial constraints.

SpaceX adopted an iterative approach to development, conducting numerous test flights of the Falcon 1 to gather data and learn from each attempt. These test flights provided valuable insights into the performance of various components and systems, helping engineers identify weaknesses and opportunities for improvement.[73]

After each test flight, SpaceX engineers analyzed the data, identified areas for optimization, and made iterative improvements to the rocket design. This iterative process allowed SpaceX to gradually refine the Falcon 1's performance, reliability, and safety over time.

Simultaneously, SpaceX encountered unexpected challenges and setbacks, such as engine and launch failures. However, instead of being deterred by these setbacks, the company used them as learning opportunities, incorporating lessons learned into future iterations of the Falcon 1.

Through continuous iteration and refinement, SpaceX eventually achieved success with the Falcon 1, becoming the first privately funded company to successfully launch a liquid-fueled rocket into orbit in 2008. This milestone marked a significant achievement in the commercial space industry and paved the way for SpaceX's future successes with the Falcon 9 and other rockets.

SpaceX could have chosen a diametrically opposite methodology. It could have taken years to figure out the (on paper) optimal design and engineering for every part and system of the Falcon 1 and all resources been invested into the singular design judged best. True, it likely would have performed better than the initial first few Falcon 1 test launches, but SpaceX would not have benefited from all the failures to create the ultimate success. In the meantime, the make-it-perfect-all-at-once process would have eaten up resources and time, with no guarantee of getting it right.

Instead, SpaceX chose iterative decision-making in the face of extreme uncertainty. By embracing a test-and-learn approach, continuously improving its designs, and adapting to challenges along the way, SpaceX overcame technical hurdles and achieved success in a highly complex and uncertain environment.

As mentioned previously, one of the most famous models for iterative decision-making is the OODA loop (observe, orient, decide, and act). These four phrases reoccur in a loop, one following the other as the decision-maker adjusts to new environments.

Such iterative approaches provide greater flexibility and agility. Iterative decision-making helps keep options open to mitigate risks associated with uncertainty. Organizations can test assumptions, gather data, and identify potential pitfalls before committing to a full-scale strategy by breaking decisions into smaller, incremental, and manageable steps.

Pivot fast. Iterative approaches allow organizations to pivot quickly in response to unexpected developments, to take advantage of emerging opportunities, and to correct its course as needed. Each iteration offers an opportunity to learn from previous decisions and their outcomes. This learning process contributes to improved decision-making over time and the development of more effective strategies.

Also, deciding iteratively allows organizations to allocate resources incrementally. This conserves resources until a decision's feasibility and viability become clearer, reducing the risk of resource wastage. In uncertain environments, data is valuable. Not all data or expertise resides within the organization; involving external stakeholders in the decision-making process at multiple points can lead to better-informed and more robust decisions. It ensures that diverse perspectives and expertise are considered.

Experiment. Uncertain environments often require experimentation and innovation. Iterative decision-making encourages experimentation and allows organizations to test hypotheses and refine strategies over time without risking too much. The alternative, too often, is that organizations may struggle with overanalyzing and delaying decisions in highly uncertain situations. An iterative approach encourages action and experimentation rather than paralysis by analysis.

Iteration also enables organizations to make decisions based on actual data and feedback in close to real-time rather than relying on assumptions. Iterative decision-making enhances an organization's strategic resilience. It is better equipped to withstand shocks and disruptions because it can adapt and evolve in response to changing circumstances.

Avoid the sunk cost fallacy. One caution about using an incremental, iterative strategy: Iteration allows changes in direction, but only if you treat the amount of time and resources already expended as a good investment in decision-making, not a determinant of the direction your organization should take. As with financial options, real options give you the right, but not the obligation, to continue down any one path. Sooner or later – and the advantage of iteration is that it can be later – you will need to decide.

Unending. The principle of deciding iteratively in uncertainty is a practical and effective approach for navigating complex and uncertain environments. It acknowledges that decision-making is an ongoing process that refines and adjusts as conditions change, ultimately leading to more informed, flexible, and successful outcomes.

Lesson Worth Learning: Take intelligent, necessary risks while minimizing or avoiding unnecessary risks

> All organizations must learn to embrace risk-taking in order to thrive.
> *The Directors and Chief Risk Officers (DCRO) Institute*[74]

Risk is the potential for an unwanted difference between actual and expected performance, regardless of cause. People are usually concerned about downside risk. But sometimes performance can be "too good to be true" (e.g., Madoff, Theranos, FTX).

Enterprises must be risk intelligent.[75] They must take necessary, calculated actions that create potential risk if they are to create, deliver, and capture new value and overcome inertia. They must adapt while avoiding or mitigating unnecessary risks, such as ethical shortcuts and operational failures. Avoiding all risks can lead to missed opportunities, inertia, and stagnation. Innovation demands a willingness to fail but also requires the ability and willingness to learn from it.

SpaceX's decision to develop reusable rockets was a calculated risk. The idea was to create rockets that could be launched, returned to Earth, refurbished, and then relaunched, significantly reducing the cost of access to space. The development of reusable rocket technology has transformed the space industry, making it more sustainable and cost-effective. It required a commitment to innovation, rigorous testing, and perseverance in the face of severe technical challenges.

Smarter. Better. Faster. Risk assessment and management are integral to strategic decision-making. This requires smarter, faster collective decision-making that demands the board's involvement. The board's understanding of the risks of inaction, not just the risks of action, and their role in defining the organization's risk tolerance levels are crucial in preparing to take calculated, necessary risks.

The truth is that all courses of action – and inaction – involve risk. It's a fundamental reality for any organization, whether for-profit or not-for-profit. The general bias, however, is to become comfortable with the risks that we have always taken and, therefore, to underestimate the risk of continuing to do what has worked in the past. This understanding can help us navigate the uncertainties of the business world more effectively.[76]

Shift happens fast. Organizations that remain inert and resist change will eventually become obsolete. Eastman Kodak, once a photography industry pioneer and leader, failed to adapt to the digital photography revolution in the late 20th century and early 21st.

Despite having early research into digital imaging technology as far back as the 1970s, Kodak hesitated to embrace digital photography fully. The company's primary revenue came from selling film and chemicals, and they were hesitant to cannibalize this profitable business. Kodak's reluctance to disrupt its existing film-based business model ultimately led to its downfall. Kodak came face-to-face with a changing environment of its own creation and seemed to close its eyes and wish that it could stop it instead of embracing it and trying to benefit.

Taking intelligent, necessary risks allows organizations to adapt to new market conditions and customer preferences and is essential for a business's long-term sustainability. Calculated risks keep businesses dynamic and forward-thinking. Intelligent risk-taking is essential for driving innovation and fueling growth by embracing new technologies, products, or markets that can lead to competitive advantages and increased market share.

Lesson Worth Learning: Not taking calculated risks is very risky

> There are risks and costs to action.
> But they are far less than the long-range risks of comfortable inaction.
> *John F. Kennedy, 35th U.S. President*

Xerox developed the graphic user interface that Apple later commercialized to become one of the most important companies in the world. In fact, in 1973, Xerox produced a computer, the Xerox Alto. It was the first computer to feature a graphic interface and a mouse. However, Xerox management was focused on copy machines and missed the opportunity to dominate the nascent computer field. In 1979, Apple founder Steve Jobs visited Xerox and incorporated those innovations into Apple's Macintosh computers. The rest is history for Apple and what might have been for Xerox.[77]

New is risky. Seizing the opportunities to enter new markets, whether regional or global, or developing new products or services involves risk.

But as the Xerox example shows, so does ignoring those opportunities. Top talent is often drawn to organizations that encourage innovation and growth. Companies that take calculated risks are more likely to attract and retain talented employees who seek dynamic and challenging work environments.

Organizations willing to take intelligent, necessary risks tend to be more resilient in the face of economic downturns or industry disruptions and more attuned to transformational opportunities. Intelligent risk-taking allows businesses to learn from both successes and failures. It contributes to ongoing improvement and informs decision-making. This principle encourages the development of contingency plans and risk mitigation strategies to address potential adverse outcomes and strengths, weaknesses, opportunities, and threats (SWOT) or other types of analyses to discover opportunities.

Lesson Worth Learning: One size fits one!

We all face a changing world, but how it changes will differ for each organization and individual. The principle of "one size fits one" emphasizes customization and individualization. It recognizes that not all organizations and situations are the same. As organizations vary, so will the solutions, even compared to other organizations in the same situations facing similar challenges. These must be tailored to meet each organization's specific mission, needs, preferences, skills, strengths, resources, circumstances, and culture rather than trying to apply a single solution to all.[78]

Mass customization. Mass customization is a manufacturing and marketing strategy that combines elements of mass production with those of customization. It aims to provide customers with products tailored to their specific preferences and needs while still achieving the efficiency and cost advantages associated with mass production techniques.

The wealth management industry has taken that lesson to heart. Most financial advisors use "model portfolios," pre-set selections of investments put together by a home office but customized for specific issues, such as the investor's age and the level of volatility the investor desires. The financial advisor then adjusts the portfolio within the allowable parameters of both the home office and the individual investor. Goldman Sachs calls this type of mass customization "Sophisticated investing. Made simpler."[79]

The move toward personalized medicine, particularly in pharmaceuticals and healthcare, is also an example of "one size fits one." In personalized medicine, treatments and medications are tailored to individual patients based on their unique genetic makeup, medical history, and specific needs. Some cancer therapies are now designed to target specific genetic mutations in a patient's tumor cells.

These treatments are not a one-size-fits-all solution but are customized to the genetic profile of each patient, offering a more effective and targeted approach to cancer treatment. This approach recognizes that each patient's condition is unique, and treatments should be tailored to address their specific characteristics and needs rather than applying a standardized treatment to all patients. Personalized medicine is made possible through advances in genomics, data analysis, and medical technology, and it represents a shift away from traditional, one-size-fits-all medical treatments.

The way an organization governs should depend on its specific circumstances. One style does not fit all circumstances. Effective governance requires adaptability and the ability to tailor governance approaches to your organization. While boards may have much in common, they are also unique, as are each organization's circumstances.

Lesson Worth Learning: Stakeholder relationships are essential

> When you are dying of thirst, it's too late to start digging a well.
> *Japanese proverb*

Relationships. Relationships. Relationships. Strong relationships with stakeholders (e.g., customers, suppliers, investors, regulators, and partners) can lead to increased support and access to resources. This support can be financial, in the form of investments or loans, or non-financial, such as knowledge sharing and expertise or a more productive regulatory environment.

Building positive relationships with customers can result in higher customer loyalty and brand reputation. Satisfied customers are more likely to return for repeat business, refer others to the company, and provide valuable feedback for improvement.

Employees are key stakeholders, too. A positive workplace culture and good relationships with management can lead to higher employee engagement, productivity, and retention and lower recruitment and training costs. Strong relationships with stakeholders can enhance an organization's reputation and build trust, attracting more customers, partners, and investors.

Collaborative relationships with stakeholders can improve innovation. By working closely with suppliers, partners, and even competitors (in a legal, allowable manner), organizations can access new ideas and technologies. Good stakeholder relationships can also help manage risks. When an organization faces a crisis or challenge, having a network of supportive stakeholders can buy time, and the reservoir of goodwill makes it easier to navigate and recover.

Organizations often need to comply with various regulations and standards. Positive relationships with regulatory bodies can facilitate compliance and reduce regulatory risks. They can also help turn what is often an adversarial relationship into a mutually beneficial one, wherein regulatory exams are viewed not only as compliance but also as a chance to get a knowledgeable third party's opinion about some of your operations.

Positive relationships with local communities and a commitment to social responsibility can enhance an organization's standing. Ultimately, good stakeholder relationships can lead to a loyal customer base, innovative products or services, efficient supply chains, and strong financial backing.

Don't wait. It will be too late if you wait to try to build relationships until you need them. Strong and positive relationships with stakeholders provide competitive advantages, including support, trust, innovation, and resilience in facing challenges. Those relationships can create goodwill (in the colloquial, not accounting sense), an invaluable resource in a crisis. Therefore, organizations should prioritize building and nurturing these relationships as part of their business strategy.

Lesson Worth Learning: Fiduciary duties are full-time responsibilities even though directors are part-time

> Don't be sloppy, and don't be sleazy.[80]
> *Charles Elson, Corporate Director*

Corporate officers and directors are bound by several fiduciary duties to ensure the organization's best interests are served. The two primary fiduciary duties are the duty of care and the duty of loyalty. Volumes have been written about these duties, which are well-known to corporate directors and their legal counsel.

In the context of corporate governance, the fiduciary duties of directors and officers play a vital role in ensuring the stability and integrity of organizations. These duties help prevent corporate misconduct, fraud, and mismanagement, which can have far-reaching economic consequences. Fiduciary duties encourage a focus on long-term sustainability and responsible stewardship of assets. This perspective is critical for achieving financial stability and prosperity over time.

Applying these fiduciary duties can be challenging, as situations often lack clear-cut answers. Therefore, fiduciaries should seek legal counsel to ensure they understand the extent of their legal responsibilities and fulfill their fiduciary duties effectively in any specific uncertain situation. That said, there are courses of action that fulfill fiduciary duties and make boards effective and adaptive.

How can a board fulfill these duties? How can a board develop consensus under conditions of extreme uncertainty? How can they make the highest and best use of their limited time? One answer is through the prudent exercise of the five essential powers common to all boards.

Lesson Worth Learning: Exercise the board's five essential powers to enable organizational success

An adaptive board enables the achievement of its purpose and mission despite extreme uncertainty and inevitable adversity. It does this by relentlessly focusing on the most important issues that a board can address – how it spends its time and exercises its five essential powers – and by adopting a disciplined process for adaptation (Figure 2.2).

Adaptive Governance

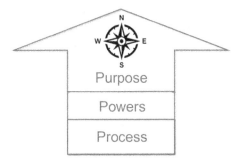

Figure 2.2: Adaptive Governance: Purpose, Powers, and Process of the Board.

Purpose and Mission. Adaptive governance starts with purpose. What have you chosen to accomplish? Is your purpose clear? Your purpose, mission, and your values are your North Star. Governance answers: What are the key decisions? Who gets to make them? Are they aligned?

The purpose of governance is to enable:
- better and faster organizational adaptation through the highest and best use of resources
- better and faster decisions through the highest and best use of time

Five Essential Powers. The board has five essential powers to enable the organization's successful adaptation (Figure 2.3). These powers require a disciplined process to continuously improve the organization's adaptive capabilities.

Figure 2.3: The Five Essential Powers of the Board.

1. Conduct the business of the board and its committees.
Effective board processes focus discussions on strategic priorities; ~build trust; create and demonstrate accountability; identify, assess, and mitigate risks; and promote constructive dialogue, collaboration, and diversity of thought. Corporate culture starts in the boardroom.

2. Set direction and policy.
The goal of strategy is to enable rapid adaptation to achieve the mission despite extreme uncertainty and inevitable adversity. Strategic thinking enables the

board to make informed directional and resourcing choices. The best plans are situationally aware and cross-functional, cutting across the entire enterprise. They define the existential opportunities, challenges, and risks, the resources needed, and what various parts of the organization must do to successfully achieve the mission. Boards oversee the development of key policies that define the expected behavior and choices of the people who lead and work for the organization. Strategy is the steering wheel and the gas pedal. Policies are the brakes.

3. Approve key decisions, then prudently delegate.

Boards cannot delegate responsibility, so they need mechanisms to ensure that the enterprise is being managed within approved policy, and the power to "Approve" is among the most powerful. "Approve" occupies the space on the spectrum between "Set direction and policy" and "Oversee," whereby the board reserves final authority over a decision to itself, but with "Approve" the board is involved at the end of a due diligence process. It also should have approved the process and the criteria for due diligence before considering a recommendation.

4. Oversee the execution of direction within policy.

The power to oversee allows the board to be reasonably assured that its directions are being executed within policy. This includes financial (budget, planning, risk management, reporting) and operational (services/products) oversight, compliance with laws and regulations, and corporate culture. Through its oversight power, boards can track organizational performance trends and policy implications against expectations and quickly understand whether actual performance remains within established policy ranges.

5. Verify the reliability of advice and information before trusting.

Consistent and repeated verification builds trust and helps prevent fraud, mismanagement, and unethical behavior. It creates an environment and context where trust flourishes as verifications consistently prove the board's and management's trustworthiness.

Together, these five essential powers are interdependent. They help directors act prudently and demonstrate it when required. The next five chapters dive deep into how these powers work, how they should work, and what happens when they're not used properly.

As mentioned at the outset, despite the vast literature on management and governance, there is no comprehensive framework for board governance, so we developed one. Think of the five essential powers of the board as the pillars of governance. These are the powers of every board to enable organizational adaptation.

Adaptive governance framework. Figure 2.4 shows the five essential powers interwoven with the 5 steps of an adaptive governance process, just like the warp and weft of a fabric. This combination provides a 5x5 adaptive governance frame-

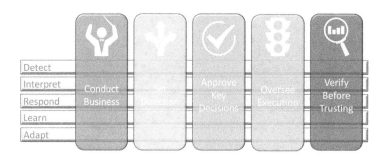

Figure 2.4: The 5 x 5 adaptive governance framework (AGF).

work which presents a way to better understand and exercise the board's powers, combined with a disciplined adaptation process that gives the organization flexibility and strength to achieve its purpose.

Throughout this book, we will discuss each of these five essential powers in the context of the adaptive governance framework. Let's start with the power of the board and its committees to "conduct business."

Conduct

There's no shortage of remarkable ideas,
what's missing is the will to execute them.
Seth Godin, American Author, and former dot com Business Executive

Chapter 3
Conduct the business of the board

1. Do we have a high-performing culture that promotes value creation, ethical behavior, transparency, and accountability?

- Inspire people.
- Constructively engage employees.
- Diversity beats groupthink.
- Catch them doing it right!
- Embed ethical behavior.
- Say what you mean. Mean what you say. Don't be mean about it. Be consistent.

2. Do our board dynamics enable consensus building and make the highest and best use of everyone's time?

- Adaptive boards create processes that encourage effective and efficient dynamics for decision-making and consensus-building.
- The board needs its own change management processes.
- The board must innovate. Conventional governance processes have not kept pace with the rate of change.
- Agenda setting is strategic.
- Decision discipline is essential, especially when there is little time.
- Executive sessions don't involve executives
- *Robert's Rules of Order* may have outlived their utility.
- Consensus is better than majority rule, even though it may take longer.
- The role of the chair is to determine the will of the board.
- Conventional board reporting, information sharing, and board books/portals often end up data-rich but insight-poor.
- Constructive challenge serves everyone.

3. Do our committee assignments and board members' expertise effectively address the organization's specific issues and challenges?

- The board's expertise and skills, as well as the committee structure and membership, should align with the organization's mission and strategic plan.

4. Do we effectively plan director succession, including the nomination and compensation processes?

- Director succession is strategic.

5. Do we do a good job of selecting, evaluating, compensating, and planning for the succession of the CEO?

- The selection, compensation, and planning for the CEO's succession are among the board's most important decisions.
- Know what you need. Be patient and be willing to compromise but recognize that you can't turn a canary into an eagle if an eagle is what you need.
- Succession planning matters.
- Evaluating – Just do it! Broaden your focus. Look ahead.
- When compensating, hire a specialist.

https://doi.org/10.1515/9783111344027-003

Introduction

Breathing is not the purpose of life, but life would be impossible without it. Any difficulties in breathing decrease one's ability to live fully. Conducting the board's business is like breathing; it's not the purpose of the board (which is driving performance with acceptable risk), but it would be impossible without it. Any difficulty in conducting business puts creating, capturing, delivering, and preserving value at risk.

The way a board conducts its business is essential because:
- Clear agendas and structured meetings lead to efficient decision-making.
- Concentrating on strategic priorities helps the board use its time effectively and efficiently.
- Aligning board discussions and decisions with the company's strategy guides management toward long-term goals.
- Transparent decision-making processes demonstrate accountability to all stakeholders, including executives, employees, shareholders, and regulators.
- Robust processes help identify, assess, and mitigate risks, safeguarding the organization's interests.

Most importantly, the way a board conducts its business sets the tone for board dynamics and corporate culture. Respectful and inclusive board processes promote constructive dialogue, collaboration, and diversity of thought, leading to better decision-making and a more positive boardroom environment.

Conducting the business of the board applies to all its powers to set, approve, oversee, and verify.

This chapter asks five critical questions and offers answers based on lessons worth learning from the successes and failures of others about the ways a board conducts its business:
1. Do we have a high-performing culture that promotes ethical behavior, transparency, and accountability?
2. Do our board dynamics enable consensus building and make the highest and best use of everyone's time and talents?
3. Do our committee assignments and board members' expertise effectively address the organization's specific issues and challenges?
4. How well do we plan director succession, including the nomination and compensation processes?
5. How well do we select, evaluate, compensate, and plan for the succession of the CEO?

1 Do we have a high-performing culture that promotes ethical behavior, transparency, and accountability?

A culture is not a set of beliefs. It's a set of actions. What you do is who you are.
It's not what you believe, it's not what you think, it's not what you tweet, it's not the values
you that you have. That's not who you are. Who you are is what you do.
The behaviors are the culture, not the values.
Ben Horowitz, Cofounder and General Partner at the venture capital firm
Andreessen Horowitz[81]

One of the board's most important roles is to instill a high-performing culture that promotes ethical behavior, transparency, and accountability. There must be a strong "tone at the top" as well as at the middle and bottom.

Table 3.1 provides some of the main characteristics of a high-performing, ethical culture. The board should instill these behaviors through their actions and regularly assess the extent to which these are present in the organization. As the following pages demonstrate, their presence or absence can have significant impacts on organizational performance and risk.

Table 3.1: Characteristics of High-Performing Ethical Cultures.

Inspire People	Everyone understands "why."
	"True north" is clear.
	Relentless focus on results.
	Non-stop improvement, learning, and experimentation.
Constructively Engage Employees	Genuine concern for employee well-being.
	Diversity beats groupthink.
	Catch them doing it right.
Embed Ethical Behavior	Ethical behavior is the cornerstone of trust.
	Bad news must travel fast. Self-reporting is key.
	A culture of ethics and transparency is attractive to top talent.
	No blind eye. Ethics have lasting effects.
	Ethical organizations are often more resilient in times of crisis.
	If it was easy, everyone would do it.

Lesson Worth Learning: Inspire people

> The most important thing is to try and inspire people
> so that they can be great in whatever they want to do.
> *Kobe Bryant, basketball legend*

Everyone needs to understand why. Effective and inspirational leadership sets a positive example and motivates employees. It can inspire selflessness and a commitment to achieving the mission. Good leadership tells everyone how; great leadership inspires with why.

A culture that encourages innovation, adaptability to change, and a willingness to take calculated, necessary risks tends to suffer fewer "preventable surprises." Constant change in the environment may or may not require corresponding changes in strategy, business model, tactics, and/or talent; these need to be conscious choices. Today's world is too fluid and too complex for any organization to "set it and forget it." An adaptive culture bends and rebounds when stressed, while an inert culture breaks easily and often.

True north is clear. Adhering consistently to core principles and values, even in challenging situations, goes to mission. Having a true north for any organization is a great way to align the entire organization. When CEO Kathryn Minshew first co-founded The Muse, a recruitment agency, one of the first big corporate customers who signed up for The Muse's recruiting services started to abuse the agency's junior staff.

As a recruitment agency that tries to place employees in companies that "fit your life and goals," Minshew knew just how much of an issue that was. What she did sent a signal to all her employees. She fired the client, even though her company was young and needed the cash. "I didn't realize how relieved my team was – and how much they appreciated it – until after it was all done," she said. "I think backing your team in situations like that is really important, but it's not always easy. Especially when you're early stage."[82]

Relentless focus on results. A relentless focus on strategic goals and objectives keeps everyone aligned on what's important. When well designed, metrics are a great way of aligning everyone with the mission and breaking down the mission into achievable parts. It is not just what is achieved but also how it is achieved.

Non-stop improvement, learning, and experimentation. Waves of productivity made possible by technology or other improvements, such as computerization and digitization, drove productivity improvements for virtually every enterprise at the end of the 20th century.

Artificial intelligence (AI) has the potential to do the same a quarter of the way into the 21st century. On a day-to-day basis, a culture that encourages constant improvement of efficiency and productivity and employee empowerment makes employees feel safe sharing new ideas and taking calculated risks to achieve organizational goals.

A commitment to learning and development, with opportunities for skill-building and growth, also creates adaptive resiliency against obsolescence. This applies equally to directors.

Board members are nominated for their skills and experiences. But those have all been achieved in the past; in a changing world, those skills need continuous updating. While it may be evident that board members need to keep up in technology areas like cyber-security and AI, where change is constant, this is also necessary in fields such as marketing, finance, and geopolitics. In fact, we can't think of a single experience set that, when held constant for any extended period, will remain up to date.

Lesson Worth Learning: Constructively engage employees

A constructive, collaborative, and cooperative environment encourages cross-functional teamwork. High levels of constructive employee engagement, satisfaction, and a sense of ownership in the organization's success are both input into and a contemporaneous measure of a performance culture.

High-performing organizations engage their workforce through vision, leadership, and two-way communication. Workers who feel engaged, valued, and included innovate and engage in new value-enhancing behaviors, creating a virtuous upward spiral.

Google is an example of collaboration. It is also known as a creative workplace.[83] That's not an accident. Anyone who has ever participated in producing a play, opera, concert, or movie intuitively understands how collaboration makes the ultimate production far superior to anything an actor, director, set designer, stage manager, or anyone else could have produced on their own. It turns out that bouncing ideas off one another combines the benefits of the above attributes – transparent communication, diversity and inclusion, innovation, etc. – and supercharges them.

Genuine concern for employee well-being. Concern for the well-being of employees and initiatives promoting work–life balance and a healthy workplace helps attract the best workers. Ford Motor Company's "2024 Trend Report" found that more than half of all workers globally would trade 20 percent of their compensation for better balance. "It shocked us . . . A 20% pay cut is a big deal," said Ford's Jennifer Brace, who also noted that younger workers were even more willing to make that trade.[84]

Of course, different people react to different positive incentives, but virtually everyone reacts negatively to being dehumanized. People give their best to leaders whom they believe care about them.

Lesson Worth Learning: Diversity beats groupthink

> The leader, or the guide, is there to help the team make the right decisions. They don't actually lead in a very direct hierarchical way. As an individual within that group, your leadership ability is how you influence and address the group. Individuals have to step up, and that can be in anything, not just climbing. People have different styles. There's definitely a responsibility for them to step up and contribute.
>
> The teams that have been a disaster, and I mean a real disaster, is when you get a group that is actually more similar than dissimilar. I think the least successful expeditions I've been on have been when they've been predominantly similar because they assume too much in terms of others' understanding.
>
> Successful teams come from lots of different backgrounds. Because we've had no common language, there's lots of room for disagreements. When you look at the individuals going in, you ask yourself, 'Is this really going to work?'
>
> So, you have to spend the time to figure it out, and you can't make the assumption that everyone is on the same page. You have to develop a common understanding. You have to work at it. You have to really watch and read each other, and you become very aligned that way. That's what leads to a very, very successful expedition team![85]
>
> *Esther Colwill, the first woman to climb Mt. Everest and the world's seven highest mountains*

Embracing diversity and inclusion in a workforce or team that reflects varied backgrounds and perspectives allows for the diversity of viewpoints that form a consensus to be as robust as possible. Let us be very clear – consensus is not groupthink.

In groupthink, everyone thinks the same because they have been exposed to similar contexts and think similarly. So, even if there are 20 people in the room, you don't get the benefit of 20 independent thinkers; instead, you get one set of thoughts 20 times. By contrast, consensus takes the best of 20 different sets of thoughts and forges them into a stronger, coherent path for action.

Lesson Worth Learning: Catch them doing it right!

Doing it right has to make a difference because it's usually harder. Most managers are familiar with progressive discipline, a structured approach used by organizations to address employee performance or behavior issues and deter undesirable performance.

The purpose of progressive discipline is to:
- **Correct Behavior**: Encourage employees to improve their performance or behavior through a structured approach.
- **Provide Clear Expectations**: Clearly communicate the standards and expectations for performance and behavior.

- **Offer Opportunities for Improvement**: Give employees multiple chances to correct their behavior before more severe actions are taken.
- **Ensure Fairness and Consistency**: Apply a consistent and fair process for all employees, ensuring that discipline is not arbitrary.
- **Document Issues**: Create a record of disciplinary actions taken, which can be useful for future reference, or in legal situations.
- **Protect the Organization**: Help maintain a productive and respectful work environment and protect the organization from potential legal issues.
- **Support Development**: Assist employees in their professional development by identifying areas for improvement and providing support to address them.
- **Maintain Morale**: Address issues consistently and fairly to help maintain overall team morale and trust in management.

Disciplining poor performers sets a standard, encouraging all employees to meet or exceed expectations. It also helps to ensure that all employees are held to the same standards and promotes a sense of fairness and equity within the team. Disciplining poor performers emphasizes accountability, encouraging employees to take responsibility for their work. Discipline can also boost team morale by showing that everyone is expected to contribute equally.

Disciplinary actions clarify expectations and provide a clear framework for acceptable behavior and performance. Constructive discipline can motivate poor performers to improve and develop their skills. Maintaining high standards helps protect the organization's reputation and ensures consistent quality of work.

While progressive discipline is necessary and appropriate for accountability, it works best when combined with progressive motivation (Table 3.2).

Table 3.2: Five Steps in Progressive Discipline and Motivation.

Progressive discipline when you catch people doing it wrong	Progressive motivation when you catch people doing it right
1. Verbal warning	1. Verbal praise
2. Written warning	2. Written recognition/appreciation
3. Probationary period	3. Cross-training, job rotation
4. Suspension or fines	4. Pay increases and bonuses
5. Termination	5. Promotion

Research shows that people are motivated to act by rewards; rewards inspire good choices, while punishment merely deters bad ones.[86] Less well-known and practiced is progressive motivation for when people are "caught" doing things right. The benefits of catching people doing things right include:

- **Boosts morale**: Recognizing positive actions enhances employee morale and job satisfaction.

- **Encourages positive behavior**: Positive reinforcement encourages repeat behavior and sets a standard for others to follow.
- **Increases motivation**: Recognition and praise motivate individuals to maintain and improve their performance.
- **Builds confidence**: Acknowledging achievements builds confidence and self-esteem in employees.
- **Enhances productivity**: When people feel appreciated, they are more likely to be productive and engaged in their work.
- **Strengthens relationships**: Positive recognition builds a supportive and collaborative work environment.
- **Improves retention**: Employees who feel valued are more likely to stay with the company, reducing turnover rates.
- **Cultivates a positive culture**: Regular recognition of good work contributes to a positive organizational culture.

While the board is not involved in the organization's day-to-day management, it should keep a hand on its pulse and treat executives in a similar way.

Lesson Worth Learning: Embed ethical behavior

> Integrity is doing the right thing, even when no one is watching.
> *Unknown, but often misattributed to C. S. Lewis*

There is a reason that "tone at the top" is a cliché. Because it's true. How board members act and treat one another, the executive team, the staff of the organization, and others sets the tone for the entire organization. Ethical violations are not only morally troubling, but they are bottom-line costly, increasing litigation costs, fines, reputational damage, lost sales, product recalls, supply chain disruptions, shareholder lawsuits and settlements, and brand value destruction.

Ethical behavior is the cornerstone of trust. When employees, customers, shareholders, and other stakeholders trust that the organization and its leadership act with integrity, it enhances the organization's reputation and credibility. It also reduces costs and increases effectiveness and efficiency.

As Nobel Laureate Economist Kenneth Arrow wrote:

> Trust is an important lubricant of a social system. It is extremely efficient; it saves a lot of trouble to have a fair degree of reliance on other people's word. Unfortunately, this is not a commodity that can be bought very easily. If you have to buy it, you already have some doubts about what you have bought.[87]

Ethical behavior is a component – perhaps the key component – to earning trust.

Ethical behavior and a culture of compliance help organizations avoid legal and regulatory pitfalls. Organizations that fail to adhere to ethical standards and regulations may face severe legal consequences, fines, penalties, and reputational damage. Indeed, federal sentencing guidelines try to encourage ethical behavior, providing reduced penalties for those companies that self-report violations and have robust ethics and compliance policies and procedures.

"Bad news must travel fast," says Norman Augustine, former CEO of Lockheed Martin and the American Red Cross.[88] Airline safety offers an excellent example of why this is so. As of this writing, no major airline in the U.S. has had a crash in almost 15 years despite flying 100 million miles and 10 billion passengers. "High-level safety officials . . . and leaders of the U.S. industry's main trade group reported that if accident rates remained the same (as in the 1990s) while global passenger traffic continued growing at projected rates on average, there would be at least one major jet crash a week by 2015."[89]

Things needed to change, and fast. Among the industry improvements was a change that allowed bad news to be shared widely and quickly. Penalties for self-reporting safety issues and errors were removed, self-reporting increased, and crashes were prevented.[90] Unfortunately, airplane manufacturers such as Boeing are a different story.

In early July 2024, Boeing pled guilty to one count of "conspiracy to defraud the United States."[91] This related to two fatal crashes involving the 737 MAX's Maneuvering Characteristics Augmentation System (MCAS). The company was found to have prioritized production speed and cost-saving efforts over thorough safety evaluations.

Boeing violated the terms of a 2021 deferred prosecution agreement by failing to implement an adequate compliance program to prevent and detect fraud. Reports suggested an entrenched perspective at Boeing that production speed and cost-saving efforts were given precedence over detailed safety evaluations. At Boeing, bad news did not travel fast. Clearly, culture matters.

A culture of ethics and transparency is attractive to top talent. One study found that employees were virtually unanimous in saying that ethics matter; some 94 percent said working for a company with good ethics was either "critical" or "important." Perhaps more impressively, almost as many – 82 percent – said they would be willing to be paid less to work at a company with high ethical standards. In addition, employees are also more likely to stay with an organization that aligns with their values.[92]

An ethical culture promotes responsible performance risk management since cutting corners is discouraged. Organizations that prioritize ethical behavior are more likely to identify and address risks early and reduce the potential for costly crises and reputational damage. Of course, just having ethics policies in writing doesn't necessarily equate to a truly ethical culture.

No blind eye. The board of Enron waived its ethics rules to allow CFO Andrew Fastow to be on the other side of deals that the company was making with a private partnership.[93] Those private partnerships and the loose ethical culture that allowed them were major causes of the scandal that saw Enron implode from being the seventh largest company in the U.S. to bankrupt in just over a year.

The very idea that your CFO would suggest creating a structure wherein his interests could be antithetical to that of the organization should have been a very bright flashing red light warning the board to examine the corporate culture. That they turned a blind eye to it says a lot about why the company became synonymous with corporate fraud and bankruptcy.

Ethics have lasting effects. Ethical conduct and transparency contribute to the long-term business sustainability of an organization. Repeated ethical behavior builds enduring relationships with stakeholders, maintains customer loyalty, and may give suppliers or donors (at non-profits) confidence to stick with the organization through the inevitable down periods.

In good times, it can result in increased investment, stronger partnerships, reduced costs, better terms, and less employee turnover. Trustworthy ethical organizations may even have their choice of better business partners, as most prefer to do business with those they perceive as trustworthy and responsible.

When ethical considerations are at the forefront of decision-making processes, leaders are more likely to make choices that align with the organization's long-term interests. Ethics tend to prevent private agendas (e.g., Enron's special purpose vehicles) and therefore reinforce alignment to the organization's mission – its "true north."

The media loves bad news. Today's boards need to deal with another contextual issue: The internet loves accusations of ethical lapses, so severe reputational damage occurs rapidly. In 2018, 39 percent of all forced CEO departures were due to scandal, up from just 10 percent ten years earlier.[94]

Not only are ethical organizations less likely to suffer such damage, but when it does happen, they are better equipped to respond and recover. They can show what they have done.

Ethical organizations are often more resilient in times of crisis. A culture of transparency and accountability facilitates crisis management and recovery efforts, helping the organization bounce back from setbacks. According to the LRN Benchmark of Ethical Culture, companies with the strongest ethical cultures outperform – by approximately 40 percent – across all measures of business performance, including levels of customer satisfaction, employee loyalty, innovation, adaptability, and growth.[95]

To embed ethical behavior, develop and communicate a comprehensive code of conduct that outlines the organization's values, ethical principles, and expected behaviors for all employees to follow. Demonstrate ethical behavior starting from the top leadership levels. When leaders consistently model ethical conduct, it sets a positive tone for the entire organization and reinforces the importance of ethical behavior.

Offer regular training sessions and educational programs on ethics and compliance to ensure that employees understand the organization's ethical standards and know how to apply them in their daily work. Create systems for monitoring and enforcing ethical standards, such as whistleblower hotlines, anonymous reporting channels, and disciplinary measures for misconduct.

Create internal newsletters highlighting employees' ethical behaviors and have top management or the board comment on the situation. Conversely, hold employees accountable for their actions and promptly address ethical violations.

Clear expectations, individual accountability, and a culture of responsibility for one's actions and outcomes are companions to open communication. People need to be accountable for both problems and successes, and others need to know that their compatriots are held accountable for their actions.

If it was easy, everyone would do it. Nothing in today's world works easily or in a straight line. Transparent and open communication channels encourage collaboration, feedback, and idea sharing. If we've seen one constant in high-performing enterprises, it's that news – especially bad news – travels quickly and without blame attached. Norm Augustine would be pleased.

Getting news quickly transmitted, understood, analyzed, and catalyzed is situational awareness in action. It enables problems to be solved and puts an organization back on course. Open communication enables organizations to practice continuous improvement . . . and discontinuous improvement when needed.

Encourage open communication and empower employees to speak up about ethical concerns or dilemmas they encounter. Foster a culture where employees feel safe raising questions, reporting misconduct, and seeking guidance without fear of retaliation. Creating a culture of ethical behavior, transparency, and accountability is both a moral principle and a strategic imperative. Here are two examples of companies: one that did it right and the other that did not.

Patagonia. Privately owned Patagonia proudly wears its ethics on its sleeve (no doubt a responsibly sourced sleeve made from recycled materials). Patagonia's commitment to environmental and social responsibility and its workforce aligns with the outdoor clothing and gear retailer's day-to-day business and contributes to its business success. The company understands this well.

In 2022, as it approached its 50th anniversary, Patagonia decided to revamp its core values statement (Table 3.3).[96]

You may or may not like Patagonia's core values, but there's no doubt about the culture the company is trying to foster. Everything is aligned. And it is mainly consistent in practice and on paper. The company expresses its concern for its workforce, concretizes it into specific actions, and reminds everyone that Patagonia

Table 3.3: Patagonia's Core Values.

Quality	Build the best product, provide the best service, and constantly improve everything we do. The best product is useful, versatile, long-lasting, repairable, and recyclable. Our ideal is to make products that give back to Earth as much as they take.
Integrity	Examine our practices openly and honestly, learn from our mistakes, and meet our commitments. We value integrity in both senses: that our actions match our words (we walk the talk), and that all of our work contributes to a functional whole (our sum is greater than our parts).
Environmentalism	Protect our home planet. We're all part of nature, and every decision we make is in the context of the environmental crisis challenging humanity. We work to reduce our impact, share solutions, and embrace regenerative practices. We partner with grassroots organizations and frontline communities to restore lands, air, and waters to a state of health; to arrest our addiction to fossil fuels; and to address the deep connections between environmental destruction and social justice.
Justice	Be just, equitable, and antiracist as a company and in our community. We embrace the work necessary to create equity for historically marginalized people and reorder the priorities of an economic system that values short-term expansion over human well-being and thriving communities. We acknowledge painful histories, confront biases, change our policies, and hold each other accountable. We aspire to be a company where people from all backgrounds, identities, and experiences have the power to contribute and lead.
Not bound by convention – innovate	Do it our way. Our success – and much of the fun – lies in developing new ways to do things.

designs its clothing for fun, active pursuits while valuing the natural capital of the planet.

According to Patagonia's HR chief, turnover at its corporate office is only about 4 percent, compared to the U.S. national average of 27 percent. A total of 97 percent of Patagonia employees say it's a great place to work, compared to the average American company, where only 57 percent of employees say that.[97]

Table 3.4 shows what Patagonia does to "walk the talk."

Table 3.4: Patagonia's Values in Action.

Patagonia Inc.	
Ceaselessly create value	
Clear vision and values	Patagonia actively works to reduce its environmental footprint through using recycled materials, reducing water usage, and promoting responsible manufacturing processes.[98] Perhaps most pointedly, Patagonia famously declines any orders for co-branded products – a major business line – from companies the firm deems to be "ecologically damaging," like fossil fuel companies and some financial firms.[99]
Long-term view	Patagonia's founder, Yvon Chouinard, often emphasizes the importance of values-aligned decision-making and long-term sustainability. His vision: "Patagonia is trying to build a company that could last 100 years." Patagonia was the first California corporation to be certified as a Benefit Corporation in 2012, aligning its corporate form and corporate governance with its long-term aspirations and mission statement.[100]
Adherence to core principles	Patagonia designs and manufactures products with a focus on longevity, quality, and repairability. The "Worn Wear" program encourages customers to buy used Patagonia gear, and the company provides repair services to extend the life of products and reduce waste.[101]
Inspire people and embed ethical behavior	
Charitable giving	Not only does Patagonia donate 1 percent of its sales to efforts to preserve and restore the environment, but it has created the "1 percent for the Planet" initiative, which is open to other businesses. It has donated more than $140 million through early 2024.[102]
Activism and advocacy	Patagonia uses its platform to advocate for environmental and social causes. The company has taken public stances on issues like climate change, public lands protection, and sustainability.[103]
Transparency	Patagonia is open and transparent about its business practices, sustainability efforts, and challenges. The company publishes its environmental and social impact on its website, detailing its progress and areas for improvement. This transparency builds trust with customers, employees, suppliers, and other stakeholders.[104]
Fair labor practices	The company emphasizes fair labor practices and has adopted a strong supply chain responsibility program. Patagonia conducts audits of its suppliers to improve labor conditions. It aims to ensure fair wages and safe working environments as well as to combat child labor and modern slavery.[105]

Table 3.4 (continued)

Patagonia Inc.	
Constructive Employee Engagement	
Employee well-being	Patagonia closes all its stores for a week between Christmas and New Year's Day: "We're out for the holidays so our employees can spend time with loved ones and chase some much-needed fun. We'll be back on January 2nd, hopefully with sore legs and a few great stories."[106] Patagonia also offers employees paid time off for environmental volunteer work and encourages a work–life balance that aligns with its values.
Accountability and measuring impact	The company uses a data-driven approach to help make informed decisions and improve its ethical practices. Here is an example of how granular Patagonia's data are: "For Spring 2024, 98% of our styles use recycled materials. Switching to recycled allowed us to avoid 8,500 metric tons of CO_2e [carbon dioxide equivalent], enough to power more than 1,070 homes for one year in the United States, according to the EPA."[107]

Wells Fargo & Company. Of course, you can also embed or passively tolerate unethical behavior. That usually leads to value destruction.

Wells Fargo & Company is an American multinational financial services firm that operates in 35 countries and has more than 70 million customers worldwide. The Financial Stability Board recognizes it as a systemically important financial institution.[108]

From 2002 to 2016, to meet aggressive sales goals, Wells created millions of false accounts and reaped hundreds of millions in fees from them. Often, customers were unaware. In other cases, bank employees simply lied to them.

Not only did bank management turn a blind eye to the illegal and unethical situation, but it encouraged it by "pressuring employees to meet unrealistic sales goals that led thousands of employees to provide millions of accounts or products to customers under false pretenses or without consent, often by creating false records or misusing customers' identities," according to the U.S. Department of Justice.[109]

> Many of these practices were referred to within Wells Fargo as "gaming." Gaming practices included forging customer signatures to open accounts without authorization, creating PINs to activate unauthorized debit cards, moving money from millions of customer accounts to unauthorized accounts in a practice known internally as "simulated funding," opening credit cards and bill pay products without authorization, altering customers' true contact information to prevent customers from learning of unauthorized accounts . . .[110]

The U.S. Department of Justice described the result of that pressure in its announcement of the $3 billion fine: "The Community Bank's onerous sales goals and accompanying management pressure led thousands of its employees to engage in unlawful conduct – including fraud, identity theft, and the falsification of bank records – and unethical practices to sell products of no or little value to the customer."[111] The impact on the bank was huge (Table 3.5).

Table 3.5: Consequences of Wells Fargo Sales Practices.

Financial	It paid a $3 billion fine on top of a $185 million settlement. Between the January 2018 high of $322 billion and October 2020, market capitalization crashed by $234 billion – a loss of almost 73 percent.[112]
Internal	Some 5,300 employees were fired, 1 in every 50. More than 500 were bank branch managers or even more senior officials. Former CEO John Strumpf lost his job and was forced to pay $175 million personally to settle charges. The board also clawed back a record $180 million.[113] Between 2016 and 2021, there have been four CEOs.[114] CFO James Strother was later fined $3.5 million by the Office of the Comptroller of the Currency (OCC).[115]
External	For years after, Wells operated under Federal Reserve supervision that limited its growth and then a deferred prosecution agreement.[116] Increased regulatory scrutiny also incurs increased compliance costs.[117]
"Soft" impacts	Wells Fargo's reputation tanked. In just two months, the number of people who viewed the bank positively crashed from 60 percent to 24 percent, while negative perceptions soared from 15 percent to 52 percent.[118] Prospective customers stayed away.

As the Comptroller of the Currency Thomas Curry said, "This is a culture issue. You cannot, as a bank, abuse your customers' trust."[119] The high-profile fake account scandal didn't just expose a flawed compliance system but also a toxic corporate culture that violated virtually every rule of how to create a positive culture. The bad news did not travel fast; people were not held accountable; short-termism was rampant; and employees were not valued.

The scandal spotlighted cultural problems that Wells had kept in the dark. Exposed and examined, Wells' culture was incompatible with either ethics or long-term sustainability. Failure was an inevitability. At Wells, however, instead of taking accountability and control, they blamed the lower-level employees who had been responding to the sales culture and incentive. CFO John Shrewsberry told a New York audience that "it was really more at the lower end of the performance scale, where people apparently were making bad choices to hang on to their job."[120]

CEO John Strumpf initially denied any systemic problem and asserted "there was no incentive to do bad things." He was tone-deaf at the top. *The Wall Street Journal* headline on that article read, "Wells Fargo CEO Defends Bank Culture, Lays Blame with Bad Employees." The attempt to use the "few bad apples" defense was itself a rotten apple.

As Melissa Arnoff, the head of the reputation practice at communications consultant Levick, told *The Washington Post*, "Yes, it is the employees who created the accounts. But there's something wrong with the internal system if this went on for five years and involved at least 5,300 employees."[121] As two commentators wrote at the time, corporate leaders should assume responsibility, execute accountability, and earn their compensation and stakeholder trust by saying the buck stops with them (Table 3.6).[122]

Table 3.6: Causes of Wells Fargo Sales Practice Failures.

Short-termism	Putting short-term profits above long-term business sustainability. At the heart of the scandal were aggressive – actually unobtainable – sales goals for cross-selling. The only way for bank employees to meet those goals was to cheat, so that's what they did.
The customer is the mark not "the king"	Customers had their personal information stolen, their credit ratings affected, their cars lost, and their homes foreclosed.
Bad news didn't travel at all.	The culture at Wells Fargo did not appreciate or even tolerate whistleblowers. One bank manager, who had been promoted ten times in a decade, was fired three weeks after she called the ethics hotline to complain about the sales practices.[123] Officials within the bank first noticed the problem in 2002. By 2004 an internal investigator called it "a growing plague." Yet the cancer was allowed to grow for more than a decade.[124]
Lack of constructive challenge	Blinded by profits. The board seemingly did not question or challenge the results that were "too good to be true." As a result, there were still no changes in the bank's culture.[125]
Lack of a "true north" combined with bad leadership.	CEO John Strumpf admitted that he had been having weekly calls about the issue with Carrie Tolstedt, the bank official in charge of the program, for years. Instead of firing her, or just stopping the deceptive practices, he effectively doubled down. Not only did he allow her to retire in 2016, but this is what he said of her at that time. She was, he said, a "principled" banker. He credited her with "reinforcing a strong risk culture."[126]
No accountability	CEO John Strumpf said he never thought of firing Carrie Tolstedt. That fits perfectly with the lack of accountability elsewhere in senior management and at the board.

Where was the board?

It strains credulity to think that the Wells Fargo Board wasn't aware of the situation. However, it did not act to end it. Instead, it seems that directors were willfully blinded by the short-term profits and the "sunny disposition of the CEO."[127]

Were the strong profits pre-scandal too good to be true? The board wasn't asking the right questions. Internal investigators questioned the practice 12 years before the scandal; why did no one pay attention? In 2002, an internal report to the Wells Fargo audit committee identified "gaming" as a problem.[128]

In 2005, the board was informed that most of the calls (more than 700) to the ethics hotline and most firings were related to sales practices. The *Los Angeles Times* reported on the bank's aggressive sales practices in 2013.[129] Apparently, the board found out that 5,300 bankers were fired for practices related to the scandal, including pressure to hit unrealistic goals, only after the settlement with authorities hit the news.[130]

Instead, the company's 2013 annual report, signed by the board, reassured shareholders about risk management, stating:

> Our risk culture also depends on the "tone at the top" set by our Board, CEO, and Operating Committee members. Through oversight of the three lines of defense, the Board and the Operating Committee are the starting point for establishing and reinforcing our risk culture and have overall and ultimate responsibility for oversight of our risks, which they carry out through committees with specific risk management functions.[131]

In 2014, management told the board that the sales were a "noteworthy" risk.[132] An internal report post-scandal found that directors should have moved faster to fix the flawed "decentralized structure."[133]

The company's own quarterly reports bragged about the volume of cross-sales it was making, which were consistently two to three times better than the best others in the industry could do.[134] Did no one ask why Wells could achieve what JP Morgan Chase, Citibank, and Bank of America could not even come close to doing? It smacks of a passively accepting board that was "going along to get along" rather than practicing constructive challenge. Or any type of oversight.[v]

Of course, the Wells Fargo scandal was unique, but that doesn't mean it was unusual. From Enron and WorldCom to Wells Fargo and Volkswagen to Theranos, FTX, and Boeing, the last quarter century has been littered with companies and other organizations that cut corners, cheated, or were absolute frauds. They all suffered. Some survived, some did not. But it's fair to say that no one wants to be on a board blamed for either creating an ethical crisis or letting one fester. So, what can you do?

Lesson Worth Learning: Say what you mean. Mean what you say. Don't be mean about it. Be consistent

> Be who you are and say what you mean
> because those who mind don't matter and
> those who matter don't mind!
> *Dr. Seuss, American Author*

---

v As discussed in "Oversee," results that are "too good to be true" should be a warning to boards of directors.

Make sure the board's desire for an ethical culture is clear and communicated throughout the organization from top to bottom. Establish and keep updated a comprehensive set of board governance policies and enterprise-wide rules to help set the tone of cultural expectations. Among those policies that every board should consider are the ones shown in Table 3.7.

Table 3.7: Key Governance Policies.

Conflicts of interest/Code of ethics/Expectations of professional conduct	Ex parte communications during bidding processes
Insider trading/Personal trading/MNPI[vi]	Communications and social media
Anti-harassment	Related party transactions
Gifts and loans	Anti-discrimination
Foreign Corrupt Practices Act (FCPA)	Lobbying and social media
Ethics hotline procedures	Contacts with vendors
Whistleblower protection	Record retention policies

These are some examples; your organization may require other policies, but all must be adapted to suit your organization. Most importantly, it's imperative that such policies are reflected in actual practice and reinforced by the system of internal control.

Enron and others

As noted, Enron's conflicts of interest policies looked fine, but they did not work. In fact, the board sent the opposite signal – those short-term profits outweighed ethics – when it voted to suspend them. Most of us don't work for someplace like Enron. But smaller inconsistencies, like senior executives who exempt themselves from travel expense rules, build resentments that sometimes can cause an employee to steal or otherwise violate the company's trust with the justification that, "Well, if they can do it, then so can I."

Here's an example. Jon Lukomnik, one of the authors of this book, was once appointed to serve on an equity holder's committee for a regional retailer trying to emerge from bankruptcy under court supervision.

The CEO's draft employment contract included a provision that included a definition of "cause" for dismissal as theft of more than $50,000. Lukomnik was infuriated and asked why the company proposed endorsing the theft of $49,999. The company's bankruptcy lawyers told him that he wasn't being "collegial." "I told them they were crazy; that tone at the top mattered, and the tone at the top of that company sucked." Lukomnik petitioned the court and left the committee. Sure enough, the company never emerged from bankruptcy and was liquidated shortly thereafter.

---

vi Material Non-Public Information

Walk the talk. Ethics must be more than a poster campaign. In the end, say what you mean. Mean what you say. But don't be mean, or bad news won't travel fast. Do what you say. Make sure you comply with laws, regulations, and your internal rules.

Simply put, make your expectations as clear, transparent, and concrete as possible throughout the organization and, in today's world, outside the organization. Then, live up to them.

Finally, be adaptive. Ten years ago, few organizations had social media policies. Today, it's de rigueur. We have all seen companies fire employees for offensive social media posts or go to great lengths to convince suppliers, customers, and other stakeholders that an offensive post does not represent the organization's culture and thinking.

2 Do our board dynamics enable consensus building and make the highest and best use of everyone's time and talents?

> Lost time is never found again.
> *Benjamin Franklin, one of the Founding Fathers of the United States*

Lesson Worth Learning: Adaptive boards create processes that encourage effective and efficient dynamics for decision-making and consensus-building

Consensus is a process that optimizes diverse opinions. It ensures all opinions are heard, resulting in the best decision under the circumstances.

The job of the board is to ensure the organization achieves its mission despite extreme uncertainty, high-velocity change, and inevitable adversity. The single most limited resource of any board is the time of the board members, both individually and collectively. Conducting the board's own business effectively, efficiently, and ethically is critical to driving value.

Effective boards make an essential contribution to achieving the organizational mission. Efficient boards make the highest and best use of everyone's limited and valuable time. Board members at large public companies typically spend 245 hours or six weeks per year on their board work.[135]

"How much time does your board spend?" is an often-asked question. But the follow-up questions – "Where does your board spend its time?" and "How should it spend its valuable time?" – are the real keys to improving effectiveness and efficiency.

Even if your board members have unlimited time to devote to your organization, brute force – more and longer meetings – can only take you so far.

Lesson Worth Learning: The board needs its own change management processes

> To improve is to change; to be perfect is to change often.
> *Sir Winston Churchill, twice former Prime Minister of Great Britain*

Boards need to adapt their governance styles to focus on the essentials of performance and risk to meet the demands of rapid change and extreme uncertainty. Conventionally, change management has primarily focused on executive leadership. However, more attention must be paid to the board's role as a necessary enabler and amplifier of major internal change and overcoming inertia.

How do board processes enable or inhibit adaptation? The board cannot delegate its responsibility or its requirements for collective decision-making to the organization. Delays in the board's decision-making process can impair response times. Early signal detection, pattern recognition, and timely interpretation are critical. Boards need better, faster escalation of policy implications to keep pace with and even get ahead of the external rate of change. Conventional governance methods and processes are no longer up to the task.

Lesson Worth Learning: The board must innovate. Conventional governance processes have not kept pace with the rate of change

> Change happens when the pain of staying the same is greater than the pain of change.
> *Tony Robbins, American Author and Coach*

On the following pages, we examine three of the most common governance processes to illustrate how they have not kept pace with contemporary needs and to make suggestions as to how they should evolve:
1. Agenda setting
2. Reporting/Information sharing/Board books
3. Rules of order and majority rule

Lesson Worth Learning: Agenda setting is strategic

Conventionally, board agendas are too often treated as administrative tasks rather than as one of the most strategic decisions about the highest and best use of the board's limited time. Seemingly simple tasks, like creating the board agenda and information packet, can enable or impair efficacy and efficiency. Unfortunately, many agendas leave little time for in-depth discussions of strategic options.

Too often, the creation of the board agenda is treated like a routine, repetitive task that gets little serious thought. Many organizations use their last agenda as a model without thinking about what's changed. This routine and mundane approach to setting agendas has major negative impacts on a board's effectiveness.

To be fair, many boards send advance notices to board members asking if they have additions or changes to that initial agenda. And many provide updates to keep current with a calendar of required actions. Those are productive practices. But they tend to be the entirety of most enterprises' focus on the board agendas. That's a missed opportunity, for the agenda governs how the enterprise will use one of its most limited resources: board members' time.

Think of it this way: The agenda is like a musical score. Both meeting agendas and musical scores are structured formats. They create a choreographed sequence of events, provide clarity and direction, assign parts to the players, suggest what is important, and determine timing, tempo, and emphasis. While musical scores create a composition, agendas drive the achievement of meeting objectives.

Scores allow musicians to interpret. Jazz allows for much improvisation, allowing the musicians to call, respond, and cue one another to create an entire musical composition. Agendas arrange the topics and reports and cue individual board members to create the discussion and drive toward the decision on any individual item.

In essence, meeting agendas and musical scores serve as guiding documents that help facilitate communication, coordination, and collaboration, whether in the context of a business meeting or a musical performance. They provide structure, clarity, and direction, enabling participants or performers to work together effectively toward a shared goal or outcome.

Of course, there are differences, but rethinking the agenda, making it every bit as valuable as a well-orchestrated score, is a great first step toward improving board efficiency and effectiveness.

The process of setting the agenda should be led by the chair (or lead director) in coordination with the CEO or executive director. There should be an efficient method to solicit agenda items from executive management and the members of the board to produce a draft agenda. This should be done far enough in advance of a board meeting so that the chair can solicit any proposed changes or additions in a timely manner so that executive management can prepare for changed/added agenda items.

An annual work plan from each committee and executive management, creating an annual calendar for the board, can help keep long-term focus. While the annual work plans should keep the committees and management on track, there should not be barriers to new or revised tasks resulting from changes in the operating environment.

The annual calendar serves as the core for board meetings, though the agenda is almost always expanded to include other issues. An annual calendar routinizes periodic regulatory requirements so that the appropriate resolutions can be passed on schedule and the appropriate actions taken, such as board approval of disclosure submissions. The same applies to committee chairs in setting their committee agendas.

One partial fix is to put Oversight items later in the agenda rather than first, to allow discussion of the harder issues earlier in the meeting, and to hold an executive session both at the beginning and end of each meeting.

Exception-based reporting (discussed in Chapter 6, "Oversee the Execution of Direction within Policy") can save time and help to focus the board, thereby freeing up time for items needing extended discussion.

More impactful is an alternative agenda structure based on the powers reserved. An agenda based on the five powers of a board could be organized as follows. Notice that it splits up the routine items, putting those later, rather than first, to allow the items that require policy action more discussion time closer to the beginning of the meeting when people are fresher and their eyes aren't on the clock or the door (Table 3.8).

Table 3.8: Powers of the Board and Related Agenda Items.

Conduct the business of the board
Executive session
Call to order
Roll call
Approval of prior minutes
Consent agenda
Set direction and policy by topic/committee
Check strategic direction and change course if needed. Approve and update policy based on recommendations of board committees. (Note: Recurring policy decisions, such as setting the annual dividend, should be established in a multi-year calendar.)
Build in flex time – time allocated on each agenda for unforeseen policy issues
Approve key decisions
Recurring decisions
One-off decisions
Oversee the execution of direction with policy by topic/committee
Exception-based reporting
Committee reports
Any related policy issues suggested by the exception and committee reports
Verify by topic/committee
Independent reassurance of the reliability of advice received and reports to be issued by the board

Table 3.8 (continued)

Conduct the business of the board
Comments/Announcements
Any other business
Next meeting date and location
Executive session
Adjournment

While some aspects of agenda-setting are universal, every organization is unique. Agendas should play to the organization's and board's strengths and provide support for overcoming weaknesses. Are you a for-profit public company? A private company? A not-for-profit? A governmental body? Do you have a large board or a small one? Are you mature or a start-up? Do the board members understand their roles, or do they trip over one another and the executive officers?

It would make little sense to give a group of jazz musicians a score that annotates every note and rest, leaving little room for improvisation. Certainly, they could replicate the notes, but such a score would literally not play to the ensemble's strengths.

Their ability to both solo and to feed off each other, improvising notes and riffs that touch on the main musical themes in some way and yet stay within the structure of the composition, would be lost. The fact that jazz encourages improvisation within the rules leaves room for the players to create value for themselves and their audiences. Constraining them to reproduce a score note-for-note would be an utter waste.

By contrast, the score for a world-class classical orchestra or chamber music ensemble seems, at first, to be more buttoned down. There is interpretation, but it exists within a different structure – how a note or phrase is approached, how it is allowed to build and fade, how loud or soft, or the tone.

The structure encourages a certain set of emotions and virtuosity that is every bit as value-creating as the jazz performance. They're just different because the scores they follow are designed to produce valued performances in the most effective way possible for that group of musicians.

Is your board's best structure for value creation best served by a jazz-style approach to the agenda and, thus, more time for less structured discussion? That's typically the case for smaller, younger, less mature organizations in lightly regulated industries (though not always so).

Remember, a jazz-like approach doesn't mean there is no structure; it means giving more flexibility to the board to reach productive answers within broader goals but always playing together toward a common goal.

That implies that all board members and key executives must have certain expertise and skill sets. It might also suggest some unstructured board time with no agenda item to be discussed specifically but a robust discussion guided by the organization's overall goals, mission, and current position. In many organizations, executive sessions or board dinners fulfill that function.

Or is the best structure for your board a more buttoned-down, note-by-note agenda, wherein everyone knows what everyone else should be doing, similar to the scores used by a major classical orchestra?

In general, that works better for larger, more mature organizations, particularly those with major compliance needs in highly regulated industries and where specific reports and board actions may be legal requirements. Certainly, there are still allocated soloist spots – the CEO for sure, but also others, like the chair of the audit committee on financial reporting, for example – but areas for board improvisation are more constrained.

Of course, few boards are at one extreme or the other. Most are somewhere in the middle. Still, it's worth asking the question and thinking about what that implies for how you structure your meetings: Is your board more like a jazz ensemble or an orchestra?

One of this book's authors, Rick Funston, chairs the board of a start-up company. Like most start-ups, it is experiencing rapid change, multiple opportunities, and, of course, inevitable adversity. To deal with the high velocity and uncertainty, the board meets at least bi-weekly for an hour to act as a sounding board for the CEO and chief operating officer (COO) to explore issues and options in an unstructured way.

Once a month, the board meets formally, as a board, to review new business opportunities and review the related due diligence procedures, which have been clearly defined in advance. For this meeting, management prepares a one-page summary scorecard that describes the overall status of critical performance with drill-down capability. In these ways, the board acts as both a jazz ensemble (in the informal bi-weekly meetings) and an orchestra (in the formal monthly meetings). The frequency and agenda of the meetings will evolve with changing circumstances.

Lesson Worth Learning: Decision discipline is essential, especially when there is little time

> You make business decisions every single day. Every once in a while, a decision comes
> along with the potential to be a game changer for your organization. Maybe your company
> is considering mergers and acquisitions. Maybe you're trying to decide whether to expand
> operations, enter a new joint venture, build new facilities or invest in a new large-scale
> research and development project.

The last thing you want to do is make these decisions on the fly using nothing more than gut instinct. Even when big decisions require us to be quick to avoid being left behind, it's critical that we still have discipline to give our businesses the best chances for success.

One of the most important parts of careful analysis is to have the discipline to clearly document all of the assumptions. This ensures that when we choose an alternative and move forward, we know the critical variables or assumptions that make the decision a good one.[136]

Allan Gray, Director of Purdue University's Center for Food and Agricultural Business

Decision discipline at Purdue University refers to a systematic approach to decision-making to ensure effective, efficient, and transparent governance across the institution. It involves a set of principles, processes, and practices designed to foster accountability, collaboration, and strategic alignment in decision-making at all levels of the university.

Table 3.9 shows an overview of Purdue's Decision Discipline.

Table 3.9: Decision discipline at Purdue University.

Principle	Example
Data-driven decision-making	Decisions at Purdue University are informed by data and evidence-based analysis whenever possible. This includes gathering relevant data, conducting thorough research, and utilizing quantitative and qualitative information to support decision-making processes.
Strategic alignment	Decision discipline ensures that all decisions align with the university's strategic goals, mission, and values. It involves regular review and assessment of decision outcomes to ensure they contribute to advancing the university's overall objectives.
Inclusive and collaborative decision-making	Purdue University emphasizes inclusivity and collaboration in decision-making processes. This involves soliciting input and feedback from relevant stakeholders, including faculty, staff, students, and external partners, to ensure diverse perspectives are considered.
Clear accountability and responsibility	Decision discipline clarifies roles, responsibilities, and accountabilities within the university governance structure. This includes defining decision-making authority, establishing clear lines of communication, and holding individuals accountable for their decisions and actions.
Transparent communication	Purdue University prioritizes transparent communication throughout the decision-making process. This involves sharing relevant information, rationale, and decision outcomes with stakeholders in a timely and accessible manner to promote understanding and trust.
Continuous improvement	Decision discipline is an ongoing process of continuous improvement. Purdue University regularly evaluates decision-making processes, solicits feedback from stakeholders, and implements changes to enhance effectiveness, efficiency, and transparency.

Overall, Purdue University's decision discipline reflects a commitment to creating a culture of accountability, collaboration, and strategic alignment in decision-making processes across the institution. By adhering to core principles and practices, Purdue aims to ensure that decisions are made thoughtfully, responsibly, and in the best interests of the university community.

Applying these principles to the adaptive governance process can be a powerful tool for the adaptive board.

Lesson Worth Learning: Executive sessions don't involve executives

Ironically (from a semantic perspective), executives aren't present at board executive sessions, except by invitation of the board. In this context, the word "executive" refers to the powers delegated to the session, not the titles of those present. In a typical session, the CEO (but no other executives, except by invitation of the board) is present at the beginning of the meeting, and then the independent board members meet without anyone else present.

Many high-performing boards hold executive meetings of independent directors both before and after each board meeting. The meeting before the formal board meeting highlights issues that may arise. The following meeting allows the board members to make sure they heard the same thing and to surface any new issues for follow-up.

Holding executive meetings routinely, rather than on demand, removes any idea that the meeting is being held because of dissatisfaction with executive management or that the board is "hiding things." Indeed, on many boards, the chair or lead director will debrief the CEO following the executive session, particularly if executive management needs to follow up.

Lesson Worth Learning: *Robert's Rules of Order* may have outlived their utility

Conventionally, decision discipline was more about structure and rules of order and less about enabling collective decision-making processes. Originally developed almost 150 years ago by U.S. army officer Henry Roberts, Robert's Rules of Order are a widely accepted framework for conducting meetings and making decisions, especially not-for-profit, as that was their original purpose. They have been revised several times, most recently in 2020. The latest edition is more than 800 pages.[137]

According to Robert's Rules,[vii] meeting agendas are organized first to conduct board business (e.g., call to order, roll call, minutes approval); second, oversight; third, recurring approvals; and finally, policy items. There is often an executive session at the end. A consent agenda saves time by grouping routine approvals for a vote without discussion. Any board member can request that an item be removed from the consent agenda so it can be discussed individually.

While these rules can be helpful and may even be required under some Sunshine laws (such as meetings of local government commissions or homeowners' associations), they aren't well-suited to 21st century boards.

Robert's Rules are premised on majority rule rather than consensus building. They can be rigid and inflexible, leaving little room for creativity or innovation in decision-making processes. This rigidity may stifle productive discussion and hinder the exploration of alternative solutions. Adhering strictly to Robert's Rules can make meetings time-consuming, especially when debating procedural motions or parliamentary points. This can lead to frustration among participants and detract from the meeting's objectives.

Members well-versed in parliamentary procedure may have an advantage over others, potentially dominating discussions and decision-making processes. This imbalance can marginalize less experienced or less-process-oriented members. Strict adherence to procedural rules may also prioritize the form of decision-making over the substance of the issues being discussed. As a result, important decisions may be delayed or overlooked in favor of following procedural protocols.

Robert's Rules may not be conducive to promoting inclusivity and participation among all members, particularly those who are less assertive or confident in parliamentary procedure. Also, the hierarchical nature of Robert's Rules, with its emphasis on the authority of the chair and formal roles such as president and secretary, may reinforce power dynamics that marginalize differing opinions.

Despite these shortfalls and criticisms, *Robert's Rules of Order* remain a widely used framework for conducting meetings and making decisions in many organizations, particularly in the public and non-profit sectors. Thosese organizations tend to have larger boards and engage more stakeholders. Larger boards make it more difficult to reach a consensus, and thus use Robert's Rules more often.

For meetings of for-profit corporations still using Robert's Rules, it may be time for a change to keep pace and make meetings more productive, inclusive, focused on achieving the organization's goals and making the highest and best use of everyone's time. Consider that the first place to start is with an agenda ordered, as shown in Table 3.8 ("Powers of the Board and Related Agenda Items"), prioritizing the most impactful issues that need discussion and consensus-building.

---

vii Robert's Rules uses more general terminology, like "reports" and "new business," but this is how many boards have implemented the agenda order.

Lesson Worth Learning: Consensus is better than majority rule, even though it may take longer

> I once asked [Bertrand] Russell if he was willing to die for his beliefs.
> 'Of course not,' he replied. 'After all, I may be wrong.'
> *Leonard Lyons*, New York Post, *June 23, 1964*

Consensus is a collective decision-making process where all members of a group accept and support a decision, even if it is not their preferred outcome. It involves cooperation and compromise, ensuring that the group's decision reflects a shared understanding and mutual consent rather than a majority rule. It starts with diverse opinions; emphasizes collaboration, inclusivity, and collective responsibility; often requires discussion, negotiation, and compromise; and aligns the board's diverse perspectives and interests to a common cause.

Consensus is not merely a majority vote. Nor is it groupthink evidenced by a quick unanimous vote. Nor is it the least common denominator. Instead, consensus seeks to address and incorporate the concerns and viewpoints of all board members to the greatest extent possible. The goal is to arrive at decisions supported by all and not actively opposed by any member. This may not even require a formal vote. A colleague who knew the famed Sir Adrian Cadbury said that when she mentioned a board vote, he looked at her in horror: "Boards don't vote. They achieve consensus." He nailed it.

In practical terms, consensus can be challenging to achieve, especially in larger or more diverse boards, due to differing opinions, goals, and values. However, when successfully reached, consensus can lead to a stronger commitment from all members to the final decision, as it reflects collective ownership and agreement.

Consensus is a key concept in various fields, including business, politics, social sciences, and technology (notably in blockchain and distributed systems, where it refers to agreement on the state of a network among distributed nodes or participants). Each context may apply different methods and standards for achieving and validating consensus tailored to the specific needs and goals of the group or system involved.

Consensus building. Constructive challenge takes center stage, of course. Boards should also be willing to utilize facilitation techniques such as brainstorming, group discussions, and consensus-building exercises to encourage collaboration and participation from all stakeholders. When the board has a vigorous discussion of diverse perspectives, carefully considers the policy implications, and is respectful of those diverse opinions, then it is more likely to be effective.

By focusing on finding mutually acceptable solutions and resolving conflicts constructively, directors improve their chances of finding common ground and reaching a consensus.

Lesson Worth Learning: The role of the chair is to determine the will of the board

> The great leaders are like the best conductors –
> they reach beyond the notes to reach the magic in the players.[138]
> *Blain Lee, American Author*

While we are not fans of Robert's Rules' hierarchical nature, we are huge supporters of board chairs and understand their difficult – and sometimes conflicting – roles. Good governance begins with an adaptive board, and an adaptive board begins with an effective chair. If the agenda is the musical score, the chair is the conductor/musical director. Both positions involve orchestrating the efforts of multiple individuals to achieve a harmonious and productive outcome.

The "what" of being a chair. The principal roles of the chair are to determine the will of the board and to maintain decision discipline. The chair needs the support of the board to do this effectively. The chair typically has seven major duties:

1. Preside over meetings and maintain order in conducting the business of the board.
2. Oversee the setting of the strategic agenda and priorities.
3. Oversee board communications and collaboration with the chief executive.
4. Ensure the board receives adequate and appropriate materials in a timely fashion.
5. Monitor and assess board performance and coach board members.
6. Appoint and rotate terms of committee members and chairs. (At some boards this is a full board decision.)
7. Act in coordination with the chief executive as a spokesperson for the board and as an ambassador to stakeholders.

The chair also has a vital continuity role, ensuring that follow-up items are, in fact, followed up on and that recommendations made at board meetings are timely implemented within policy.

Finally, the chair may also be tasked with creating or overseeing the board's ongoing education program, with input from the CEO or executive director and the board's committee chairs (who should each have their annual work plans). Education sessions should be scheduled to inform board members about the context and nuances of upcoming strategic discussions so valuable board time can be spent on analysis and decision-making, not getting up to speed on a particular issue.

Education sessions are also the place to upskill the board on emerging issues; cyber-security, artificial intelligence, sustainability, and regulatory change are examples of such recent emerging issues as of the time this book was written. One tip: Corporate law firms, accounting firms, and various consultancies frequently provide emerging issue updates. You don't have to be a client to get them. Circulating them to board members is a good first step, even before a board education session.

The list of a chair's responsibilities is the "what" of the job. What is a chair supposed to do? Of course, your organization may have more or less than those seven functions. The list is likely in the board charter and can be looked up. But what differentiates great chairs from mediocre ones is not what they do but how they do it.

The "how" of being a chair. Great chairs share several characteristics. Chairs:
1. Maintain order and decision discipline in board meetings.
2. Elicit diverse opinions, then find common ground and build on it.
3. Build a cohesive, problem-solving, respectful board.
4. Be patient, diplomatic, and emotionally intelligent.
5. Are always prepared.

Maintaining order and decision discipline is the number one role of the chair. Notwithstanding our concerns about Robert's Rules, the chair must be fully conversant with the board's rules of order for conducting meetings, as there is nothing more embarrassing for a chair than to be caught off guard by rules of procedure. Board members typically are not well versed in parliamentary procedure, and process issues can create problems.

However, knowing the rules is a necessary but not sufficient condition. Process is not a stand-alone goal. Effective chairs make the process a tool to achieve substance. They embody a sense of purpose and rally all board members to put the organization above each individual at the table.

Effective chairs make all board members feel heard. That doesn't necessarily mean calling on each board member to speak like some professor testing whether those sitting in the back row have read the board book. Different people impact collective decisions in different ways. Often, this involves soft skills to put each board member in a position to contribute.

The chair plays a very important role in establishing the board and entity culture and should encourage constructive challenge and try to help the board find the common ground and build consensus.

Last, and probably one of the chair's most challenging roles, is dealing with difficult board members because they can negatively affect the entire board and the organization itself. An effective board chair should also be capable of introspection to ensure that opportunities for improvement in fulfilling his or her chairmanship duties are also captured.

Second, an effective chair finds the common ground and builds on it. That begins by encouraging diverse opinions and constructive challenge. The chair should facilitate getting all board members involved in the board's work, ensure it focuses on its key tasks, and engage the board in assessing and improving its performance.

The chair should be the last – not the first – to express their opinion. The chair needs to make sure everyone is heard and remains impartial to the extent practical. It may be frustrating, but it is far better to let board members arrive at a conclusion on their own than for them to feel one was forced on them.

This can be time-consuming and challenging, but the results are well worth it. Diversity of opinion that evolves into unity of direction is powerful.

Third, an effective chair does not provide the solution but builds a cohesive, problem-solving, respectful board.
Leadership in this context differs from what we normally think of a center-stage do-er, someone charismatic who gets people to do things their way or the "highway." Instead, the effective chair helps others to do and grow; avoids the use of the word "I" and instead focuses on "we." Stanislav Shekshnia succinctly states, "The role of the chair is to provide leadership to the board, not to the organization."[139] That may be a challenge if the chair is also used to being the CEO.

Fourth, an effective chair is patient, diplomatic, and emotionally intelligent.
In most cases, the issues that come before the board are complex and have long-term implications. Chairs need to be able to distinguish between issues that are truly important and those that are merely urgent.

The board must be able to focus on the long-term and "see the forest despite the trees." The chair's role is to try to ensure that the board does not rush to judgment and instead thoughtfully considers the issues, the full range of options available, and the related pros and cons to make an informed decision.

Obviously, some issues will arise that demand immediate attention. In those cases, a high-performing board skilled in constructive challenge, consensus building, and decision-making is even more important. Those boards act like athletes under pressure – they stay calm and stick to their decision-making process because it's become ingrained and instinctual.

One key to finding common ground is emotional intelligence. Effective chairs do not respond abruptly or in kind to an offensive remark but are quick to end any personalized attacks on other directors, staff, or consultants. This is the ability to recognize your emotions and those of others, hear spoken words, observe body language, and recognize and understand their underlying motivation.

Being seen as fair allows a chair to use gentle persuasion rather than dominating or exercising the authority of the gavel. Of course, order must be maintained at the same time. The chair's goal should be to ensure that all understand that their opinion has been heard by focusing on the process.

Finally, an effective chair is always prepared.
This requires a level of commitment. Effective chairs often schedule check-in calls between board meetings with key executives, committee chairs, outside advisors, and sometimes with all board members. Those check-ins surface issues

that might arise, allowing preparation. "No surprises" is a good rule for any chair.

Effective chairs also use informal methods to boost enterprise performance. For example, a chair may schedule a board dinner and invite the senior executives in charge of a certain area to attend so that they can chat informally with board members interested in that aspect of the enterprise.

It's not just the other board members with whom the chair must have a respectful relationship. Elise Walton, long-time organizational observer and a Board Leadership Fellow of the National Association of Corporate Directors, also notes that the relationship between the chair and the CEO or executive director in organizations where the same person does not hold those positions is critical. "Good communication is the fabric for creating and sustaining the right tone of the relationship (between a chair and the CEO)."[140] Walton advises that the best chair–CEO relationships are close but not personal.

Make no mistake about it: Chairing a board is a skill. Just as the culture of the organization starts with the board, the culture and effectiveness of the board start with the chair.

Bad chairs embody the old metaphor that a fish stinks from the head. It is very difficult to be an effective organization if the governing body is run poorly. For instance, Jon Lukomnik (one of the authors of this book) was an independent board member of a leading retailer from 2006 to 2010. The company was a "controlled company." In other words, the controlling shareowner had enough of the stock of the public company that it could elect whomever it wanted to the board, ensuring that it ultimately got what it wanted. If not, it could replace the board members. There are numerous controlled companies worldwide, and in some jurisdictions, particularly in emerging markets, controlled companies (often family-owned) are the norm.

Also, companies with differential voting rights – like many Silicon Valley technology companies where the founders or management own shares with super-voting rights – may be controlled companies. Many controlled companies have good governance; some don't.

Aware of those issues, the controlling shareowner recruited Lukomnik to the board to be a good governance influence. "It's a little like getting a new doctor who tells you to exercise and lose weight," Lukomnik recalled. "The first year, it's a new doctor, so you do it. You grumble the second year but still try. You get tired of it in the third year and don't even try. The fourth year, you get a new doctor."

He says that for two years, he was effective. Together with the chair, he made sure that independent directors were heard and that issues were robustly debated. The retailer made it through the global financial crisis of 2008–2009 in relatively healthy shape.

However, by year three, Lukomnik recalls being ignored; by year four, the chair wasn't even pretending to allow debate. "I had an off-site meeting with the chair. I explained that the leading practice for boards with controlling shareholders was for the chair to wait to express an opinion. That way, the independent board members could air the issues. That would give everyone the benefit of hearing differing viewpoints. The chair's response? 'No. If we've already decided on a course of action, why should we waste all this time debating it.'" Lukomnik soon resigned from the board.

Within eight years, the company failed. Lukomnik noted that the rise of online shopping characterized the era and that many brick-and-mortar stores failed. "But the decision to view the board as a bother rather than a resource certainly didn't help," Lukomnik said.

Lesson Worth Learning: Conventional board reporting, information sharing, and board books/portals are often data-rich but insight-poor

Board books often bury board members in detail rather than provide information. Today, board books are delivered electronically and securely, but that hasn't helped. If anything, it may have exacerbated the problem.

Most board books are still electronic versions of what they were unfortunately when they were printed and often run into hundreds of pages. Occasionally, board books top 1,000 pages. While it's not always true, the most voluminous tend to be "data dumps," burying board members in detail while missing the big picture and its implications.

As a result, board members are drinking from the proverbial fire hose. Reports are detailed but without intelligent analysis. The result? The decision-making process bogs down as the board drowns in detail about what J. M. Juran called the "trivial many" rather than the "vital few."[141] We call these voluminous board packets "DRIP"; that is, they are **D**ata **R**ich, but **I**nsight **P**oor.

The result? Boards suffer from information overload when what they really need is analysis that leads to insights into the policy implications. And, as a double irony, drowning board members in details may increase the board's legal liability because, after all, they were "informed."

Board reports are like most conventional board processes; they were designed for a time when boards had less on their plates, when the outside (and inside) context of their organizations changed at a much slower pace and less substantively, and when the chief executive or executive director was, at many organizations, an overwhelming center of gravity and power and the board an afterthought.

As Figure 3.1 shows, there is a hierarchy from data to information to intelligence to insight. Too much of what is presented to a board is at the data and information level. As a result, boards suffer from data overload. They then must

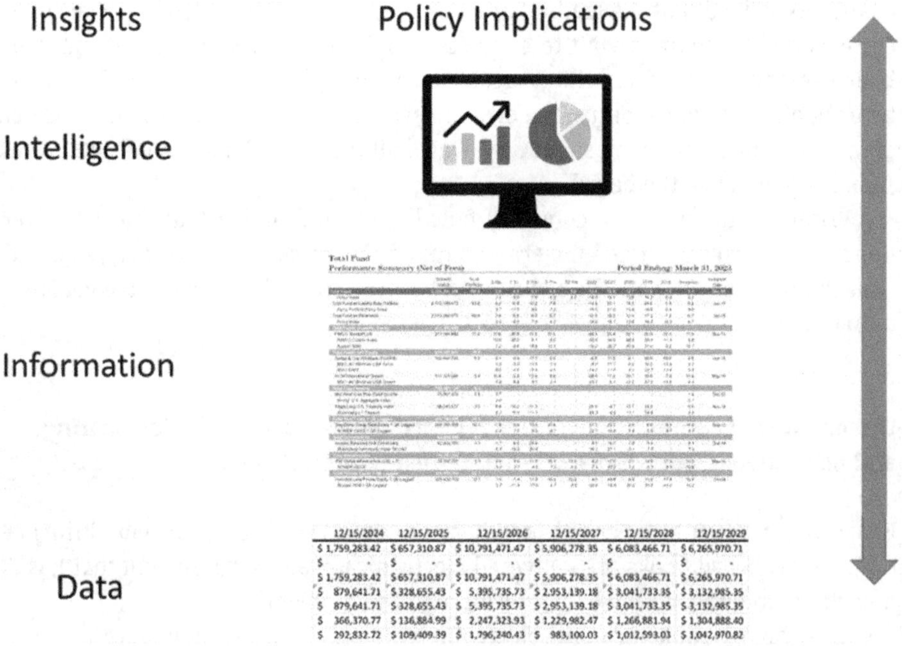

Insights

Intelligence

Policy Implications

Information

Data

	12/15/2024	12/15/2025	12/15/2026	12/15/2027	12/15/2028	12/15/2029
	$ 1,759,283.42	$ 657,310.87	$ 10,791,471.47	$ 5,906,278.35	$ 6,083,466.71	$ 6,265,970.71
	$ -	$ -	$ -	$ -	$ -	$ -
	$ 1,759,283.42	$ 657,310.87	$ 10,791,471.47	$ 5,906,278.35	$ 6,083,466.71	$ 6,265,970.71
	$ 879,641.71	$ 328,655.43	$ 5,395,735.73	$ 2,953,139.18	$ 3,041,733.35	$ 3,132,985.35
	$ 879,641.71	$ 328,655.43	$ 5,395,735.73	$ 2,953,139.18	$ 3,041,733.35	$ 3,132,985.35
	$ 366,370.77	$ 136,884.99	$ 2,247,323.93	$ 1,229,982.47	$ 1,266,881.94	$ 1,304,888.40
	$ 292,832.72	$ 109,409.39	$ 1,796,240.43	$ 983,100.03	$ 1,012,593.03	$ 1,042,970.82

Figure 3.1: From Data to Insights Hierarchy.

search for how to turn that into intelligence: What do the data and information mean? What are the insights into the policy implications?

In our experience, few organizations optimally leverage technology to create timely insights. Instead, they use technology to deliver more and more data faster, leading to overload and impaired signal detection and pattern recognition.

In the chapter "Oversee the Execution of Direction within Policy," we provide a more in-depth discussion of how to develop a "Board's Eye View" that moves the board up in the hierarchy from data to information to intelligence and, ultimately, to insight.

Lesson Worth Learning: Constructive challenge serves everyone

We discussed the principles of constructive challenge in Chapter 2. What turbo-charges constructive challenge is building it into each board power. While constructive challenge is touched upon in each relevant chapter – it's that important – Table 3.10 provides a summary for board members to consider how to conduct board meetings.

Table 3.10: Constructive Challenge Tools for Powers of the Board.

Power Reserved	Examples of Constructive Challenge Tools
Conduct the business of the board	– Diverse board composition – Annual retreats, board self-evaluation – Individualized feedback/coaching from the chair – Mentoring – Statement of core values/beliefs – Board orientation – expected behavior – Continuing education, including access to outside experts – Critical questions that should always be asked
Set direction and then prudently delegate	– Decide iteratively in uncertainty – Discontinuous improvement/Challenge of underlying assumptions – Develop asymmetric signal detection – Set risk parameters – Policy option summaries include diverse stakeholder opinions with a hierarchy of options (least to most) and related pros/cons – Critical questions that should always be asked
Approve key decisions	– Due diligence (committee, staff, advisors) to demonstrate care, checks, and balances in the management recommendation process – Delegations of authority – Prudent use of experts – Critical questions that should always be asked
Oversee the execution of strategy within policy and advise	– Vital signs for vital functions – Exception-reporting with drill down – Critical questions that should always be asked
Verify before trusting	– Independent verification – Questions a committee should always ask (depending on mandate)

When conducting board and committee business, constructive challenge can be enabled:

– Have board members from diverse backgrounds, including different industries, professions, cultures, genders, ethnicities, and ages. This diversity brings a range of perspectives and insights to board discussions and decision-making processes and helps avoid groupthink. The diversity of perspectives should reflect the current and future needs of the organization. Ensuring real diversity among the board is a key responsibility of nominating committees.
– Adopt inclusive governance practices that actively encourage participation from all board members, regardless of their background or perspective. Fos-

ter an environment where every voice is valued and respected and where diverse viewpoints are considered in board deliberations. To encourage dialogue and provide time for consensus building, the board should consider annual retreats and other formal and informal settings for collaboration, such as board dinners.

- Board self-evaluations should include a component on how well the board constructively challenges itself and others. The chair can reinforce this through individualized feedback and coaching. Board orientation can also describe expected and desirable behavior, as can a statement of core values and beliefs. Assigning an experienced board member to mentor new board members can help reinforce a positive culture.
- As noted, law firms, consultancies, accounting firms, and even this book provide lists of questions appropriate to various constituencies (e.g., "questions an audit committee should ask") or topics (e.g., "questions boards should ask about cyber-security"). Informally circulating those questions among the board members can help them hone their own questions, adapted to their specific organizations.

3 Do our committee assignments and board members' expertise effectively address the organization's specific issues and challenges?

> The only place where success comes before work is in the dictionary.
> *Vidal Sassoon, British Hairstylist and Businessman*

Lesson Worth Learning: Board expertise and skills, as well as committee structure and membership, should align with the organization's mission and strategic plan

Maintain strategic focus. High-functioning board committees can significantly enhance a board's efficiency and effectiveness. Each committee should have a strategic focus as defined by its charter and be able to exercise important oversight functions. Insight is essential to both effective direction setting and oversight.

In reality, most boards (acting as a full board) do not have the time to dig into complex issues and fully understand the options and the related pros and cons. At the same time, boards need to avoid simply rubber-stamping staff and consultant recommendations with minimal board discussion or debate. Committees can enable broader trustee engagement in understanding the due diligence and deliberation process that management uses to make its recommendation, thus leading to greater board confidence.

Boards delegate to committees to research and bring back recommendations for the review and approval of the full board and to oversee the work of staff and consultants. Committees should perform work that is not practical for the board as a whole; e.g., the investment committee of a pension fund would monitor investment due diligence processes and vet investment recommendations from staff.

Committees enable directors to dig deeper into key issues and better understand the range of options available to the organization. Committees make insightful recommendations to the board about preferred options, their related pros and cons, and the risks of action and inaction. That way, the full board benefits from the more in-depth discussion and analysis that can typically take place in a committee.

Identify needed expertise. Committee members should collectively broadly define the range of expertise required for the task. Such expertise may or may not reside within the board. If not, a board has the authority and responsibility to retain such expertise for the committee.

Typical independent expertise includes compensation experts for the compensation committee, lawyers for ad hoc committees with investigative needs, executive search firms for the nominations/governance committee, etc. Standard practice is to allow committees to select external advisers without executive management involvement (e.g., a compensation committee may select a compensation consultant without going through management). A leading practice is for the committee to review the performance of its advisers annually.

Many organizations create a skills matrix and gap analysis when they embark on the search for a new director, but a skills matrix/gap analysis is important for multiple reasons. Creating such a document identifies the relevant skills and experiences of each board member and of the board cumulatively. The matrix is then compared to a list of desired skills and experiences, given the organization's mission and strategic plan (i.e., a geologist likely would be desired for a mining company board but not necessarily for a hospitality company).[142]

While the most obvious use for the skills matrix and gap analysis is in searching for a new board member, adaptive boards also use it to inform what the board education program should be ("Where do we need to upskill?"), and to determine whether the board should hire an outside consultant to help inform key discussions to address gaps.

One note: The skills matrix and gap analysis should be refreshed periodically. Emerging issues, contextual changes, new competitors, and evolution in organizational strategy change the analysis. Also, specific skills don't stay relevant. For instance, the best marketer in the world from just a few years ago may or may not have skills honed for today, when social media dominates (as opposed to traditional print and electronic media), influencers matter (they didn't exist a generation ago), and streaming has replaced traditional, cable, and satellite television.

Strike the right match. Board members should be assigned to committees based on skills, experiences, and their ability to help fulfill the committee work plan. Some boards rotate some committee members periodically to refresh perspectives and expose board members to different issues and the senior managers responsible for them. Adaptive boards review committee assignments periodically, resetting them as required.

Keep it real. Committee charters are living documents. A leading practice is to have each committee review its charter annually. Well-defined charters outline the committee's purpose, scope, responsibilities, and any special expertise needed, such as financial or scientific expertise.

Committees can be incredibly useful, but, at their heart, they are creations of the board, and they wield authority delegated from the board. They are not fiefdoms. The full board should receive reports of what was discussed and decided in committee meetings.

Many boards allow non-committee board members to attend but not to participate in a committee meeting. The transparency engendered by reports and open meetings helps to validate the board's trust in the committee's work and allows the board to make informed decisions. Also, where necessary, committee chairs and committees should consult with each other when issues overlap their respective areas of expertise.

Nothing is permanent, but everything is long-term. Boards concerned about sustainability (in every sense of the word) know that not only does the organization have to adapt, but so does the board itself. They update their skills matrices and gap analyses. They track potential future directors and CEOs, even when they're not searching for anyone. They ask whether the current board committee structure and composition continue to be appropriate. They use education sessions and board advisers to understand what's changed and how it affects them. And then they adapt.

Finally, a word about board evaluations.

Some jurisdictions, such as the New York Stock Exchange (NYSE Rule 303A. 091), require the boards of directors of all listed companies to conduct a self-evaluation at least annually. In addition to the various regulatory rules, "leading practice" is to conduct periodic evaluations. Self-evaluations should be useful and not simply viewed as compliance exercises. There are as many varieties of board evaluations as there are boards.

Adaptive boards use evaluations as an opportunity for improvement, not as a check-the-box requirement. They use self-evaluation as an opportunity to question everything from the structural – "Do we have the right committee structure?" – to the procedural – "How is the agenda created?" and "Do we get the board documents with adequate time to review them?"– to the substantive contribution of the individual board members. Peer evaluations are designed to improve group performance rather than attack individual members.

Some boards, concerned about the discoverability of board evaluations, run a legalistic process utilizing outside counsel. Others run an informal process. But whatever process best fits your situation, the highest value will be achieved if the evaluation encourages positive evolution rather than devolution into a gripe session.

4 How well do we plan director succession, including nomination and compensation processes?

> If we get the right people on the bus, the right people in the right seats . . .
> we'll figure out how to take it someplace great.
> *Jim Collins, American Author*[143]

Lesson Worth Learning: Director succession is strategic

Where do you begin to make sure the board can conduct its business effectively? With the people who sit around the board table.

Nominating committees have expanded their purview to include the governance of the board itself, including areas such as board education. Indeed, many, if not most, are now titled the nominating and governance committee. Notwithstanding that useful broadening of the committee's charter, the traditional, principal role of the nominating committee – to identify candidate(s) for election to the board– is still central to the nominating committee's role.

The composition and overall structure of the board may be determined in part by the jurisdiction(s) in which the enterprise is legally domiciled due to either regulatory requirements or dominant local practice. There is no globally accepted structure for effective governance and no academic evidence that any one structure is "the" solution and better than the rest.

One size does not fit all. Some jurisdictions require a dual or bicameral structure composed of a supervisory board and a management board, while others demand a unicameral board. Similarly, there are differing requirements/norms for size, the inclusion of insiders and non-executive directors and/or independent directors, election policies and proxy voting, length of board member terms, the composition of committees, mandatory committees such as audit, and the separation of CEO/chair responsibilities.

Sometimes, the differences are due to function. Not-for-profit boards often are larger than for-profit boards, reflecting their need to raise funds. Sometimes, they are due to maturity levels; new, founder-led organizations often have smaller boards of affiliated advisors/directors.

In some regulated industries, director candidates must pass muster with the regulator before taking office. Proactive provisions in shareholder agreements or even bond covenants may also affect composition and structure.

So, who should the nominating committee nominate? Simply put, the people they think will be most effective – in combination, as a board – at driving performance. Personal conduct issues – character issues – are universal and paramount. Every board member should exhibit high character and honesty.

Guts and courage. Corporate governance expert Charles Elson adds a practical requirement enabling directors to demonstrate integrity at the most difficult times:

> Guts. Courage. That's the hardest thing about being a director. Sometimes, dissent and hard discussions need to be had. And I think people have to have the guts to do it; not just to have integrity but to demonstrate it at the most difficult times . . . No one wants to raise tough issues, but sometimes they have to.[144]

One early indicator of whether a prospective board member will commit to the time and effort necessary is during the nominating process. If a prospect doesn't indicate that s/he has independently researched the organization and, therefore, has questions for the chair and CEO (or executive director), be wary. Serious candidates have as many questions about the entity as the organization has about them.

Time and focus are limited qualities. Various organizations have guidelines on "overboarding"; they set a maximum number of boards on which any individual can serve. For example, CalPERS, the largest public pension fund in the United States, has a policy of voting against any sitting CEO who serves on the board of more than one other company and against non-CEOs who hold more than four board positions.[145]

As importantly, there should be a clear linkage between a nominee's (or a director's) experience and skills and the organization's strategic thinking and planning. For that reason, a nomination committee typically evaluates an organization's strategic plan with an eye toward the skills and characteristics required of the board. The committee then evaluates the board's current composition to create a gap analysis before seeking qualified candidates to fill the identified gaps and future needs.

In many cases, particularly at larger organizations, the committee may be assisted by a professional search firm to find appropriate candidates beyond the existing board's personal networks. Or it may use one of the many networks that have been started to facilitate the consideration of non-traditional candidates.

Increasingly, it's recognized that a wide diversity of backgrounds, experiences, and qualifications enables boards to respond more effectively to a range of issues because the directors can analyze them from different points of view, both professionally and in terms of experience.

In addition to recommending candidates, the nominating committee typically recommends director compensation. There are myriad reasons why people serve on boards – and most not-for-profit boards do not pay at all – but competitive compensation is generally regarded as necessary in for-profit situations.

There should be a clearly delineated process for determining director compensation. This often involves benchmarking against peers, considering whether the workload has increased/decreased, and analyzing whether compensation has affected the organization's ability to attract desirable candidates.

Size matters. Larger enterprises pay directors more than smaller ones. In theory, that's because they are more complicated organizations, and the directors do more, but the reality is that size is almost an independent variable.

For example, in 2022, the average compensation for a director serving on a mutual fund board where the fund complex had less than a billion dollars in assets under management (AUM) was $59,477. However, for directors overseeing investment complexes with AUM of $5–10 billion, it was $158,273. And for those overseeing funds with AUM of $300 billion or more, it jumped to $427,567.[146]

Those factors are just data points to help inform the committee's judgment. Despite the obviously self-serving nature of determining your own compensation, the fiduciary obligation to the organization still rules.

The nominating committee is also typically responsible for the structure of director compensation, although in some cases the compensation committee determines this. In general, consistent with the board's role as an "oversight" rather than an operational board, there has been a steady migration away from perquisites such as retirement pay and other perks,[147] and meeting fees have become increasingly rare. There is a trend to have "all-in" pay via an annual retainer in stock and cash.

As jointly responsible fiduciaries, directors are paid identical amounts. There are no "stars" who can drive performance individually. The only variation is based on role (chair, lead director, committee chair) – not company performance.

As a result of such changes, in major public companies today, you won't see director pension benefits or perquisites such as product discounts and spousal travel. You will see increased use of stock and cash as the form of currency in retainers for board service, increases in compensation for board and committee leaders (lead director/independent chair, committee chairs), and fewer payments for attending meetings.

Furthermore, again linked to the oversight role, there is an increasing use of minimum stock holding requirements for public company board members (usually some multiple of their total annual compensation).

That compensation structure makes sense for a board primarily focused on oversight. However, in some private equity and early stage companies, the board serves more of an active role, for instance, by making introductions to potential clients, suppliers, and financiers.

Such boards often feature equity investors in the company (either individuals or representatives of venture capital and private equity firms), and compensation at those boards is sometimes laden with incentives directly related to the company's success. This might be anathema at a larger, widely held public company where independence is valued. In other words, when it comes to director compensation, form should follow function.

Similarly, while public company boards in the Anglo-American model are composed overwhelmingly of independent directors, private company boards include more affiliated directors, consistent with their more active business roles.[148]

5 How well do we select, evaluate, compensate, and plan for the succession of the CEO?

> In my opinion, board members who are adept at picking CEOs do four things others don't:
> They work painstakingly to clarify the essential qualities needed to succeed in the job;
> they keep an open mind about where the best candidate will come from;
> they go deep to understand which candidate is the best fit; and
> they allow for imperfections in the chosen candidate.
> *Ram Charan, Author*[149]

Lesson Worth Learning: The selection, compensation, and planning for the CEO's succession are among a board's most important decisions

Many board members say selecting the CEO or executive director is the single most important task they have. To that, we add compensating the CEO and evaluating the CEO as tasks that enable the leader of your organization to be successful and aligned with the board's priorities. Finally, succession planning protects the organization should anything untoward happen in the short term and prepares it for the long term.

Being prepared is necessary: The median CEO tenure for large American companies was just 4.8 years in 2022, a more than 20 percent decline from the six-year median just nine years earlier. The mean had declined only 5.3 percent and stood at 7.2 years. It skewed longer than the median because of the number of long-tenured CEOs who had served for 10, 20, or even 30 years.[150] One way to think about those numbers: Most CEOs don't stay long, but those who do succeed and stay have a generational effect on your organization.

We describe the examples of two outstanding organizations: Microsoft and Apple. Each used a systematic approach to the search, selection, and transition of its new CEOs.

Microsoft

Steve Ballmer announced his retirement in August 2013, prompting Microsoft to begin the search for his successor. Ballmer's tenure had seen successes but also challenges, particularly in adapting to mobile and cloud computing trends. There were also growing tensions between Ballmer and Microsoft founder and former CEO Bill Gates about the company's future. At that time, it was a $300 billion company with 100,000 employees. Its stock price had languished as the company repeatedly missed opportunities in burgeoning new technology markets.

1. **Search.** Microsoft's board of directors formed a search committee led by board member John Thompson. The committee also included other board members, including co-founder and chair Bill Gates. The board identified several key criteria for the new CEO, including strong leadership skills, a deep understanding of technology and innovation, and the ability to drive cultural and organizational change quickly. They also realized that no single person would have all the skills they needed and understood they would need to compromise.[151]

   They started with a list of more than 100 internal and external candidates. External candidates included high-profile industry leaders like Ford CEO Alan Mulally and former Nokia CEO Stephen Elop. Several external candidates withdrew because of concerns about potential boardroom dynamics, with both Ballmer and Gates being on the board.

   Internal candidates included executives such as Tony Bates, Satya Nadella, and Kevin Turner, highlighting the importance of assessing both insider knowledge and outside perspectives.[152]

2. **Selection.** The board assessed the pros and cons of an outsider versus an insider. At one point, they even considered the position of executive chairman. After months of deliberation involving major time commitments from the search chair, John Thompson, the board selected Satya Nadella.[153] Nadella had been with Microsoft since 1992 and was leading the company's Cloud and Enterprise group. Nadella's vision for cloud computing and his deep technical expertise were considered critical factors in his selection.

3. **Transition and support.** The transition was managed smoothly, with Ballmer stepping down and Nadella taking over in February 2014. Bill Gates also stepped

down as chairman to provide Nadella with six months of additional support and guidance as a technology advisor, which the committee believed would be necessary for a successful transition. Thompson became board chair, replacing Gates.

It paid off. The Microsoft board's methodical approach to selecting Satya Nadella, including forming a dedicated search committee, considering a diverse pool of internal and external candidates, and focusing on strategic criteria, exemplifies a successful corporate search process for finding the right CEO. This thorough and strategic approach ultimately led to Microsoft's significant resurgence and growth.

Under Nadella's leadership, Microsoft underwent and continues to undergo significant transformation, focusing on cloud computing, AI, and other innovative technologies. As of June 2024, Microsoft had a market capitalization of approximately $3.32 trillion, more than ten times what it was at the time Ballmer announced he was leaving. The company employs in the region of 221,000 people globally, a number that has remained consistent over the past year. Microsoft's substantial market cap reflects its dominant position in the technology sector, driven by its cloud services, software products, and ongoing innovations.[154]

One thing to note is that it appears that Microsoft didn't begin the search for Balmer's replacement until he announced his retirement. Having a succession planning process already in place could have made the task easier. In our next example, Apple had no choice. Steve Jobs' declining health was well-known for years.

Apple Inc. How do you find someone to replace Steve Jobs?

1. **Succession Planning and Search.** Apple's board had been engaged in succession planning for several years, recognizing the importance of identifying a capable leader to succeed Steve Jobs. Here are Apple's search criteria at that time:
– Operational Excellence
– Steady Leadership
– Cultural Continuity
– Global Perspective
– Vision for the Future
– Investor Confidence

In preparation, the board had been grooming Tim Cook, who had served as Apple's COO since 2007, as a potential successor. Cook was known for his operational expertise and leadership skills, having overseen Apple's global supply chain and manufacturing operations. He played a crucial role in streamlining Apple's production processes, improving efficiency, and ensuring product quality.

During Steve Jobs' medical leaves and absences, Cook served as interim CEO multiple times, demonstrating his ability to lead the company effectively. His steady leadership and strategic decision-making earned him the trust of Apple's board and senior executives.

Having worked closely with Steve Jobs for years, Cook was deeply ingrained in Apple's culture and values. He shared Jobs' passion for innovation, design excellence, and customer focus, which were core to Apple's identity and success. Cook's experience in managing Apple's international operations and expanding its presence in key markets worldwide were essential considerations. His understanding of global business dynamics and cultural nuances positioned him well to lead Apple's continued growth and expansion.

Cook articulated a clear vision for Apple's future, emphasizing innovation, sustainability, and customer experience. He recognized the potential of emerging technologies and new markets, charting a strategic course for Apple's continued success and relevance in the rapidly evolving tech industry.

2. **Selection.** In 2001, Cook's appointment as CEO was well-received by investors, who viewed him as a capable and trustworthy leader to steer Apple through its next growth phase. His transparent communication style and commitment to shareholder value instilled confidence in Apple's long-term prospects.

Overall, Tim Cook's selection as CEO validated the selection criteria, exemplifying the importance of strategic succession planning, operational expertise, cultural alignment, global perspective, visionary leadership, and investor confidence.

It paid off too! Under Cook's leadership, Apple has continued to innovate, launch new products and services, and deliver strong financial performance, maintaining its position as one of the world's most valuable and influential companies. As of June 28, 2024, Apple's market capitalization is approximately $3.28 trillion.[155] As of September 30, 2023 (the most recent official data), Apple had 161,000 employees.[156]

Lesson Worth Learning: Know what you need. Be patient and willing to compromise but recognize that you can't turn a canary into an eagle if an eagle is what you need

Selecting a CEO is a critical decision for any organization, and several key aspects should be considered in the process:

Leadership skills and vision

The CEO should possess strong leadership qualities, including the ability to inspire and motivate others, make tough decisions, and communicate a compelling vision for the organization's future. They should clearly understand the company's mission and goals and the strategic acumen to drive growth and innovation.

Industry experience and expertise

Industry-specific knowledge and experience can be invaluable in guiding the organization through challenges and opportunities. The ideal CEO candidate should deeply understand the industry landscape, market trends, and competitive dynamics, enabling them to make informed decisions and capitalize on market opportunities.

Track record of success

Candidates should have a proven track record of success in executive or leadership roles, demonstrating their ability to deliver results, drive profitability, and create value for stakeholders. Previous accomplishments, such as revenue growth, market expansion, successful product launches, or turnaround efforts, can serve as indicators of future performance.

Cultural fit

The CEO should align with the organization's culture, values, and mission. They should embody the desired cultural traits and behaviors, enabling a positive and inclusive work environment and building strong relationships with employees, customers, and other stakeholders. Cultural fit is essential for ensuring alignment and cohesion across the organization.

The easiest way to guarantee cultural fit is to select an internal candidate who has been steeped in the organization's culture. We note that both Nadella and Cook were internal, though both had ideas that differed from their predecessors in material ways.

Strategic thinking and innovation

A forward-thinking CEO who can anticipate market trends, identify emerging opportunities, and drive innovation is crucial for long-term success. The CEO should be able to develop and execute strategic initiatives that position the organization for growth and sustainability in a dynamic and competitive business environment.

Effective communication and stakeholder management

A CEO must have strong communication skills to effectively convey the organization's vision, strategy, and expectations to internal and external stakeholders, including employees, investors, customers, regulators, and the broader community. The CEO should also excel in stakeholder management, building and nurturing relationships to support the organization's objectives.

Ethical and Transparent Leadership

Integrity, ethics, and transparency are fundamental qualities for a CEO to uphold trust and credibility within the organization and with external stakeholders. The

CEO should demonstrate a commitment to ethical conduct, corporate governance best practices, and responsible decision-making, creating a culture of accountability and compliance.

Adaptability and resilience

In today's rapidly evolving business landscape, the CEO must be adaptable and resilient, able to navigate uncertainty, overcome challenges, and capitalize on opportunities. They should demonstrate agility in responding to market changes, technological advancements, regulatory developments, and other external factors that impact the organization's operations and strategy.

By considering these key aspects in CEO selection, organizations can identify candidates with the qualities, skills, and experience needed to lead effectively and drive sustainable growth and success.

Lesson Worth Learning: Succession planning matters

A leading practice is having a succession plan, just as Apple did before it was needed. That plan identifies either one potential CEO or several candidates for the board to consider when the time comes. Often, the plan is drafted by the current CEO. Identified successor candidates may be internal or external. Some boards go a step further and tie part of CEO compensation to career development and succession planning of the next tier of executive management.

Far-sighted boards also have an emergency succession plan in case the unexpected happens. Ideally, the plan should be updated annually as potential CEO talent matures and the situational context changes. That is a leading practice; unfortunately, nearly half of the corporate board directors surveyed admitted they did not have a plan, and 82 percent of those without plans had little confidence that they knew what they would do when confronted by a succession situation.[157]

Inside or outside? Long before the need to search for a new CEO, adaptive boards identify internal candidates and provide them with professional development opportunities. Board members monitor their progress and performance, make sure they get time in the boardroom, invite them to board dinners, and discuss their evolution and readiness with the current CEO.

Promoting from within sends a signal to the rest of the organization: Do a good job, and you will move up. In addition, internal candidates know the corporate culture. However, hiring an external candidate also has some advantages.

An outsider can bring different and sometimes better ways of thinking and running the organization. An outsider can also change culture when that is necessary. The academic literature on inside versus outside hiring is mixed but leans toward insider hiring being less risky. As one study concluded, "In only 7.2% of instances will an outside CEO hire have a 60% chance of outperforming an insider, and in a mere 2.8% of cases will he or she have a 90% chance of outperforming an insider."[158]

Process matters. Define the search process in advance. Does it involve the whole board, a standing committee, or an ad hoc committee? Will you look both inside the organization and outside? Will you use an executive search firm? What's the expected time frame, and when during the process will the full board be informed of progress (or lack thereof)? How will you ensure that appropriate potential candidates, including non-traditional candidates, are considered?[viii]

Ensure the process is transparent and unbiased to all board members (including those not directly involved). All board members should have had an opportunity to speak with the ultimate nominee before the final selection.

This might not be possible at some charitable boards, where the number of board members can be 25 or more. Such situations are usually resolved by using an executive committee and/or the nominations/governance committee or an ad hoc search committee. Finally, once a selection is made, have a communications plan to explain it to both inside and outside stakeholders.

Lesson Worth Learning: Evaluating – Just do it! Broaden your focus. Look ahead

Many boards use the compensation committee to formally evaluate the CEO or executive director annually. The most important part of evaluating a CEO is doing it. While some people find performance management difficult, most board members know that the purpose of the evaluation is neither to praise nor to punish. Instead, it's to help the CEO or executive director improve.

Periodic evaluations using established performance goals, set in advance and agreed upon by both the board and the individual, help ensure that the day-to-day leader and the board, as the organization's ultimate fiduciaries, are aligned.

Broaden your focus. Many boards find value in a 360-degree evaluation. Board members have a particular and limited view of the CEO. Gathering feedback from other executives, employees, and key stakeholders provides a more comprehensive perspective on the CEO's performance. Also, remember the Wells Fargo example? That CEO looked great . . . until he didn't. So, always look at how the performance has been achieved. Is it sustainable? Has the CEO acted ethically within the organization's culture and values?

---

viii Non-traditional candidates includes both ethnic/gender diverse candidates and candidates with non-traditional career paths.

Look ahead. As noted under "Inside or Outside," organizations like to have internal candidates ready to succeed the current CEO or executive director. This is prudent in a succession situation and helpful in developing the second line of executives' skills. The current leadership is responsible for developing and identifying future leadership. Make that part of the evaluation performance goals.

Lesson Worth Learning: When compensating, hire a specialist

Tomes have been written about executive compensation, so we defer to those in-depth treatments rather than try to add to their expertise in a format ill-suited to doing so. However, we note that compensation needs to be linked to the evaluation process and strategy so that incentives align with the organization's overall direction. See Chapter 4, "Set Direction and Policy."

One company that has traditionally aligned its CEO compensation with both its strategy and its culture is Johnson & Johnson (J&J). Its 2023 proxy statement reveals:

– It weights financial goals at 70 percent of total compensation. Those financial goals are three-fold: operational sales, adjusted earnings per share, and free cash flow.
– It weights achieving strategic goals at 30 percent of total compensation. Those strategic goals include:
  – critical business goals, including product pipeline and innovation, oncology treatments, digitalization and talent management, and separating its consumer health business from its pharmaceutical business
  – environmental, social, and governance goals, including quality and compliance (including a reduced number of health authority actions), safety, human capital management (including succession planning), diversity/equity/inclusion, and reduction in the use of plastics and electricity[159]

In addition, J&J notes,

In assessing our named executive officers' contributions, we look to results-oriented measures of performance as well as how those results were achieved. We consider whether the decisions and actions leading to the results were consistent with the values embodied in Our Credo and the long-term impact of the decisions.[160]

Conclusion

Common to all. Even though we specifically focus on the power to conduct business in this chapter, it is also part of all the remaining powers. How the board conducts itself in exercising those powers makes a difference, as we will see in the remaining chapters.

In exercising its power to conduct business (Figure 3.2), the board needs to:

1. Enable a high-performing culture that promotes ethical behavior, transparency, and accountability.
2. Build consensus and make the highest and best use of everyone's time and talents.
3. Use committee assignments and board members' expertise to address the organization's issues and challenges effectively.
4. Plan director succession, including the nomination and compensation processes.
5. Select, evaluate, compensate, and plan for the succession of the CEO.

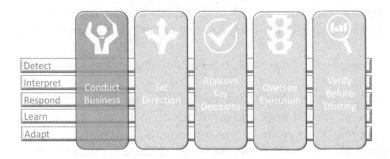

Figure 3.2: Conduct Business.

Next, we discuss the essential power of the board to "Set Direction and Policy." What are the critical issues facing the organization for the foreseeable future? What are our "life or death" assumptions? What if they are wrong? What are the options available?

One ship drives east and another drives west
With the selfsame winds that blow.
Tis the set of the sails
And not the gales
Which tells us the way to go.
Ella Wheeler Wilcox, American Author and Poet

Chapter 4
Set direction and policy

Set Direction and Policy – Critical Questions and Lessons Worth Learning

Critical Questions	Lessons Worth Learning
Role of the Board	
1. Is the board clear about its role in setting direction and policy?	– The board needs to be involved throughout the entire strategic thinking and planning process. Executives do the heavy lifting.
	– Committees usually do the research, provide oversight, and make recommendations for board approval.
Mission and Values	
2. Is there alignment on the mission and values?	– Alignment on the mission and values forms the foundation of every successful strategic plan.
3. Is the strategic plan truly strategic?	– Strategy is the plan for adaptation. Policies define the expectations.
	– Adaptive boards maintain a long-term perspective.
Detect Signals	
4. Have critical issues been identified?	– Maintain situational awareness. What's vital? What's changing? How fast?
	– Early signal detection and pattern recognition are critical to successful adaptation.
	– Look for what you least expect.
Interpret	
5. What are the existential opportunities and threats?	– Symmetric strategies and rules are the way the game is played today.
	– Asymmetric strategies change the game and the rules.
	– A straight line isn't always the shortest route.
Respond strategically	
6. What are our strategic options?	– Think "out-of-the-box" – it's the key to radical innovation and anticipating asymmetric competition.
	– Start by defining the box. Make life-or-death assumptions explicit.
	– Iterate. Have a range of real options ready for uncertainty.

https://doi.org/10.1515/9783111344027-004

(continued)

Critical Questions	Lessons Worth Learning
Respond strategically	
7. Have strategic options been systematically evaluated?	– Take intelligent, necessary risks. Understand your options and the rewards and risks of action and inaction. – Performance and risk are inseparable. – Understand your risk appetite. – Prioritize resources.
8. Have strategic goals and metrics been agreed upon?	– Goals need to be relevant, measurable, and balanced. – The choice of vital signs (metrics) is strategic.
9. Is the organization aligned with the strategy?	– Don't underestimate the power of organizational inertia. – Misalignment of compensation and incentives causes inertia and resistance to change.
Learn and Adapt	
10. Are we on track? (Also, see feedback loop in Oversee)	– Are expectations being met or exceeded? – What are the policy implications? – Should the organization stay, adjust, or change course?

Introduction

If I had asked people what they wanted, they would have said faster horses.
Henry Ford, Founder Ford Motor Company

The purpose of the organization is to ceaselessly create, deliver, capture, and protect value. High-performing organizations are driven by a focus on value to customers. You can't shrink or financially engineer your way to greatness. Without customers, an enterprise has no real economic purpose. Neglecting the needs of customers inevitably puts an enterprise at risk. But does the customer know what they really want?

Who knows what customers want? For instance, Apple is known for its culture of celebrating product design to create a unique customer experience. However, the late Steve Jobs, Apple's CEO, said, "People don't know what they want until you show it to them. That's why I never rely on market research. Our task is to read things that are not yet on the page."

Like Ford and Jobs, Harvard professor Clayton Christiansen said this was the "Innovator's Dilemma." If you just listen to what your current customers want, you will miss what future customers will need.[161] By 2012, Apple's relentless focus on the customer made it the most valuable company in the world, a position it would hold (other than for brief periods) for more than a decade. The company that replaced it as number one is Nvidia.

In 2009, its CEO Jen-Hsun "Jensen" Huang said essentially the same thing.[162]

> Sometimes you have to ignore your customers. The reason for that is because they don't know the nature of your business. While the industry is being created, before there's common sense about the rules of that business, there is no way they can possibly know. 3D Graphics was insatiable. It was insatiable that if I made something twice as good every year, even if the customer never asked for it, even if the customer told us it was too expensive, even if the customer told you that they're not interested.
>
> I took our products back to Dell, HP, IBM, and Gateway. They all told me it was too much money. They said, "You're well outside of the boundaries of what we are willing to pay for." When your customers all tell you not to do something, the question is, what do you do?
>
> In our case, because we had this unique perspective that the demand for 3D graphics would be insatiable, and Moore's Law was our friend, therefore, we decided should make our graphics processors twice as good every year.[163]

Beware of short-termism. Short-termism focuses on the short-term to the detriment of long-term value. It is the sugar high of corporations; it tastes great but is full of empty calories that add fat, not muscle. Short-termism has many manifestations.

One danger is the desire to protect the current profit and loss (P&L) by hanging onto a lucrative but dying cash cow. For example, engineer Steven Sasson created the world's first digital camera in 1975 while working for Eastman Kodak. But Kodak chose to protect its film franchise, which was minting money at the time.[164]

The result was one of the worst performance choices ever, as others jumped on the digital bandwagon and left analog film behind. By January 2012, Kodak had filed for bankruptcy.[165] Focusing on long-term sustainability and growth rather than short-term gains prevents mistakes that seem so tempting at the time.

Kodak's decision to forego digital took a short-term view to put its existing P&L first, not the customers. As Peter Drucker wrote, "The purpose of a business is to create a customer . . . and has two – and only these two – basic functions: marketing and innovation."[166]

Discontinuously improve. Discontinuous improvement, also known as breakthrough improvement or radical improvement, refers to a significant and transformative change in processes, systems, products, or services that results in substantial gains in performance, efficiency, and effectiveness. Unlike incremental improvements, which involve small changes over time, discontinuous improvement involves revolutionary shifts or breakthroughs that fundamentally alter how things are done or perceived. It doesn't just apply to new technologies.

Discontinuous improvement often requires thinking outside the box, challenging existing norms and assumptions, and embracing innovative ideas and approaches. It may involve adopting new technologies, redesigning processes, restructuring organizations, or creating entirely new business models. Discontinuous improvement aims to achieve breakthrough results that propel the organization forward and create a significant competitive advantage. It may even involve cannibalizing an existing profit center to create a bigger one, as Kodak only learned in retrospect.

Lesson Worth Learning: Setting direction and policy is an essential power of the board

> One small step for man, one giant leap for mankind.
> *Neil Armstrong, Astronaut, upon landing on the moon on July 20, 1969*

The board plays a critical role in setting the strategic direction. The executives do the heavy lifting, but the board needs to thoroughly understand and embrace the strategy. If an organization's purpose is to achieve its mission by ceaselessly creating, delivering, capturing, and protecting value, then the purpose of strategy is to enable rapid adaptation – in good times and bad.

All strategy is based on the mission and values. They are the North Star of the organization. The measure of successful adaptation is whether the organization thrives, with longevity, and learns from the effectiveness of its strategies. Strategic thinking enables the board to make informed choices about direction and resource allocation in the face of uncertainty to increase resilience to adversity and the agility to seize opportunities.

An effective strategic plan starts from the organization's vision, mission, and values. The best plans are also situationally aware and cross-functional, cutting across the entire enterprise. What are the opportunities, challenges, and risks of the strategy under consideration? What resources are needed (leading practice is to perform a gap analysis of what is missing)? What do all departments have to achieve for the enterprise to be successful in achieving its mission?

Resources may be reallocated from one business line or operating department to another, capital raised, or through changes in the capital structure, talent management, partnerships, outsourcing, insourcing, mergers/acquisitions/divestitures/joint ventures, etc.

Applying the adaptive governance process to setting strategy

Strategy thinking and development begin with detecting signals that can affect strategic direction (Figure 4.1). These include external vital factors such as competition, stakeholders, geopolitics, social and economic conditions, technological breakthroughs, legal and regulatory rules, and environmental issues. Internal vital factors include people, finances, operations, other resources such as intellectual property and brand, and cyber-security. Detection of a change in the environment often changes objectives or strategies; however, much less frequently does even today's volatile landscape affect mission and vision.

Figure 4.1: An adaptive governance process.

Strategic thinking is a continuous, not an intermittent process. The purpose is to identify what's vital, what's changing, and how fast it's changing. Most organizations are set up to identify symmetric signals but aren't very good at detecting asymmetric signals.

Asymmetric signals are those coming from unexpected origins; think of industry disruptors. For example, for retailers at the turn of the 21st century, symmetric threats were coming from Walmart, which had fine-tuned conventional store retailing. But asymmetric threats were coming from Amazon, which largely did away with stores, replacing them with logistics and virtual shopping experiences.

The next step is to interpret those signals. Are they threats or opportunities? What are the strategic implications for the existing business model and for the future business model? Are the "rules" of the game-changing? Or is the "game" itself changing? Which of these are existential opportunities or could become existential threats if not acted upon?

Next comes developing strategic responses. What is the range of real options available? What is the least to the most that could be done? What are the associated risks and rewards of each action and inaction? What are the risks of the strategy itself? What are the risks to the strategy's successful execution? Is the organization aligned to accomplish the strategy, including compensation and incentives?

Once executed, the board must oversee how the strategy is working. What can be learned from actual performance compared to expectations? Should the organization stay the current course, adjust the course, or change course? To enable an adaptive response, there must be a feedback loop between the oversight of actual performance compared to strategic and policy expectations and the direction and policy-setting process. Likewise, there must be feedback loops between Approval and Setting Direction and Oversight.

The idea is to understand:
- How may the environment (competition, regulation, stakeholders, etc.) accelerate or inhibit progress?
- What needs to be accomplished to achieve the mission?
- What key milestone goals and metrics are needed to judge whether the enterprise is making progress?

–   What capabilities and resources do the enterprise require to achieve those milestones, and how to build them where and when needed?
–   Who is accountable for what?
–   What is needed for successful adaptation?

What is strategy? Strategy and its execution can be complex. Strategy aligns an organization's aspirations with the practical steps needed to achieve its mission and vision.

Let's begin with a structured hierarchy (Figure 4.2) to describe the relationships between an organization's vision, mission, values, strategies and policies, goals, objectives, and metrics. Each of these elements is integral to overall success. They are more interwoven than shown here and are separated only for discussion purposes.

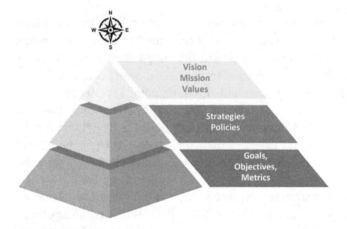

Figure 4.2: A Strategic Framework.

Vision, mission, values. The vision is the broadest and most future-oriented articulation of what the organization aspires to become or achieve in the long term. It sets a clear, idealistic direction based on its ambitions. In effect, the vision statement defines the organization's "soul" – its immutable characteristics, its DNA (or at least its desired DNA).

More specific than the vision, the mission statement describes what the organization does, whom it serves, and how it serves them in creating, delivering, capturing, and protecting value. The mission supports the vision by outlining how the organization seeks to move toward that future state.

Values are the principles or ethical standards that guide the organization's behavior and decision-making processes. They support the vision and mission by ensuring that all actions and strategies are culturally and ethically aligned. While nothing is forever in an ever-changing world, vision, mission, and values should be long-term and will change much less frequently than, for example, objectives.

Strategies. Strategies reflect priorities, risk appetite, and resource allocation. Strategies are the broad approaches the organization will use to adapt, achieve its mission, and move toward its vision. Strategies are developed in response to and in anticipation of critical issues (opportunities and challenges). Strategies need to specifically acknowledge and then enable adaptation to an ever-changing environment. Strategies outline how the organization will act to meet its objectives effectively and thereby adapt.

That said, strategies are not detailed blueprints. Organizations must choose which strategic options they will pursue and which they will not. The door also needs to be left open to choose other options as conditions inevitably change. The more uncertain and volatile the environment, the more flexibility and adaptability matter. Later in this chapter, we discuss methods and tools to deal with flexibility, such as real options and critical issue and options summaries (CIOS).

Goals. Goals are the targets the organization sets within the strategic framework to achieve part of its mission or strategy. They can encompass multiple areas or activities. Objectives are specific, measurable targets that, when combined, should achieve one or more goals. They are concrete, often short-term, and achievable. Metrics or vital signs measure the success of achieving objectives and, by extension, the progress toward goals, the effectiveness of strategies, and the overall advancement toward the vision and mission.

In summary, vision sets the long-term outcome, mission directs present activities, values ensure alignment, strategies define the approach, goals set specific targets, objectives break down these targets into actionable steps, and metrics evaluate the success of all endeavors. Each component builds upon the previous one, creating a cohesive and focused organizational plan. And, of course, all this needs to occur within the context of high situational awareness.

Project Apollo. In 1962, when John F. Kennedy said the United States would land a man on the moon by the end of the decade, that was the mission statement. The vision and values were implicit but universally understood at the time – America would lead the world to a better place – and American values, understood as democracy, improved living conditions, etc., were considered integral to America's ability to lead.

That may now seem naïve, but they were strongly held beliefs at the time. President Kennedy was also reacting to the external environment – the space race with the then Union of Soviet Socialist Republics (U.S.S.R.), whose early success and communist ideology were viewed as a threat to that vision and the free world.

The goal was specific – by the end of the decade. The objectives were myriad – to form the National Aeronautics and Space Administration (NASA), build a rocket with all the subsystems (propulsion, life support), create a ground control organization, recruit astronauts, etc. Each objective was measured for progress toward success. Less than seven years later, the U.S. landed a man on the moon.

Ten critical questions the board should always ask about strategy

*Designing a winning strategy is the art of asking questions, experimenting, and then
constantly renewing the thinking process by questioning the answers. No matter how good
today's strategy is you must always keep reinventing it.*
Constantinos Markides, Author of Game-Changing Strategies

The "moonshot" was such a success that it lends its name to any ambitious mission
statement, strategy, or goal that initially looks unachievable. But, as Microsoft
founder Bill Gates said, "Success is a lousy teacher. It seduces smart people into thinking they can't lose."[167] If everything always goes smoothly, then there is no learning.

As Gates implies, there are many times when smart people – really smart people like those who sat around the board tables at Theranos, Wells Fargo, Enron,
WorldCom, and so many other organizations – fail miserably. So, what are the
hallmarks of failure? And what can we learn from them?

Remember when organizations fail, especially catastrophically, one of the
first questions asked is, "Where was the board?" One of the first answers is usually that they weren't asking the right questions. Here are ten critical questions
the board should always ask during the direction and policy-setting process:

Role of the Board
1. Is the board clear about its role in setting direction and policy?
Mission and Values
2. Is there alignment on the mission and values?
3. Is the plan truly strategic?
Detect Signals
4. Have critical issues been identified?
Interpret
5. What are the existential opportunities and threats?
Respond
6. What are our strategic options?
7. Have strategic options been systematically evaluated?
8. Have strategic goals and metrics been agreed upon?
9. Is the organization aligned with the strategy?
Learn and Adjust
10. Are we on track?

The following pages describe the lessons worth learning in answer to these questions based on the successes and failures of others.

1 Is our board clear about its role in setting direction and policy?

The basic governance issues are those of power and accountability. Nowhere are the issues of power and accountability more clearly in evidence than in the working out of a strategy for an organization.

A firm's strategy determines the course it will try to pursue over several years; strategy guides the allocation of resources . . . financial, physical, and human. And strategy often determines how well or poorly a company fares and what its return to shareholders will be.

Clearly, strategy must be a subject that engages the interests of all the members of a firm's strategic apex – top management and the board of directors and, of course, the pivot point between the board and management, the Chief Executive Officer.[168]

Sir Adrian Cadbury, late UK governance icon and Chairman of Cadbury and Cadbury Schweppes

Lesson Worth Learning: The board needs to be involved at key points throughout the entire strategic thinking and planning process

From beginning to end. Boards have the power and responsibility to determine the organization's vision, mission, and values and to set clear direction and policy. They need to decide if they have the necessary expertise and, if not, whether to recruit or retain it. Ultimately, the board is the responsible and final decision-maker. It can say yes or no.

Boards often delegate strategy and policy development to committees and/or the executive. The board should be kept apprised throughout the planning process at key junctures to build a shared understanding, acceptance, and commitment at the full board. The board should decide how it wishes to participate. Many organizations hold special strategy or planning sessions, sometimes even "off-site." That's for good reasons. Strategic retreats or special strategy meetings ensure the board and management are not distracted by the normal business of a regular board meeting.

Spend the time. An effective strategy takes preparation, time, and focus, and the board should be prepared to commit that time. The committee presents its recommendations at the end of the planning process. However, the CEO is the de facto chief strategy officer, and collaboration between the committee and executive management is key. There is one exception worth mentioning. In a crisis, especially one involving management, more of the workload can shift to the board.

Commit. Without strong board support, pressures to prematurely abandon the strategy may emerge when inevitable "bumps in the road" are encountered. Milestones – agreements on when progress is acceptable or when to change course – should be agreed upon in advance. Once a strategy is determined, authority, resources, and accountability should be prudently delegated to the executives and staff for execution.[i]

Lesson Worth Learning: Board committees do the research, provide oversight, and make recommendations for board approval, while executives do the heavy lifting

While the balance between committee input and management's development of the plan and policies will vary by organization, strategic plans are typically developed by management – they do the heavy lifting.

The committee's role is to oversee the planning process, review, constructively challenge, refine, and then recommend that the board ratify and, ultimately, resource the approved plan. By agreeing on those roles in advance, misunderstandings can be avoided.

Ideally, no strategic plan should ever be totally rejected. If that happens, then there has been either a fundamental disagreement about vision, mission, and values between the executive and the board or a communication breakdown. In either situation, the dysfunction between management and the board is likely deeper than the disagreement on a strategy (Table 4.1).

Table 4.1: The Role of Committees in Strategy.

Adaptability and flexibility	Committees can be standing or ad hoc. Ad hoc committees can be formed or disbanded as needed to address evolving strategic priorities and challenges facing the organization.
Efficiency and focus	Committees allow a smaller group to dive deep into specific issues and develop detailed recommendations. This allows for more efficient use of the board's time and resources and helps prevent overburdening the full board with every detail of strategy and policy development.
Expertise	Committees can be composed of board members with relevant expertise in particular areas and can retain additional expertise as needed. This allows for more informed and nuanced development of strategies and policies.
Thorough analysis	Committees have the time to conduct in-depth research and analysis on complex topics that the full board may not be able to do. This results in more thoroughly vetted recommendations.

---

i The board may reserve final authority over certain key decisions, as discussed in the chapter: "Approve Key Decisions, then Prudently Delegate."

Table 4.1 (continued)

Preparation for board decisions	By developing strategies and policies at the committee level first, the full board is presented with well-formulated options to consider rather than starting from scratch.
Stakeholder engagement	Committees may be better positioned to engage with relevant stakeholders (management, shareholders, etc.) during the development process.

Strategies are the gas pedal and the steering wheel. Policies are the brakes. Policies are written statements of intent or guidelines that describe the board's mandatory standards, expectations, and rules. They define what is expected and acceptable behavior. Policies direct decisions and actions to achieve specific outcomes. Policies are generally broad in scope and address major functions or issues. They state what can and can't be done, what should be done, and why rather than how to do it. Policies tend to change infrequently compared to procedures and guidelines.

The purpose of policies is to:

– communicate the organization's values, philosophy, and culture
– require compliance with laws and regulations
– promote consistency and efficiency in operations
– reduce risk and liability
– empower decision-making at various levels

While committees (with staff and advisory support) do the detailed work in strategy and policy development, the full board still retains ultimate responsibility for approving and overseeing strategy and major policies. Committees make recommendations, but final decisions rest with the entire board.

Effective use of committees requires clear charters and good communication with the full board. The board still needs to be actively engaged and needs to thoughtfully review and approve or reject committee recommendations.

2 Are we aligned on the mission and values?

> Building a visionary company requires one percent vision and 99 percent alignment.
> *Jim Collins and Jerry Porras,* Built to Last[169]

Lesson Worth Learning: Alignment on the mission and values is the foundation of every successful strategic plan

Align, align, align. In our experience, the biggest risk to a strategic plan is a fundamental misalignment with an organization's mission, values, and compensation (more on the latter shortly). In "Conduct Business," we discussed the Enron and Wells Fargo scandals from an ethical point of view. Another way to think about them was that the strategy they adopted conflicted with the mission and values those companies espoused.

Open AI. More recently, there was the curious case of OpenAI, where confusion about the mission affected the board and the strategy. Even the organization's capital structure was confused. The structure was designed to serve two masters – a non-profit mission with the capital needs of a multi-billion-dollar for-profit company. What was the lesson learned? Alignment and agreement matter. Get that wrong, and even the smartest people will stumble.

OpenAI was founded in December 2015 by Elon Musk, Sam Altman, Greg Brockman, Ilya Sutskever, Wojciech Zaremba, and John Schulman. Its mission was to be an artificial intelligence research organization that develops and promotes AI to benefit humanity, with a focus on ensuring AI technologies are used safely and ethically.

On November 17, 2023, OpenAI's Board fired CEO Sam Altman, ostensibly because of concerns about his commitment to the company's mission of safe and beneficial AI development. The decision was influenced by disputes over how the company should balance profitability and ethical considerations regarding AI technology deployment.[170]

Altman's firing led to major turmoil. More than 700 of OpenAI's employees signed a letter demanding the board's resignation, and a significant number indicated they would leave the company if changes were not made.[171] This internal revolt highlights a significant discord between the board's decision and the perspectives of the company's employees and other stakeholders.[172] Over the following weekend, Altman was immediately hired by Microsoft to lead a new AI research unit, further complicating the situation and indicating potential shifts in the competitive landscape of AI development.[173]

Given the backlash, OpenAI quickly rehired Altman, and the board was reconstituted.

A critical board responsibility is to ensure alignment of the mission, vision, values, vital functions, and compensation (Table 4.2). This is essential for organizational coherence and successful adaptation. The odds of creating and executing a successful strategy without alignment are daunting; it's like trying to build a skyscraper on a shaky foundation.

Table 4.2: Mission Alignment – Lessons Worth Learning.

Clear and coherent mission and values	Clearly articulate the mission, vision, and values to all stakeholders, including employees, shareholders, and customers, to maintain alignment across the organization. Every board decision and action should support the sustainable creation, delivery, capture, and protection of value as defined by the mission, and continuing adaptation.
Stakeholder engagement	Require ongoing constructive engagement with stakeholders to gather diverse perspectives on how the organization's mission and values are perceived externally and internally and on how well the organization is "living" that mission.
Strategic choices	Strategies need to be both symmetric and asymmetric. Symmetric strategies are characteristic of conventional competitors using similar conventional approaches to create, deliver, capture, and protect value. They play by the same rules. Think of conventional brick-and-mortar stores as standing armies in uniforms as compared to e-tailers, who are initially the asymmetric special forces. Asymmetric strategies change the rules and attack the weaknesses of the conventional symmetric players because they are initially at least too big and well-resourced to attack directly, i.e., symmetrically. Netflix vs. Blockbuster until the tables are turned.
Regularly review for alignment	Be situationally aware if the environment has changed in a way that demands changes to the organization's mission, vision, and values. Are they still relevant? Are the board's decisions, strategies, and performance metrics consistent with them?
Performance metrics	Set performance metrics directly linked to the mission, vision, and values. Specify if the metrics evaluate organizational performance, individual contributions, or both.
Compensation alignment	Compensation structures (including salaries, bonuses, and other incentives) should align with the organization's mission and values. Reward behaviors and results that advance the organization's goals and discourage those that do not. Be vigilant for adverse incentives and monitor for unintended consequences.

Clearly, even when there is alignment, there will always be challenges. However, without alignment, if the strategy is untethered from the organizational mission and values, it is doomed.

3 Is our plan truly strategic?

> Strategy is not the consequence of planning, but the opposite: Its starting point.
> *Henry Mintzberg, Cleghorn Professor of Management Studies, McGill University*

But what is a strategic plan? That's not as naïve a question as it first appears. All good strategic plans have two things in common. They answer two simple, high-level questions: "What is the organization trying to accomplish? How?"

Lesson Worth Learning: Strategy is the plan for organizational adaptation

Many enterprises have so-called "strategic" plans, which are anything but. Rather, they are collections of tactics, resources, opportunities, and challenges bounded by business lines. For instance, there may be an annual plan for IT, sales goals, new product/service goals, etc. Those are not strategic plans; strategic plans allocate focus, resources, and risk across the organization toward a longer-term goal.

Siloed plans, even if they verge on strategic for the various operating departments, are not a strategic plan for the enterprise overall, especially not when they are designed to be revised annually. Equally insufficient, in the other direction, is a goal or aspirational statement without an associated and well-designed "plan," such as being the leader in a particular market. That's not a strategy; it's wishful thinking.

Such wishful thinking can be dangerous. Consider all the companies that have made climate-related pledges without concurrent strategies, goals, objectives, or metrics and how they are now criticized and sometimes penalized for "greenwashing."

Lesson Worth Learning: Adaptive boards maintain a long-term perspective

> Time is the friend of the wonderful company, the enemy of the mediocre.
> *Warren Buffet, American Businessman*[174]

It's your choice. If you are asked to choose between two courses of action, one short-term and one long-term, something interesting happens in your brain. Thinking about "now" versus "later" causes neurological activity in both your limbic system and pre-frontal cortex. Evolutionarily, the limbic system is one of the older parts of the brain and is generally considered more "emotional." That is, it has less cognitive power. By contrast, the pre-frontal cortex is associated with more rational, analytic thinking.[175]

In other words, when asked to make a choice over different time periods, human brains create tension. The "sugar high" of short-term, impulse-driven reaction competes emotionally against the analytical conclusion that acting long-term could be more important and, ultimately, more successful. Moreover, human beings seem to be genetically wired to "hyper-discount" the future. For example, Bank of England Chief Economist Andrew Haldane notes that investors value cash flows that are 5 years ahead as if they were 8 years away and cash flows 10 years out as if they will only occur 16 years away. "Investment choice . . . is being re-tuned to a shorter wavelength."[176]

Something similar happens in organizations. Short-termism – choosing to maximize short-term results even when that may hurt long-term interests – may be a very human failing, but it is one that poses a flashing danger sign to a board that is setting strategy. Agreeing on a time frame can be the key to aligning strategy across the board and in the executive office. Short-term performance pressures can result in an over-emphasis on quarterly earnings, with less attention paid to strategy and long-term value creation, protection, and sustainability.

By focusing narrowly on short-term financial metrics, organizations may miss opportunities for long-term growth, innovation, and mid- or long-term threats. They may starve the organization of needed resources. This can result in lost market share, competitive disadvantage, and, ultimately, stagnation, decline, or extinction as competitors with a more long-term focus seize opportunities.

Short-term solutions such as lean manufacturing, just-in-time, and some types of offshoring and outsourcing can offer short-term benefits but create long-term problems, such as strategic vulnerabilities caused by loss of core competencies and susceptibility to supply chain disruptions. Likewise, short-term incentive compensation and turf protection can result in devasting long-term consequences. Boeing's 2024 decision to buy back Spirit AeroSystems, which it spun off in 2005, is a belated recognition of the problems that go with outsourcing core competencies.[177]

Adaptive boards maintain a long-term perspective. Admittedly, "long-term" is a fuzzy time increment. It varies with the facts and circumstances of each specific situation. Among the factors to consider are the pace of innovation in the industry, the knowledge and ability of the board and executive to forecast, the stage of evolution of the entity itself, and the clarity and effectiveness of metrics to measure interim progress.

Longer periods are preferable; true transformation takes time. Depending on where you mark the start of the process, it took Apple three to five years to create the smartphone. All during that time, the company diverted resources – including some of its best engineers – to the secret project, creating short-term costs with no matching revenues.[178]

There are exceptional cases where strategic plans may be short-term. For example, a special purpose enterprise formed to create an event – such as a music festival occurring in a matter of months – will obviously have a shorter time horizon.

Another example of taking the long-term view is the Seventh Generation Principle adopted by some First Nations, based on an ancient Haudenosaunee (Iroquois) philosophy.[179] Simply put, the decisions made today should result in a sustainable world seven generations into the future.

But whether it is three years, five years, or even seven generations will depend on several factors: Your mission? How rapidly is your industry changing? Do you really know what's not changing? How good is your intelligence? How quickly can you ramp up, wind down, or change direction? What are the constraints: money, people, or regulation? Or are they internal, such as an unclear plan or a mismatch between your risk tolerance and what is needed to achieve the strategy?

Pick your planning horizon wisely. Some may argue that a long-term view is impractical given the unpredictable environment, even while a horizon that is too short can lead to myopia and underinvestment. In practice, most organizations use a combination of planning horizons to balance long-term vision and strategy with short-term performance and flexibility.

This often involves creating rolling plans that are regularly updated to reflect changes in the external environment and the organization's performance. A layered approach – incorporating strategic (long-term), tactical (medium-term), and operational (short-term) planning – is commonly used to ensure alignment and adaptability.

4 Have critical issues been identified?

> Anything less than a conscious commitment to the important
> is an unconscious commitment to the unimportant.
> *Stephen Covey, Author*

What critical issues will the organization need to address for the foreseeable future? Adaptive organizations conduct environmental scans for four reasons:
1. Learn from hindsight.
2. Detect signals and recognize patterns.
3. Gain insight into current and future critical issues.
4. Anticipate as best as possible inevitable uncertainties and opportunities.

Remember to avoid DRIP. Sportscaster Jon Miller said, "It's not about big data; it's about translating big data into clear insights." Unfortunately, conventional scans are DRIP (data rich but insight poor) for several reasons.

Scans are often subjective and, therefore, subject to bias. They can result in information overload, and in a rapidly changing environment, they can quickly become outdated. Also, most scans are designed to identify symmetric or conventional risks because they look at conventional or symmetric competitors and traditional markets and constraints. Therefore, they miss asymmetric or unconventional opportunities or threats. Finally, there are often perverse incentives to ignore unwelcome information from the scans.[180]

In most organizations, an attitude of "if it's not broke, don't fix it" creates disincentives to change and a comfort level with a status quo plan to "stick to the knitting."[181] However, the question isn't whether the current mode is broken or not but whether someone or something else outside the organization has developed an entirely new mode of operating – or if the environment has changed so much – that the current mode is not just broken but obsolete.

1. The printing press: In 1492, scholar Johannes Trithemius predicted that the printing press would never last, arguing that handwritten books were superior and would outlast printed ones. Ironically, his criticism was widely disseminated thanks to the printing press.[182]
2. The telephone: When Alexander Graham Bell debuted the telephone in 1876, it was met with skepticism. *The New York Times* warned that it could be "a device of the enemies of the Republic." Western Union, the telegraph giant, famously rejected the opportunity to buy Bell's patent, a decision that rivals the worst in business history.[183]
3. The airplane: Many experts believed heavier-than-air flight was impossible. In 1903, *The New York Times* predicted that it would take 1 to 10 million years to develop a flying machine, just days before the Wright brothers succeeded in their first flight.[184]
4. Automobiles: Early cars were seen as noisy, dangerous novelties. In 1899, *The Literary Digest* predicted, "The ordinary horseless carriage is at present a luxury for the wealthy; and although its price will probably fall in the future, it will never come into as common use as the bicycle."[185]
5. The Internet: In its early days, the Internet's potential was vastly underestimated. Even Microsoft initially undervalued its importance.[186]
6. Tablets: Microsoft's early tablet efforts in the early 2000s failed to gain traction, with many seeing them as unnecessary. It wasn't until Apple's iPad in 2010 that tablets became widely adopted.[187]

Shifts happen fast. All of these analyses share a common trait: They are rooted in the familiar, day-to-day context of the time they were conducted, even as they looked toward the future. As discussed in Chapter 2, inertia is a powerful and problematic force that can seriously hinder an organization's ability to adapt.

Real situational awareness is an unbiased ability to detect signals from noise and receptivity to unconventional and asymmetric risk signals. A board must proactively set direction and policy focusing on long-term value creation rather than short-term gains. Truly adaptive boards understand the changing landscape and thoughtfully consider sustainability, innovation, and resilience in strategic decision-making.

When organizations lose situational awareness, ignore the signals they see, choose the wrong metrics, or fail to adapt rapidly, they quickly fail despite prior success.

According to the Christensen Institute, "data is a poor judge of opportunity."[188] In each of the cases outlined in Table 4.3, the board and executive missed critical opportunities or threats. They often either did not see the signals, failed to recognize the patterns, ignored warning signals, or failed to anticipate their direction until too late, often with fatal consequences.

Table 4.3: Missed Opportunities that Became Threats.

The Company	The Signal	The Board's Response
Kodak (bankrupt 2012)	Growth of digital photography[189]	Stuck with film. Missed digital photography despite having invented it in 1975.[190]
Blockbuster (bankrupt 2010)	Growth of mail delivery and DVDs/Declining store traffic.[191]	Twice refused to purchase Netflix for $50 million.[192]
Sears (bankrupt 2018)	Growth of e-commerce[193]	Stayed store-based and never spent enough online e-commerce to have competitive online sales presence.[194]
Excite (acquired by Ask.com 2004)	Growth of Internet search[195]	Could have bought Google for $750k in 1999.[196]
Yahoo acquired by Verizon in 2017	Growth of Internet search[197]	Could have bought Google for $1m in 1999,[198] and turned them down again in 2002 for $5 billion.[199]
Encyclopedia Britannica (discontinued print edition 2012 after 244 years)[200]	Growth of Internet search – online/Crowd sourced/Free/Mobile	Stuck with print and subject matter expert model far too long.[201] Lost essential position as general knowledge resource to Wikipedia and others online.[202]
HP	Growth of personal computers	Executives turned down Steve Wozniak's (co-founder Apple) proposals for personal computer five times.[203]
Xerox	Growth of personal computers[204]	Stuck with copiers despite developing the Alto, the first personal computer in 1973.[205]

Table 4.3 (continued)

The Company	The Signal	The Board's Response
Digital Equipment Corporation (acquired by Compaq in 1998)	Growth of personal computers[206]	Stuck with mini-computers.[207]
IBM	Growth of retail customers and software	IBM gave up personal computing software market to focus on hardware, opening easy market entry to Microsoft and Apple.[208]
AT&T	Growth of cellular	Stuck with land lines too long; delayed entry into cellular.
Nokia,[209] Blackberry,[210] Motorola[211]	Growth of multi-function phones	All three dominant phone companies stuck with conventional operating systems and hardware, crashing what had been their high market share in mobile phones.[212]
Evergrande, ordered to liquidate by Hong Kong court in 2024. Had more than $300 billion in debt.	Overcapacity and vacancy rates[213]	Ignored warning signs and interest rates, kept building and borrowing to grow its real estate business.[214]

Lesson Worth Learning: Maintain high situational awareness. What's vital? What's changing? How fast?

To properly manage any business situation, you need to perform a full and complete assessment of it. In business, you have to understand your competitors, their distribution, their economics, their innovations, and their strengths and weaknesses. You also need to understand customers and their changing preferences, along with your own costs, your people and their skills.

Then there's knowing how other factors fit in, like technology, risk, motivations . . . hope you get the point. For countries, you need a thorough grasp of their economies, strengths and weaknesses, population and education, access to raw materials, laws and regulations, history and culture. Research, data, and analytics should be at a very detailed level and constantly reassessed. Only after you complete this diligent study can you start to make plans with a high degree of success.[215]

Jamie Dimon, CEO, JP Morgan Chase. Letter to shareholders, April 8, 2024

Think back to the examples of those who failed to detect the signals, recognize the patterns, and adapt (Table 4.4). Many of those organizations exhibited some or all of the following policies, processes, and/or people and organizational issues.

Table 4.4: Potential Causes of Missed Signals.

Policy and Process Issues	
Poor situational analysis and inadequate analytics	Without the right tools to analyze and interpret data, organizations might fail to extract valuable insights from the information they collect. This is particularly an issue in today's data-rich world, where the sheer volume of data can create noise that drowns out vital signals.
Failure to effectively monitor the environment	Neglecting to keep an eye on external changes in market trends, technologies, regulations, and competitive actions and the internal environment in culture, communication, and incentives.
Linear thinking	Following a systematic and analytical thought process in a known step-by-step progression like a straight line when the problem may be non-linear, e.g., using discounted cash flows to model the value of non-linear new technology.
Poor strategic alignment	When the strategy is not clearly aligned with market conditions and organizational capabilities, it can be difficult to recognize or prioritize the most relevant signals.
Failure to challenge "life or death" assumptions	Assumptions underpin all plans. It can be very difficult to make "life or death" assumptions explicit. In 1977, Ken Olson, founder of Digital Equipment Corporation (DEC), assumed there was no need or use for anyone to have a computer in their home.[216] DEC ceased to be an independent company about a decade later.
People and Organization Issues	
Poor communication and organizational silos	An organization's lack of effective communication channels can lead to critical information not reaching the right people at the right time. Silos can prevent a holistic view of the organization's environment, creating blind spots.
Resistance to change, turf, and compensation	Organizations often resist change due to cultural inertia.
Groupthink, cognitive biases, lack of diversity, and suppression of alternative views	Groupthink suppresses different perspectives and critical analysis. Heterogeneity in analyzing the environment is imperative. Some organizations use "red" and "black" teams to elicit differing views of what the information means and how it could be used.

Table 4.4 (continued)

Policy and Process Issues	
Ineffective board and executive leadership	Leaders who lack vision or the ability to inspire and guide their organizations can fail to recognize or act upon important signals.

Lesson Worth Learning: Early signal detection and pattern recognition are critical to successful adaptation

> To understand is to perceive patterns.
> *Isaiah Berlin, Philosopher*

Signal detection, pattern recognition, and response are distinguishing characteristics of intelligence (whether animal, human, or artificial). They are essential for adaptation in a rapidly changing environment.

Fight? Flight? or Freeze? Predators have eyes facing forward for depth perception. Prey typically have eyes on either side of the head – the better to detect predators. Both need signal detection and pattern recognition to connect the dots. The faster you detect and recognize the signal, the faster you can respond and, hopefully, adapt.

Nike just didn't do it. A long-time leader in the running market, Nike recently shifted its focus to other areas, such as limited-edition sneakers. This shift allowed competitors to gain market share, leading to financial challenges for Nike and prompting a strategic reevaluation after recognizing that it missed the boom in running.[217]

In June 2024, Nike reported an unexpected sales decline for the latest quarter and reduced its annual revenue forecast due to decreased store traffic and worsening economic conditions in China. Executives acknowledged the loss of market share in running shoes and launched a new line during the Paris Olympics to regain strength in this critical category.

Proactive and decisive action by boards can significantly impact the company's trajectory, often saving them from severe crises or guiding them through turbulent times. Some of these signals seem like they were hard to miss, but that is with 20–20 hindsight. This was also true of those who failed from within the same industry (Table 4.5).

Table 4.5: Recognized and Seized Existential Opportunities and Avoided Threats.

The Company	The Signal	The Board's Response
IBM in the early 1990s	Computers had become "personal," but IBM, the leading computer hardware company, wasn't participating	The board recognized this and hired an outsider, Lou Gerstner, as CEO, who planned to shift IBM's focus from hardware to software and services.[218]
Apple in 1997	Nearing bankruptcy as new personal computers like Dell had become low-cost competitors, even while customizing computer hardware configuration	The board brought back former CEO Steve Jobs as an advisor and eventually as the CEO. Jobs streamlined the product line and introduced innovative products like the iMac, iPod, and later the iPhone. Apple later became the most valuable company in the world for a time.[219]
Starbucks in 2008	Declining sales and a diluted brand experience due to rapid expansion	The Starbucks board brought back Howard Schultz as CEO.[220] Schultz took swift action to close underperforming stores, refocus on customer experience, and expand the company's global footprint more thoughtfully.[221] These changes helped rejuvenate the brand and company performance.[222]
Xerox in the early 2000s	Severe financial issues and accounting scandal[223]	The Xerox board replaced the CEO and pushed for a transformation of its business model.[224] The new leadership focused on digital printing technology and services, which helped Xerox navigate through its difficulties and stabilize financially.[225]
Best Buy in the early 2010s	Digital sales undermined traditional retail models; Best Buy appeared to be on the brink of failure	The "Renew Blue" turnaround strategy.[226] It focused on enhancing customer experience, investing in employee training, matching online prices, and enhancing services like "The Geek Squad," which consulted on, installed, and repaired technology bought at Best Buy in customers' homes.[227]
Netflix in the late 2000s	Netflix faced significant backlash and subscriber losses due to its decision to split its DVD rental and streaming services[228]	The board quickly focused solely on streaming.[229] This set the stage for Netflix's future as a dominant player in the streaming industry and a creative juggernaut.[230]

Lesson Worth Learning: Look for what you least expect

> Inspector Gregory (Scotland Yard detective):
> "Is there any other point to which you would wish to draw my attention?"
> Sherlock Holmes: "To the curious incident of the dog in the night-time."
> Gregory: "The dog did nothing in the night-time."
> Holmes: "That was the curious incident."
> *Sir Arthur Conon Doyle,* The Adventure of Silver Blaze

What about signals you don't recognize or understand? Why do so many successful organizations miss critical opportunities and threats and end up being blindsided by failure? Why are they surprised and unprepared? Perhaps because they didn't know what to look for.

According to a 2018 survey by the U.S. National Association of Corporate Directors, boards of directors tend to be diligent in overseeing risks that management has identified. However, that can lead to blind spots and leave businesses vulnerable to disruptive risks from vectors out of management's vision. Less than 20 percent of the directors said they were extremely or very confident in management's ability to address disruptive risks.[231] "Almost three in five directors (57 percent) in a recent KPMG International survey of 700 directors in 11 countries expressed concern that their boards have blind spots and are unable to identify issues that are important to their company's future."[232]

Crises often occur surprisingly quickly, triggered by new technologies that change the way people do business, by economic and political uncertainties, or by shifts in supply and demand that disrupt seemingly stable, profitable businesses.

How do you detect a signal and recognize a pattern if you don't know what you are looking for? We will discuss this next.

5 What are our existential opportunities and threats?

> You miss 100% of the shots you don't take.
> *Wayne Gretsky, Ice Hockey Player*

Lesson Worth Learning: Symmetric strategies are the way the game is played today

Same old, same old. Symmetric strategies are employed by actors who are essentially similar in approach and often in size and resources. Symmetric actors typically dominate their domains. Their strategies are often well-known and easily discerned, and they have been successful for some of time.

Symmetric actors can miss signals about existential opportunities and threats posed by asymmetric actors because their information systems tend to measure the business environment using conventional metrics that compare to conventional competitors and conventional market factors.

Think about the oligopoly of mobile phone providers in the U.S. and how they monitor one another's offers to bundle new equipment with mobile service or to compete on price. When one finds a new wrinkle, such as a "family plan," others can copy it – just like credit card companies offering versions of silver, gold, and platinum cards. Meanwhile, encrypted Internet-based communications applications, like WhatsApp, have garnered two billion users.

Conventional scanning methods are subject to confirmation bias, which is the tendency to interpret new evidence as confirmation of one's existing beliefs or theories while ignoring contradictions.

Lesson Worth Learning: Asymmetric strategies change the game and the rules

> The capitalist economy is not and cannot be stationary. Nor is it merely expanding in a
> steady manner. It is incessantly being revolutionized from within by new enterprise, i.e.,
> by the intrusion of new commodities or new methods of production or new commercial
> opportunities into the industrial structure as it exists at any moment.[233]
> *Joseph A. Schumpeter, Political Economist*

Shift disturbers. Asymmetric strategies are typically employed by those who can't compete against the dominant symmetric actors using conventional methods. They are typically smaller, outnumbered, and under-resourced.

Symmetric players typically attack one another's strengths; organizations are typically prepared for that; the strongest wins. However, asymmetric players attack previously unexploited weaknesses, making preparation much more difficult.

The term "asymmetric strategy" is often associated with warfare. Admiral Horatio Nelson at the Battle of Trafalgar (October 21, 1805) created a classic example when he famously crossed the "T." The battle pitted the British navy against a combined French and Spanish fleet that outnumbered and outgunned Nelson.

At the time, the conventional naval battle formation was "ships of the line." Opposing fleets would literally line up in parallel and fire their cannons broadside as they passed. They would then turn and repeat until the outcome was decided, usually based on the superiority of firepower and the number of ships (Figure 4.3).

French Admiral Villeneuve used this conventional strategy, commanding his fleet through flags flown from the Admiral's ship (hence the term "flagship"). Out-

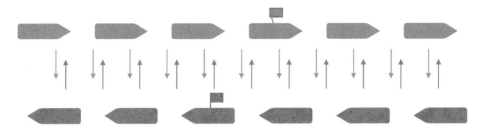

Figure 4.3: Conventional symmetric battle plan.

numbered by 33 French-Spanish ships to 27 British, Nelson sailed his fleet directly at his opponent's flank to break it into pieces, led by his flagship, the HMS *Victory* (Figure 4.4). Moreover, he decentralized command, giving each captain authority to engage independently.

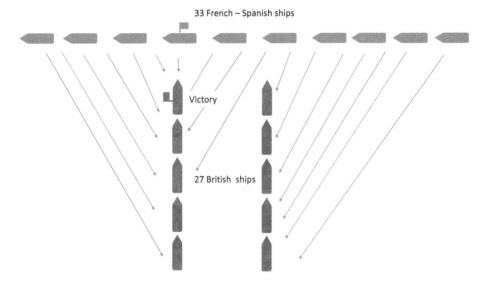

Figure 4.4: Nelson's unconventional battle plan – crossing the "T".

Amidst all the smoke and confusion, the French–Spanish flagship was unable to communicate, leaving its fleet without any direction, while the autonomous British captains were able to wreak havoc. The French–Spanish fleet lost 22 ships, while the British fleet lost none.[234]

Today, drones are asymmetric to conventional military forces. However, asymmetric strategies are not confined solely to the military. Sowing confusion and mounting many small attacks to sense weak spots is a frequent business strategy.

Not sailing into strength has been the distinguishing characteristic of radical innovators such as Morris Chang (TSMC), Steve Jobs (Apple), Jen-Hsun "Jensen" Huang (Nvidia), Jeff Bezos (Amazon), Reed Hastings (Netflix), Elon Musk (PayPal, Tesla, SpaceX, The Boring Company, Neuralink), Howard Schultz (Starbucks), and many others.

Do you have to be a founder or billionaire to radically innovate, or can a board encourage radical innovation on its own? We think the answer is yes to the latter. While the examples shown in Table 4.6 are typically characteristic of the CEO or founder, boards can help engender the same kind of radical innovation by adopting the thought process described on the following pages.

Table 4.6: Radical Innovation.

Industry	Radical Innovators	Created Opportunity/Existential Threat
Personal Computing	Apple	"Think different" about everything. Closed system of hardware and software. Design for individuals on what had been a business set of products
Retail	Amazon	Logistics as the driver of e-commerce. Real estate for distribution, not sales. Constant reinvestment.
Semiconductor	TSMC	Pure play foundry vs. proprietary in-house
Semiconductor	Nvidia	New products/New markets for graphics processing units (GPUs) to replace central processing units (CPUs)
Aerospace	SpaceX	Low cost – "Test, fail, fix, fly" vs. risk-averse and high cost
Entertainment	Netflix	Mail order then streaming vs. instore rentals and late fees, recommendation algorithms, binge watching, subscription fees, unlimited access
Airlines	Southwest	Single aircraft model, no reserved seating, no business class, regional, point-to-point routes, fast turnarounds, fuel price hedging vs. multiple types of aircraft, multiple classes of service, hub-and-spoke routes and no hedging.
Personal Care	Dollar Shave Club	Direct-to-consumer model; subscription service; simplified product options vs. retail distribution
Eyewear	Warby Parker	Direct-to-consumer model; home try-on program; vertical integration; social enterprise model to build community vs. retail distribution and advertising to build brand
Retail	Ikea	Flat-pack furniture; self-service warehouses that double as stores; a global supply chain; modular and functional design; ecosystem of ducts and services; sustainability initiatives vs. prebuilt furniture at retail with multiple supply chains and lengthy shipping wait times

Table 4.6 (continued)

Industry	Radical Innovators	Created Opportunity/Existential Threat
Hotel	Airbnb	Peer-to-peer accommodation sharing; utilization of underused private and non-corporate owned or leased assets; technology-driven platform; global reach with local experience; scalability and flexibility; regulatory navigation; dynamic pricing, variability of experiences vs. conventional hotels owned or leased at high fixed costs designed to present cookie-cutter experiences across a brand
Taxi	Uber/Lyft	Ride-sharing, utilization of underused private assets, flexible and scalable service; technology-driven platform; dynamic pricing models; driver flexibility; lower barriers to entry for drivers; market expansion; diverse service offerings vs. licensed taxis and limos
Automotive	Tesla	Direct sales model; electric vehicle (EV) technology; software-centric approach; battery innovation vs. internal combustion engine-based dealerships
Coffee shops	Starbucks	Designed as a "third space" experience and atmosphere (a hybrid of workplace and home); premium products, customization; lifestyle and cultural emphasis; global expansion and branding; retail and merchandise vs. "cup of coffee" as a commodity

What made them all such outstanding successes? They fundamentally challenged the conventions or the underlying assumption of the prevailing business model.

The Oakland Athletics and Moneyball. In the late 1990s, Billy Beane became the general manager of the Oakland Athletics, a team with one of the lowest budgets in Major League Baseball. Faced with the challenge of competing against wealthier teams, Beane sought a new approach to building a competitive roster.

Beane and his assistant, Paul DePodesta, embraced a sabermetric approach to player evaluation. This strategy emphasized so-called advanced statistics over traditional scouting metrics. It was inspired by the work of baseball analyst Bill James and considered revolutionary at the time.

Using these principles, Beane made several strategic moves that defied conventional wisdom. He acquired undervalued players like Scott Hatteberg, who had a high on-base percentage but was considered a defensive liability. Beane also focused on drafting and developing players overlooked by other teams due to their unconventional skills or physical attributes.

The 2002 season became a defining moment for Beane and the Athletics. Despite a modest payroll, the team won 103 games and made it to the playoffs, largely thanks to the contributions of players acquired through Beane's innovative methods. Their success challenged the traditional ways of building a baseball team and garnered significant attention.[235]

Leaders evolve. As their business models mature, radical innovators move from their original asymmetric antithesis to a synthetic model that combines the best of both symmetric and asymmetric models.

Amazon, for example, now owns the Whole Foods grocery chain and operates Amazon "Go" convenience stores.[236] The e-tailer, which famously started by selling books online, even ran physical bookstores for a time before shutting them down in 2023.[237]

Southwest is now considering reserved seating, seats with extra legroom, and variable pricing.[238]

Adapt or fail! It's your choice.

Lesson Worth Learning: A straight line isn't always the shortest route

So many people have this idea that you get discovered, and then you get the record deal, and then you record the song, and then the song goes number one . . . it's never like that. Very rarely is it that one thing leads to another, which leads to another end result.

It's so many dead ends, switching directions, going back and replanning and rethinking, interviews, strategy meetings, management meetings, PR meetings, and so many things that are so outside of music . . .

Taylor Swift, Singer, Songwriter, Entrepreneur

Linear vs. non-linear strategies. A conventional linear strategy in business involves a series of progressive, sequential steps leading to a specific goal without significant deviation or iteration. This type of strategy is characterized by a clear, step-by-step plan that often focuses on efficiency and straightforward problem-solving. It is most useful in a stable and predictable environment.

Consider the linear strategies many manufacturing companies use, such as Ford Motor Company's assembly line production. Henry Ford's implementation of the assembly line in the early 20th century revolutionized manufacturing by breaking down the production of an automobile into precise, repetitive, and sequential steps.

Each worker was responsible for a specific task, performed in the same order, contributing to a highly efficient and predictable process. This method significantly reduced the time and cost of production, showcasing a linear strategy's effectiveness in achieving scalability and efficiency in a stable corporate setting.

Even when complex manufacturing is roboticized, it is still a linear process.

Linear strategies fail in non-linear complexity. Unfortunately, while linear strategies are effective in stable and predictable environments, they don't work well in the conditions of high uncertainty, instability, and non-linear complexity that characterize the 21st century thus far (Table 4.7).

Table 4.7: Why Linear Strategies Fail in Extreme Uncertainty.

Inflexibility	Linear strategies rely on pre-established plans and processes that are not designed to adapt quickly to unexpected changes or disruptions. This makes it difficult for organizations to respond effectively to sudden shifts in market conditions, technological advancements, or competitor actions.
Lack of responsiveness	Because linear strategies are designed to follow a set path, they often lack the mechanisms for rapid response to new information or changing circumstances. This can result in missed opportunities or continued investment in outdated or ineffective approaches.
Over-reliance on predictions	Linear strategies are based on predictions and assumptions made during planning. These predictions may become less accurate or completely irrelevant in highly uncertain environments, leading to strategic misalignment with the current reality.
Reduced innovation	The structured nature of a linear strategy can stifle creativity and innovation within an organization. By focusing on efficiency and repetition, there is less encouragement for exploring new ideas, experimenting, or taking risks, often necessary for breakthroughs.
Difficulty in handling complexity	Linear strategies are less effective in dealing with complex situations requiring multifaceted approaches or where problems and their solutions or causes and effects are unclear. Complex environments often demand more holistic or systems-thinking approaches rather than a linear breakdown of tasks.
Reduced optionality	Linear strategies don't recognize that the organization gains knowledge while the world evolves, putting it in a different place over time. While non-linear strategies use real options (See "Iterate: Have real options ready for uncertainty," below) to adjust directionality at an appropriate cost, linear strategies rely on momentum and doing what the organization has always done.

A linear strategy with no alternatives (on or off ramps or a Plan B) is highly risky. In a 1997 *Harvard Business Review* article titled "Strategy Under Uncertainty," McKinsey describes the dangers of developing linear strategies that disregard uncertainty and develop a conventional discounted cash flow (DCF).[239] Having no choices in a world of extreme uncertainty is not advisable.

The board should question whether the proposed strategy and supporting analysis match the level of uncertainty the organization faces and whether the strategy provides sufficient flexibility to respond effectively to ever-changing circumstances.

The ability to choose. Having the ability to choose doesn't mean an organization will choose well. Perhaps the board thinks it just needs to double down and get better at what it already does. Or the board is taken by surprise, never saw it coming, and is simply unprepared to respond quickly enough. An organization or a key executive may want to protect existing territory and compensation based on existing products versus. new products, which may cannibalize profits at the expense of the leaders of the existing business units.

In "What are our strategic options" (below), we discuss methodologies and philosophies for setting strategies that overcome inertia and are therefore more attuned to the need for agility and adaptation, like "real" options that provide more degrees of freedom for longer than linear responses. Would these companies have succeeded if they had considered real options and, therefore, not assumed a linear response and traditional net present value analysis?

Stay the course, adjust course, or change course? Few, if any, strategic plans go from initiation to conclusion without modification somewhere along the line. Goals, strategies, and incentives may need realignment. Performance feedback may have identified underperformance, missed targets, or some results that were much better than expected. There may be a mismatch in the allocation of resources to priorities. The competitive environment may have changed, and new regulations or unforeseen constraints have popped up. Or a new competitor or an existing competitor has stepped up its products/services.

The reasons to adjust or change course are myriad. Tinkering, or even fully pivoting, might introduce new risks, but it could also mitigate existing ones. Strategic thinking is fundamentally about problem-solving. The options should be evaluated based on the insight gained from being situationally aware. The goal is to improve organizational resilience and agility so that the enterprise can seize opportunities consistent with its mission.

So, how do you know if you should stay the course, make a minor adjustment, or change course? Adaptive boards seek diversity of thought to avoid groupthink but in a way that allows a consensus direction to emerge. They then use a process to surface as many potential problems, opportunities, and situational changes as possible. That is incredibly valuable when setting strategy and when deciding if and how to modify it.

Equipped with these insights, the board can then thoughtfully consider the range of realistic options available to the organization.

6 What are our strategic options?

We must dare to think 'unthinkable' thoughts. We must learn to explore all the options and
possibilities that confront us in a complex and rapidly changing world.
*J. William Fulbright – Former Senator and Chairman of the United States Senate Committee
on Foreign Relations*

**Lesson Worth Learning: Think "out-of-the-box" – it's the key to radical
innovation and anticipating asymmetric competition**

All plans are based on assumptions. As mentioned, a key problem with conventional situational assessment is confirmation bias. All business models are based on assumptions, which form the conventions by which the industry operates. One way to address confirmation bias is to look for the exact opposite of what you believe are the "life or death" assumptions upon which the industry and your business model are based.

If the assumptions are proven wrong, then the plans based on them are at risk. Such assumptions must be made explicit. One of the reasons organizations and their boards are so often blindsided is that their most fundamental assumptions were invalidated, but they weren't aware of it.

Life or death? There is also a tendency to leave life-or-death assumptions unstated and unchallenged. If certain assumptions are truly life or death, shouldn't you be monitoring them very carefully? Shouldn't you be the first to recognize that conditions are changing and that your assumptions may no longer be valid? Shouldn't you have carefully considered your options in advance?

Conventional risk management fails in extreme uncertainty. One of its major weaknesses is that it tends to isolate individual risks and then assess the qualitative impact and probability of their individual rather than cumulative and/or interacting effects. Organizations can be caught off guard when shifts happen. Table 4.8 shows a couple of examples from the first quarter of the 21st century.

Table 4.8: Conventional Wisdom and Shifts that Happened.

Sector	Conventional Wisdom	Shift Happened
Retail	More stores = more customers	eCommerce prioritizes logistics over retail outlets.
Media	Knowledge is communicated in hard copy written by experts and subscription fees.	Knowledge is online, crowd-sourced, free, and now AI-enabled.

Table 4.8 (continued)

Sector	Conventional Wisdom	Shift Happened
Vaccination	Immunize through low-dose exposure to a disease.	mRNA (messenger ribonucleic acid) teaches the body to make its own protein defense.
Workforce/ Offices	People will come to work.	People will work from home or come in occasionally.
Supply chains	Lean and just-in-time promote efficiency and save money.	Lean can become anorexic and lacks resilience. When critical capabilities and competencies are offshored, they are subject to political risk and other disruptions.
Business interruptions	Local and time-limited, e.g., flu, snow/ ice storm, hurricane, IT.	Also, global and long-lasting, e.g., COVID-19, supply chain disruptions and widespread IT outages such as the 2024 CrowdStrike failed update.
Interest rates and liquidity	Interest rates will remain low indefinitely. Liquidity is easily sourced.	Higher interest rates with tightened liquidity still occur.
Peace in Europe	Peace is assured.	Russia invades Ukraine.
Global population	Ever-increasing population; Asia as a growth driver.	Peak population this century; Africa to be only continent with growing population.

Lesson Worth Learning: Start by defining the box. Make life-or-death assumptions explicit

Define the box. Boards and executives are often exhorted to think "out of the box." This is a well-intentioned but poorly designed exhortation. This "let a thousand flowers bloom" mentality often results in an unstructured and unwieldy list of possibilities. Instead, we suggest that to think "out of the box," one should begin by defining the box.

Try answering this critical question: "What are the key assumptions that define the conventional business model for your specific industry?" Then describe the exact opposite, i.e., "your worst nightmare," and then look for evidence of it.

A fish doesn't know it is swimming in water, and a bird doesn't know that flying defies gravity. This approach is simple but not easy. However, it is a highly effective tool for creating or detecting radical innovation. Defining the box requires a very deliberate approach to identifying life-or-death assumptions and their opposites, i.e., radical innovations. Describing the box and making implicit underlying assumptions explicit may be the hardest thing to do (Figure 4.5).

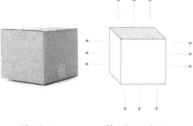

The Box   The Opposite
"Outside the box"   **Figure 4.5:** The Box and Out of the Box.

Boards should require that the critical assumptions that underpin their business model be made explicit and regularly monitored for changes.

Then, describe the opposite, which is actually relatively easy. By definition, it will be outside the box and a radical innovation. If you are a conventional, symmetric player, it could be your worst nightmare. Let's look at some other examples of how that works in Tables 4.9 and 4.10.

Table 4.9: Print Media Example.

Business Model	THE BOX Traditional	OUT OF THE BOX Internet
Medium	Print media	Non-print
Location	Stationary	Mobile
Frequency	Periodic update	Instant and continuous update
Fees	Subscription fee	Free
Sources	Specialists/Professional editors	Users/Crowd-sourced/Volunteer editors
Verification	Verified	Unverified

Table 4.10: Personal Computing Example.

Business Model	THE BOX IBM/Microsoft	OUT OF THE BOX Apple
Customer	Business/University research	Individuals/Education
Customer Experience	Unfriendly/Difficult interface	Friendly interface
	Open platform /Stand-alone	Closed/End-to-end control of experience (including retail)
Product	Rational	Intuitive
	Good enough	Quality
	Price	Product

Table 4.10 (continued)

Business Model	THE BOX IBM/Microsoft	OUT OF THE BOX Apple
	Complexity	Simplicity/Minimalism
	Details not important	Maniacal obsession with detail/perfection, packaging
	Relative quality	Absolute quality in everything
Product Development	Technology	Technology/Design/Human interface – link technology and art
	Don't cannibalize	Cannibalize yourself – or someone else will
	Incremental add on's	Apps
	Complexity comes with the territory.	Simplify through elimination, e.g., retail.
Organization	Divisions (by nature divisive)	Compulsory synergistic collaboration

Requisite conditions. The next step is to determine the requisite conditions for the commercial success of the asymmetric model. These are the conditions that must be met for the "out-of-the-box" business model to be successful. However, the requisite conditions may not yet exist. If they don't, then you should monitor the environment to be the first to know if the conditions are changing and how fast.

Netflix, for example, had to have videos in a format (DVD) that was relatively inexpensive and safe to mail. In 1997, Warner Bros. went to Blockbuster with their new format idea. Characteristically, Blockbuster turned it down mainly because they were heavily invested in the VHS rental business and did not see the immediate potential of DVDs.[240]

For the original Netflix model to work, the U.S. Post Office had to be able to handle the mail without damaging it (a requisite condition). Recall our earlier example about luck. At one point, Netflix constituted one-fifth of the total postal volume.[241]

The reverse happened with Southwest. The requisite condition forced the innovation. They had to sell one of their four jets, so they had to reduce turnaround times. This led to the famous 10-minute turnaround, which meant eliminating meal service and reserved seating.[242]

Lesson Worth Learning: Iterate. Have a range of real options ready for uncertainty

> Opportunity does not waste time with those who are unprepared.
> *Idowu Koyenikan, Author*

Options, like alliances and relationships, must be in place before you need them. A strategic real option is a realistic alternative course of action (not a theoretical one). The purpose of using real options is to optimize flexibility under conditions of uncertainty through iterative decision-making.[243]

Recall that iterative decision-making is a principle and process of adaptive governance. In this process, decisions are made through a series of iterations, allowing for flexibility, gradual refinement, and adjustment based on feedback and new information.

This approach is particularly useful in highly uncertain and complex situations where initial decisions need to be revisited as circumstances change or more data becomes available. It involves repeating planning cycles, acting, observing the results, and revising plans based on what was learned. This method helps adapt to changes and uncertainties, optimizing decisions over time rather than committing to a single, fixed strategy.

Using real options to create an iterating strategy is analogous to Bayesian statistics, where you have an assumption, called a "prior," about what will happen. Once you know what is happening, you adjust or slide your assumption (your new "prior") about what will happen the next time a similar situation occurs. Over time, you get closer to the "true" answer, knowing that you most likely will never be exactly right but that you are being "less wrong" over time until there's very little daylight between your prediction and the "true" answer.

If an option is to be exercised, it must be available before it is needed, lest it be too late or expensive. Options have a cost, but organizations should not confuse cost with value. Southwest Airlines, for example, has gladly paid premiums to create the option to hedge fuel prices, protecting itself against price volatility and helping Southwest maintain profitability and competitive fares.[244]

Insurance is another example of a real option. One can decide whether to insure or self-insure. Both options have advantages and disadvantages, costs and risks, but insurance must be in place before the loss occurs. Both commodity hedging and insurance are financial constructs used to implement real options in the non-financial world. But there are other ways to create real options.

Table 4.11 shows how real options can be applied to strategy.

Table 4.11: Real Options.

Options to delay	Organizations can view certain strategic decisions as options to delay investment until more information is available. This helps reduce the risk associated with uncertain environments. Apple, for example, delayed the launch of its first 5G phone (iPhone 12) until 5G networks were better established.[245]
Expansion and growth options	These are akin to call options in finance. After a company makes an initial investment, it retains the option to expand if the market conditions are favorable. For example, a retailer might open a few stores in a new region and, depending on their performance, choose to expand aggressively or not. Netflix expanded into proprietary content with "House of Cards." It went well, and Netflix became a major content creator and distributor.
Abandonment options	Like a put option, companies can abandon a project or exit a business segment. This allows a firm to limit losses on failing projects, much like selling a stock if it drops to a certain price. For example, Ford Motor exercised this option by abandoning sedan production, and General Motors recently discontinued the Malibu, ending its production of sedans. This leaves the sedan markets open to Honda, Toyota, and others.[246]
Switching options	Some strategies allow companies to switch between different modes of operation depending on external conditions. For example, a factory might switch between various raw materials based on price fluctuations, thereby optimizing costs. Tesla, for example, can switch its manufacturing lines between different models of its electric vehicles.[247]
Staging and sequencing options	By breaking a larger project into phases, companies can treat each stage as an option. Each phase provides an opportunity to reassess and decide whether to continue the investment. This is particularly useful in industries like pharmaceuticals, where projects are highly uncertain and costly. For example, Pfizer, in collaboration with BioNTech, employed a staged and sequenced approach to developing its COVID-19 vaccine, which is typical in pharmaceuticals due to the need to manage risk and regulatory compliance.[248]

Having strategic options helps to manage uncertainties and non-linear complexity in several ways (Table 4.12).

Table 4.12: Benefits of Real Options.

Better information/ Better decisions	Real options often trade some sort of minimal cost for more information because the option bought time or experience. If having better information enables the board to make a better decision, the cost of the option may be money well spent.
Reconciliation of differences	Board members may strongly disagree about the "best" course of action. Gaining more information before fully committing to a strategic path can significantly reduce conflict and create alignment.
Risk management	Options provide flexibility to respond to unforeseen events, reducing potential negative impacts.

Table 4.12 (continued)

Adaptability	Options allow organizations to quickly shift strategies, resources, and processes to seize new opportunities or mitigate threats.
Innovation	Uncertainty often drives innovation. Having mechanisms to explore different approaches can lead to breakthroughs and competitive advantages.
Strategic planning	Options allow for the development of contingency plans and scenario analysis.
Resource allocation	By considering multiple possibilities, organizations can more effectively allocate resources despite uncertain conditions.

Real options enable choices. In essence, real options enable organizations to be more proactive rather than reactive, positioning them to better handle whatever challenges and opportunities the future holds.

What would have been the benefit of maintaining real options for companies like Kodak, Blockbuster, DEC, Blackberry, and Encyclopedia Britannica?

Least to Most. One useful framing technique is for the executive to present a range of alternatives for the board to consider – from the least you can do to the most. Each option should include the related pros and cons, as well as key risks and stakeholder opinions.

It is obvious, but worth emphasizing, that not all options cost the same or have the same potential payoff, likelihood of success, or time frame. Starting small and scaling up when you have more information or certainty in your prognosis can lead to better outcomes. Therefore, like other strategic decisions, it may be helpful to order options from least to most in various dimensions. Table 4.13 shows some, but it is far from a comprehensive list.

Table 4.13: Least to Most that Can Be Done.

Feasibility and simplicity	Starting with the simplest or least demanding tasks allows you to quickly achieve some progress, which can be motivating. This is especially useful when time, resources, or energy are limited. Completing easier tasks first can also build momentum and confidence to tackle more complex issues.
Prioritization and planning	Evaluating tasks based on their feasibility and/or impact allows you to prioritize, especially under constraints.
Resource allocation	Proper resource allocation ensures that the most accessible tasks are handled with the resources currently available, saving more extensive resources for more significant tasks.
Risk management	Starting with less demanding tasks might reduce the risk associated with project or plan failures later. Simpler tasks are often less prone to complications and completing them "clears the underbrush" for the larger, more complex tasks that will follow.

Lesson Worth Learning: Prioritize resources

> With the level of uncertainty we see today, more people are asking, how can you develop a
> strategy in a world that keeps changing so fast? They are afraid that a set of rigid principles
> will hinder their ability to react quickly. I argue that it is precisely at such times that you
> need a strategy.
> *'Orit Gadiesh, Chair of Bain & Company*

Retain flexibility. Effective strategies anticipate uncertainties and prepare a variety of real options before they are needed. The key is flexibility. Options give you the choice but not the obligation to act, enter, withdraw, or wait (as long as you remember that waiting is a choice with consequences). Some options may never be needed.

Indeed, that is often the case. The question often is, "How many options can you afford?" Options allow you to test or learn more about a strategy before fully committing the organization's resources. But they do cost something, whether explicitly in a contract or just the cost of more study or the opportunity cost of delay.

Much has been written about real option theory since the 1990s for good reason.[249] In uncertainty, you don't want to find yourself left with no choices. But you do not want to expend resources and time fully engaging in a strategy before you really believe in it. Expending less resources and time to expand and better research your options is generally smart, provided it doesn't paralyze the board and the organization.

The committee should identify the top three or four strategic priorities within the planning horizon. This allows for focus and effective resource allocation rather than trying to do too much. Each priority should have clear ownership and accountability. Incentives should be aligned with execution. More on this in a moment.

7 Have our strategic options been systematically evaluated?

Lesson Worth Learning: Take intelligent, necessary risks. Understand your options and the rewards and risks of action and inaction

> It annoys me about the state that the world is in at the moment. No one talks about failure
> anymore. Whereas with success, everyone shouts about it, but there's nothing in success.
> Success happens from failing hundreds of times.
> *Ed Sheeran, Singer, Songwriter*

The planning process should have identified the range of options for each critical issue detected.

– Assess the pros and cons of each option, including a risk assessment and an assessment of the impacts on various stakeholders.
– The risk assessment should include the risks of action and inaction.
– Identify the risks of the strategy itself and the risks to the execution of the strategy.
– Have a plan to mitigate the risks you choose to accept.

Use CIOS. One way to do that is to use critical issue and option summaries (CIOS). CIOS is a structured approach to identifying and analyzing a critical issue and then outlining possible options to address it. Ideally, a CIOS balances thorough analysis and concise presentation. The goal is to provide decision-makers with all the information they need to understand critical issues, evaluate the options, and make an informed decision, all while being concise enough to ensure the document is accessible and actionable.

A CIOS briefly describes:
– the issue and why it is important (the background)
– the process of analysis and stakeholder engagement undertaken (due diligence)
– a list of root causes of current and developing problems (situational awareness)
– the range of real options available (hierarchy ranging from the least to the most that could be done)
– the pros and cons of those real options (addressing the dissenting opinions of all key stakeholders)
– a risk assessment of those pros and cons
– a recommended course of action based on the above

CIOSs are especially useful in evaluating options involving complex strategic and policy decisions in uncertain environments. They help enable faster decisions based on thoughtful evaluations of available real options and can also be used for strategic planning, project management, and crisis resolution. CIOS accelerates decision-making and maintains decision discipline when analyzing real options (Table 4.14).

Using critical issue and options summaries can help ensure that diverse perspectives are heard and discussed systematically and dispassionately. The tool helps separate the options and opinions from those who may hold them (even if it is well known). Those individuals do not have to escalate to get their opinion heard. CIOS also helps to promote the opinions of those who are less outspoken. In other words, CIOS creates a process for expressing diverse views and de-emphasizes personality or rank.

Using CIOS can also avoid what some boards call a "baked cake," meaning executives have already decided on a course of action and the rationale for that

Table 4.14: Critical Issue and Options Summaries (CIOS).

Clarify issues, obtain diverse perspectives, and depersonalize the discussion.	CIOS can help succinctly define and clarify the critical issues at hand. Summarizing the key problems or decisions that need to be addressed helps focus the discussion and efforts on the most pressing matters. Having diverse perspectives captured systematically and presented simultaneously can help to depersonalize issues.
Develop and compare options.	CIOS provides a structured way to present different options or solutions to the identified issues. Each option is typically accompanied by an analysis of its pros and cons, required resources, potential risks, and expected outcomes. This structured comparison aids in transparent and informed decision-making.
Accelerate decision-making.	By consolidating essential information into concise summaries, CIOS allows decision-makers to quickly understand the scenario without getting bogged down in unnecessary details. This is particularly useful in fast-paced environments or when decisions need to be made under time constraints.
Maintain decision discipline.	By requiring that all options be considered along with their respective impacts and outcomes, CIOS helps avoid bias and ensures that decisions are based on a systematic evaluation of available data.
Facilitate communication.	CIOS is a communication tool that can be easily shared among team members and stakeholders. It ensures everyone involved is on the same page with the same information, which is crucial for collaborative decision environments.
Crisis management	CIOS can be particularly effective in crises. They can help quickly identify viable courses of action and enable rapid decision-making.
Regular updates and record of due diligence	As situations evolve, the summaries can be updated to reflect new information or changing conditions, helping decision-makers adapt their strategies accordingly.

choice seems retrofitted perfectly. In contrast, other potential choices are summarily dismissed.

Describing the range of options available enables the board to better understand what the executives are thinking. It enables the board to potentially identify additional options and their pros and cons. It also provides a record of due diligence. If used systematically over time, CIOS can help embed a constructive dynamic by depersonalizing and systematizing the discussion. In that way, you can think of CIOS as the written equivalent of constructive challenge.

Lesson Worth Learning: Performance and risk are inseparable

The biggest risk is not taking any risk . . . In a world that is changing really quickly, the only strategy that is guaranteed to fail is not taking risks.
Mark Zuckerberg, CEO of Meta Platforms

What is risk? Any consideration of the pros and cons of an option must address the relationship between risk and reward. So, let's start by clarifying what we mean by risk. As mentioned, the risk is "the potential for an unwanted difference between actual and expected performance, regardless of cause." By contrast, the Committee of Sponsoring Organizations of the Treadway Commission (COSO) defines risk as "the possibility that events will occur and affect the achievement of strategy and business objectives."[250]

Risk to the strategy but not of the strategy itself. The COSO definition seems to apply to the risks to the strategy and its execution but not to the risks of the strategy itself. COSO's conventional and linear approach is widely accepted. However, as has been shown time and again, it is also problematic.

This is for several reasons:
1. Probabilities don't apply in extreme uncertainty where cause and effect relationships are unknown. There are no causes to quantify.
2. It confuses causes with effects. Performance and risk become separated when risk is really the effect or the outcome, i.e., loss, harm, or missed opportunity.
3. As Nobel Prize winners Daniel Kahneman and Amos Tversky demonstrated, subjective quantitative probability estimates are unreliable due to inevitable bias.[251]
4. It does not consider the risk of inaction. Yet inertia is one of the biggest causes of failure to adapt.
5. It does not consider the risks of the strategy itself (e.g., outsourcing, mergers and acquisitions, and supply chain).

Conventional risk definitions are primarily based on actuarial models of "risk experience" in terms of impact and probability where there are established quantified causes and effects, i.e., linear relationships. For example, many organizations create a "risk register" listing various potential causes of risk, then try to quantify how likely that cause/risk is to manifest, how material the risk would be if it does occur, and then how effective the organization believes it has been in mitigating the risk, resulting in a subjective guesstimate of residual risk listed by cause (such as cyber-security or business continuity).

But what about those risks/effects that may exist but you have never experienced? Think Taleb's black swan.[252] Europeans thought all swans were white until they discovered black ones in Australia. COSO's definition may apply to operational and ethical risk but not to strategic risk.

Performance and risk are inseparable. That is why we propose that risk be defined as "the potential for an unacceptable difference between actual and expected performance regardless of cause." Risk management is then about preventing or quickly detecting and correcting causes and mitigating effects.

As a simple example, a risk might be that the organization will not have the right people in the right numbers in the right place at the right time to execute its strategy. The risk is failure. There could be many possible causes, such as labor market conditions, a lack of apprenticeships, or a poor corporate reputation that impairs the ability to attract people. What are the most important factors that are within the control of the organization to address in terms of both causes and effects?

What is acceptable vs. unacceptable? What is necessary vs. unnecessary? What is rewarded vs. unrewarded risk? These are critical questions the board must answer. The willingness to fail in innovating is necessary and essential. The willingness to behave unethically is not.

Take intelligent, necessary risks. Not all failures are equal. Necessary risks must be taken to adapt to rapidly changing circumstances, while unnecessary risks should be avoided or mitigated.

Don't take a long time to recognize a failure. When innovating, as all organizations must, failure is to be expected. As John Maxwell said: "Fail early, fail often, but always fail forward."[253] Organizations must take intelligent, necessary risks if they are to adapt. A diet of pure risk aversion is a sure recipe for extinction.

What are the options to realistically mitigate the risks that must be taken? Conventional risk management is right about one thing: Identifying and addressing potential risks upfront is critical for robust strategic thinking. This includes consideration of both internal causes (such as operational or financial) and external causes (such as market or geopolitical).

The board should question how well the organization has identified, assessed, and mitigated key causes while seizing opportunities. This includes understanding the organization's risk appetite and ensuring that strategic decisions balance potential rewards with the risks involved.

As discussed, one way to mitigate risk is to use real options and make decisions iteratively. But those are risks *to* the strategy. Boards should also seek to understand the *risks of* the strategy itself.

Risks of the strategy itself. If the purpose of strategy is successful adaptation to changing conditions (both threats and opportunities), then the biggest risk of the strategy is failure to adapt. Typically, failure to adapt is caused by failure to act asymmetrically and discontinuously to overcome inevitable inertia or by having assumed a risk without knowing it.

For example, lean manufacturing and just-in-time (JIT) supply chain management are two closely related strategies focusing on improving efficiency, reducing waste, and cutting costs in the production processes. These strategies became very popular in the 1980s and 90s. They primarily involve outsourcing and offshoring in what became the global supply chain. However, they also created critical dependencies.

When does lean become anorexic? Supply chain disruptions significantly impact lean manufacturing (LM) and just-in-time (JIT) inventory systems. In 2011, an earthquake and tsunami in Japan had a profound impact on automotive and electronics manufacturers who relied on LM/JIT. Toyota and Honda cut production by 63 percent. The damage wasn't contained to Asia.

Parts shortages quickly rippled across global supply chains shutting down billions of dollars of production because suppliers were unable to deliver components on the strict timelines required by JIT. For example, the lack of an airflow sensor forced Peugeot-Citroën to cut production by 40–70 percent at most European plants.[254] That sensor retails for about $100,[255] and estimates of its cost to Peugeot-Citroën were as low as $30.

So, an inexpensive part that costs less than a tank of gas shut down an automobile assembly line. Separately, the U.S. has only recently woken up to the vulnerabilities of offshoring chip production and manufacturing certain pharmaceuticals.

Remember, the lack of inventory on-site at manufacturing plants is a crucial feature, not a bug of an LM/JIT system. Proponents of the strategy had assumed a risk of the strategy without fully realizing it.

More recently, the COVID-19 pandemic caused massive disruptions. Changes in trade policies or tariffs, political instability, or conflicts can also disrupt supply chains. For example, sudden tariffs on steel imports have caused production delays for manufacturers relying on JIT delivery of steel from abroad.

The point is that boards need to understand not just the risks to the strategy but the risks inherent in the strategy itself. Think of it this way: If you choose to be a Formula One race car driver, you can mitigate risk with a helmet, harness, and fire suppression system. However, the essential risk of being a racing car driver remains.

LM/JIT inventory buffers are minimal by design, so supply chain problems are an essential risk of this strategy. What you save in inventory costs and productivity is what you risk or more when conditions are not perfect. A board may choose to take that risk – and many do – but it should be an explicit decision.

CrowdStrike failure exposes critical dependency. On July 18, 2024, Crowd-Strike, a cyber-security company, released a software update that caused a global IT outage considered to be the largest in IT history.[256] The update contained a logic error in the sensor configuration, which led to system crashes and the "blue screen of death" on Windows systems.

The outage affected air travel, healthcare, and banking. Major airlines reported thousands of flight cancellations and delays, and hospitals experienced significant disruptions.[257]

The incident highlighted the interconnected nature of the global tech ecosystem (and, by extension, all global commerce), where disruptions in one critical component can have cascading effects across various sectors. For CrowdStrike, and really any software company, the event underscored the risk of software. Updates can fail, so rigorous quality control checks on software updates are needed to prevent widespread disruptions and reputational and real economic damage.

However, the CrowdStrike incident also showed that, in today's interconnected world, boards are exposed not just to the risks of their organization's strategy and execution but also to their suppliers, customers, and communities. Isolation and self-sufficiency are generally not achievable strategies. Even if they were, they would be highly inefficient. Therefore, boards need to recognize that the need for agility, resilience, and adaption has never been higher.

Missed existential opportunities that became existential threats. Boards need to understand and accept the risk of these critical dependencies. Returning to our earlier examples of organizations that missed existential opportunities and threats, these were more likely failures of the strategy itself and a lack of willingness to embrace risks necessary for successful adaptation.

Risk aversion and a linear approach to strategy likely contributed to their demise. For these reasons, leaders need to consider the risks of the strategy itself very carefully and go beyond conventional approaches that simply look at risks to their strategies' execution.

Microsoft – in search of mediocrity. Another example is the oft-recommended need to focus on your core competency by "sticking to the knitting," made famous in the 1982 book *In Search of Excellence: Lessons from America's best-run companies* by Tom Peters and Robert H. Waterman Jr.[258]

Steve Ballmer, who served as CEO of Microsoft from 2000 to 2014, emphasized sales and aggressive business tactics. This focus helped Microsoft consolidate its dominance in certain sectors, such as enterprise software and operating systems.

Under Ballmer's leadership, Microsoft continued to reap substantial profits from its core business areas, such as Windows and Office. He succeeded in "focusing on a core competency." However, the company often was criticized for being slow to recognize and invest in new technological trends. Notable examples include the rise of smartphones and tablets. Microsoft's failure to offer competitive products early on allowed Apple and Android to capture significant market share with their iOS and Android platforms.[259]

Similarly, in the search engine market, Microsoft was a latecomer with Bing, which struggled to compete against Google's already dominant search engine. This delay in entering the market and the subsequent inability to capture significant market share were partly attributed to the company's initial focus on its "core competencies."[260] Microsoft was successful in consolidating and expanding its existing software products, but that strategy gave innovating new products and services much lower priority.

The core competency strategy ultimately left Microsoft vulnerable as the tech landscape evolved. Among other sectors, the missed opportunities in mobile and search are seen as significant strategic missteps that allowed competitors to become dominant players in sectors crucial to today's technology ecosystem. During the 14 years of Ballmer's rule, MSFT's stock price fell by 14 percent.[261]

This period of vulnerability highlighted the need for a more balanced approach that valued both sales and product innovation, leading to shifts in strategic direction under Satya Nadella, Ballmer's successor. Since taking the reins in 2014, Nadella has embraced greater internal and external collaboration, introduced Microsoft Office for the iPad and iPhone, made major acquisitions such as LinkedIn and GitHub and more than 300 other deals, refreshed the board, created the position of chief technology officer, and cemented the relationship with Sam Altman and OpenAI.[262]

Risks to the execution of the strategy. This is not to say that execution is not important. It is critical, but a different lens is required. So, now let's talk briefly about risks *to* the execution of strategy.

Richard Cook, MD, said, "Complex systems fail for complex reasons."[263]

Strategies can and do fail for many reasons. Causes typically fall into several categories of external factors: people and organization, policies and processes, information and systems, and governance.

Table 4.15: Failure Modes and Effects Analysis (FMEA).

Failure Mode	Examples
External factors	Unforeseen external events (e.g., economic changes, political instability, natural disasters).
Resource constraints	Insufficient funding, time, manpower, or other resources.
Lack of leadership support	Strategies lack the necessary support to overcome obstacles and are not prioritized within the organization.

Table 4.15 (continued)

Failure Mode	Examples
Misalignment with goals and incentives	Failure to align with the organization's overall goals or the needs of the market.
Execution oversights	Lack of detail in planning, insufficient monitoring of progress, failure to establish clear accountability.
Change resistance	Internal resistance from employees or other stakeholders who are reluctant to adapt to new processes, technologies, or changes in organizational culture. Fear of cannibalizing existing revenue streams.
Poor communication	Inadequate communication can result in misunderstandings about the strategy's objectives and inconsistent implementation.

FMEA. A proactive risk assessment can benefit the analysis of strategic options. If a strategy is important enough, boards should consider requiring executives to conduct a failure modes and effects analysis (FMEA) to identify how it might fail (Table 4.15).

FMEA is a systematic, proactive method for evaluating a process to identify where and how it might fail. It assesses the relative impact of different types and magnitudes of failures to identify the parts of the process that need the most change. Think of it as an ex-ante, mirror image of a traditional root cause analysis (RCA) (Figure 4.6).

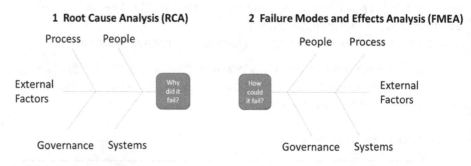

Figure 4.6: RCA and FMEA.

FMEA has been widely used in industries such manufacturing, aerospace, automotive, healthcare, and more, as part of continuous improvement initiatives ultimately leading to safer, more reliable, and more efficient operations. We believe FMEA can also be meaningfully applied to strategy because strategy is a process.

In summary, expected performance is the objective or target. Strategic risk lies in choosing the best option and metrics. Again, risk is the potential for an unacceptable difference between actual and expected performance, regardless of cause. Risk is the effect, not its causes. Therefore, performance and risk are inter-twined and inseparable.

Lesson Worth Learning: Understand your risk appetite

How much are you willing to bet? One of the authors (Rick Funston) was giving a speech to a large audience in Las Vegas. He asked, "How much would any of you be willing to bet that I can guess your birthday accurately, that is, within three days?" One immediately shouted, "I am all in!" Funston asked, "How big a bet?" "One hundred thousand," was the answer, to which Funston replied, "Wednesday." Clearly, the nature of the bet was not understood, and thus, the risk wasn't either. Whether the gentlemen could afford it or not remains un-known.

Explicitly understanding and accepting the nature of the risks *of* the strategy, goal, or objective and the risks *to* its execution sets the enterprise's risk appetite policy.

The Committee of Sponsoring Organizations of the Treadway Commission (COSO) defines risk appetite as "the amount and type of risk an organization is willing to accept in pursuit of value."[264] The board should explicitly address whether the risks are within the organization's appetite for risk. In other words, is it biting off more than it can chew?

To some extent, risk appetite depends on the nature of the enterprise. As noted, if you are a Formula One driver, it's inherently a risky business. So is new technology, moving into new and unfamiliar markets, etc. If you don't want to accept the strategy's risks, go no further.

If you do accept them, you should understand the factors that may affect your ability to be successful. Like the Formula One driver who checks all the safety equipment before every race, professional risk-taking is characterized by extraordinary preparation and calculation to de-risk it. The same is true with pi-lots who do their pre-flight circle checks. Contrast that with the amateur who says, "Hold my beer and watch this!" Your board does not want to be amateurish in taking on a high-risk strategy.

For example, SpaceX's business of launching rockets is clearly "risky." True, SpaceX has maintained a high success rate, with the Falcon 9 family achieving a historical success rate of about 99.4 percent.[265] However, the company has faced challenges with its Starship test flights.

Out of three Starship test flights conducted so far, two ended in explosions or loss of the vehicle before completing all mission objectives. The Starship test flight on March 14, 2024, made it to space but was lost on reentry.[266] These Starship flights are part of an iterative testing process, and the failures are considered part of the development and data-gathering efforts to improve the vehicle's design and performance.[267]

How much can you afford to lose? The average cost of a SpaceX Starship launch is currently estimated to be between $28 million and $90 million per flight, depending on the number of reuses and operational efficiencies achieved. As SpaceX improves its production and reusability, the goal is to reduce this cost significantly, potentially down to $2 million per flight in the long term.[268]

Clearly, the expense of a trial-and-error approach is considerable, but equally clearly, it is within SpaceX's risk appetite. After all, its motto is "Test, fail, fix, fly."

Risk appetite is distinct from the potential obstacles that may impede the execution of the strategy or the achievement of the goal or objective. Do you have the appetite for the nature of enterprise? Are you willing to accept the potential for loss?

Risk appetite represents the board's willingness (or not) to take on risks such as strategic, financial, operational, and compliance risks. While it's not normally considered a governance tool, understanding an organization's risk appetite helps maintain control, improve situational awareness, and prevent complacency. The board should understand and approve its appetite for various types of risk, from none to intelligent, necessary risk-taking.

8 Have our strategic goals and metrics been agreed upon?

> Not everything that can be counted counts, and not everything that counts can be counted.
> *William Bruce Cameron, American Author, Columnist, and Humorist*

Simply setting a strategy doesn't move an organization toward achieving it. Strategies overarch many individual goals. Boards must set goals and metrics to guide the execution of strategy, and that should be done when the strategy is adopted and modified whenever the strategy is modified.

The choice of goals and metrics is strategic for several reasons:
- They ensure the alignment of organizational efforts with the long-term vision, mission, and values.
- They measure progress toward its future direction and priorities.
- They ensure the organization has the necessary financial, human, and technological resources to achieve its goals.

Lesson Worth Learning: Goals need to be relevant, measurable, and balanced

(Goals) Objectives can be compared to a compass bearing by which a ship navigates.
A compass bearing is firm, but in actual navigation, a ship may veer off its course for
many miles. Without a compass bearing, a ship would neither find its port nor be able to
estimate the time required to get there.
Peter Drucker, Author and Management Consultant

Keep it real. The board should collaboratively and constructively engage with executive leadership to set goals and metrics that are relevant, measurable, and balanced. Benchmarked and measured goals enhance accountability, track progress, and enable ongoing strategic adjustments. This means:

- setting goals that are ambitious but achievable
- selecting relevant metrics directly tied to strategic goals to provide insights on progress
- ensuring the chosen metrics can be accurately measured and tracked over time
- incorporating a mix of financial and non-financial metrics to provide a holistic view of performance
- setting benchmarks and targets that challenge the organization to improve continuously
- holding executive leadership accountable for achieving strategic goals

Lesson Worth Learning: Metrics motivate behavior. Choose wisely

Each metric has strategic implications and can have severe consequences if not carefully selected. The choice of inappropriate goals and metrics can significantly distort behavior. Overreliance on quantitative measures can lead to unintended consequences and neglect of essential but hard-to-measure factors in business and management.[269] Unfortunately, if the goals are flawed, the metrics will be gamed. Table 4.16 provides some unfortunate examples.

The law of unintended consequences. Unrealistic or poorly designed targets can drive counterproductive behavior.[304] This happens so often that it has become a "law." But, if effective metrics are crucial for providing objective evidence of success and early warnings of areas needing improvement, how do you design them? After all, they are as important an indicator of the state of organizational health as vital signs such as heart rate, blood pressure, and temperature to monitor individual health (Table 4.17).

Table 4.16: The Consequences of Choosing the Wrong Metrics.

Organization	Goal/Issue	Consequences
Ford Pinto (1970s)	Cost and time targets for producing a low-cost vehicle[270]	Safety was compromised, resulting in a design flaw that led to deadly fuel tank explosions.[271] This caused significant financial losses and damage to Ford's reputation.[272]
Enron (2001)	Focus on stock price and earnings growth.[273]	Executives engaged in accounting fraud to meet targets, leading to the company's collapse and bankruptcy.[274]
Eli Lilly (2000s)	Sales targets for the antipsychotic drug Zyprexa[tm275]	Sales reps were incentivized to promote off-label uses, resulting in hefty fines and settlements for illegal marketing practices and reputational damage.[276]
Lehman Brothers (2008 Financial Crisis)	High-risk financial product sales and short-term profits[277]	Excessive risk-taking led to the firm's bankruptcy, significantly contributing to the global financial crisis and widespread economic turmoil.[278]
Fannie Mae and Freddie Mac (2008 Financial Crisis)	Pressure to increase home ownership rates and grow their mortgage books.[279]	Relaxed lending standards led to a housing bubble and subsequent collapse, contributing to the financial crisis and requiring a massive government bailout.[280]
AIG (2008 Financial Crisis)	Aggressive growth targets in the financial products division.[281]	Engaged in risky practices with credit default swaps, leading to massive losses and a government bailout as well as limitations on business going forward.[282]
BP (Deepwater Horizon Oil Spill, 2010)	Cost-cutting and production targets[283]	Safety protocols were neglected, contributing to one of the worst environmental disasters in history. BP faced massive fines, cleanup costs, and long-term reputational damage.[284]
Sears (2010s)	Cash flow and profitability targets	Following a failed attempt at becoming a financial behemoth (dubbed the "socks and stocks" strategy when the retailer bought broker Dean Witter), Sears' final failed strategy was to focus on cash flows and profits, cutting back on capital expenditures and store refreshes. The stores became unappealing, and the lack of resources resulted in an uncompetitive e-commerce platform.

Table 4.16 (continued)

Organization	Goal/Issue	Consequences
Takata (Airbag Scandal, 2013)	Cost reduction and production targets[285]	Produced defective airbags that caused fatalities and injuries, leading to the largest automotive recall in history to that point, significant financial losses, and reputational damage.[286]
VA (Veterans Affairs) Health System (2014)	Goals for reducing patient wait times[287]	Led to systemic manipulation of scheduling data and cover-ups of long wait times, resulting in scandals and leadership changes within the VA.[288]
Volkswagen (2015 Emissions Scandal)	Targets for market share, profitability and regulatory results[289]	Engineers installed software to cheat emissions tests, resulting in substantial fines, legal actions, and a severe blow to the company's reputation.[290]
Wells Fargo (2016 Scandal)	Aggressive sales targets[291]	Employees created millions of unauthorized bank and credit card accounts to meet unrealistic sales targets.[292] This led to massive fines, legal costs, and severe reputational damage.[293]
Uber (Various Scandals, 2017)	Rapid growth and market dominance targets	Fostered a toxic corporate culture,[294] legal issues related to regulatory evasion,[295] and public scandals, ultimately leading to the resignation of the CEO.[296]
Mattel (2017)	Focus on short-term sales targets	To meet quarterly sales goals, the company cut corners in product safety. This led to massive recalls of toys due to safety hazards, damaging the brand's reputation and incurring substantial costs.[297]
Equifax (2017)	Inadequate security metrics and targets[298]	The company failed to prioritize data security adequately, resulting in a massive data breach that exposed the personal information of more than 147 million people. The fallout included regulatory fines, lawsuits, and significant reputational damage.[299]
General Electric (GE) (2018)	Unrealistic earnings targets[300]	GE's aggressive financial targets led to accounting manipulations and an overemphasis on short-term financial performance. This resulted in regulatory scrutiny, a sharp decline in stock price, and loss of investor trust.[301]

Table 4.16 (continued)

Organization	Goal/Issue	Consequences
Facebook (2020)	Metrics focused on user engagement without considering ethical implications[302]	The company's algorithms prioritized engagement metrics that amplified harmful content, leading to widespread misinformation and negative societal impacts. This spurred regulatory actions and a Congressional hearing.[303]

Table 4.17: Considerations in the Board's Selection of Vital Signs.

Clarity on key performance indicators (KPIs)	The board must first know what it wants to measure, not what measures already exist. What metrics meaningfully monitor efficiency, effectiveness, financial stability, and strategic alignment and identify unwanted or unexpected performance.
Early detection	Vital signs should be measurable in as near real-time as possible so the board can identify potential problems early. A proactive approach allows for intervention before issues become severe, potentially saving resources and preserving stakeholder trust. It can also help assess the effectiveness of controls before they break down.
Enhanced decision-making	Vital signs provide objective data that can guide board decisions. This is especially important in complex situations where subjective judgment alone might lead to biased or incomplete conclusions.
Accountability and transparency	Regularly measuring and communicating about vital signs enables a culture of accountability and transparency within the organization. Milestones, timing, budgets, and accountabilities should be clearly defined and assigned for monitoring, mitigation, and reporting.
Adaptability	Combining effective metrics with real options enables the board to calibrate the strategy as situations change.
Alignment with strategic goal	Vital signs should be directly linked to the organization's strategic goals and objectives. This alignment ensures that all parts of the organization are moving in the same direction and that resources are allocated appropriately.
Engagement and communication	Effective boards use the insights gained from monitoring vital signs to engage with management and stakeholders actively. Stakeholder engagement would, for example, have enabled the Wells Fargo board to understand the unintended consequences years earlier.

9 Is our organization aligned with the strategy?

Lesson Worth Learning: Don't underestimate the power of organizational inertia

> Look at the companies who failed. It was because they were dumb, bureaucratic, backward, and political. CEOs should never allow that stuff, and yet they do.
> *Jamie Dimon, Chairman and CEO of JPMorgan Chase*

The power of organizational inertia should not be underestimated. An organization may have its vision, mission, and values, detect signals both symmetric and asymmetric, recognize patterns, identify critical issues, and decide on realistic options to deal with those issues. Still, if the organization is not aligned, its chances of success are greatly reduced. According to Erika Andersen, "70% of change management initiatives fail."[305]

Think back to inertia, Newton's first law of motion. An object tends to remain at rest or continue in a straight line unless acted upon by an external force. In other words, it takes intention, leadership, and often resources to adapt. Table 4.18 shows some of the common causes of organizational inertia.

Table 4.18: Common Causes of Organizational Inertia.

Cultural resistance	A culture that values rank and bureaucracy over talent and innovation or that fears failure creates resistance to change. This cultural resistance can lead to entrenchment, where new ideas are not welcomed or valued.
Structural inertia	Large, established organizations often have complex and stubborn structures. These structures include established roles, hierarchies, and procedures that can make it challenging to implement new processes or ideas quickly. Protecting one's "turf" is a strong motivator.
Past success and market dominance	Significant success with a particular business model or product can create complacency, a mindset that discourages change, believing that the existing ways are the best ways. However, adhering to the old saying "if it ain't broke, don't fix it" can leave organizations vulnerable to changes in conditions and both symmetric and asymmetric challenges.
Sunk cost fallacy	Established organizations often have significant resources invested in current processes and technologies, which makes new opportunities appear risky.
Regulatory and legal constraints	Regulatory and compliance requirements can be stringent and time-consuming, discouraging organizations from deviating from established practices.

Table 4.18 (continued)

Leadership entrenchment	Leaders who have been in place for a long time might resist changes that could undermine their historical decisions and their legacy. Or they simply do not want to make the effort to learn something new. This can lead to top management maintaining the status quo rather than seeking innovation.
Employee skill sets	An existing workforce might lack the skills needed for new technologies or methods. The cost and time involved in training can be a barrier to change.
Compensation and incentives	If compensation and incentives aren't aligned, then people are likely to resist change.

Lesson Worth Learning: Misalignment of compensation and incentives causes inertia and resistance to change

> Culture eats strategy for breakfast.
> *Attributed to Peter Drucker, Management Consultant*

Are compensation and incentives aligned with the strategy and metrics?

If the compensation structure is tightly aligned with current but not future goals or metrics, employees might resist changes that could disrupt their ability to meet these targets and negatively affect their earnings. Remember the example of Eli Lilly before the board required an overhaul of the product pipeline. The heads of existing profit centers were turning down new potential blockbuster drugs to protect their earnings.[306]

Employees who are comfortable with the status quo may view any change as a disruption. This is especially true if they perceive the change as threatening their current compensation or job security or if, in performance-based pay structures, the changes could make it harder to achieve bonuses or commissions.

Strategic plans often have nuances that call for judgment, for example, the desire to attract and maintain a skilled workforce, transition to a new strategy, and achieve certain financial results. Even if these goals are not in conflict, a typical compensation plan with x percent for metric 1, y percent for metric 2, and z percent for metric 3 doesn't handle these multiple goals well. For example, if financial goals are 80 percent of a compensation threshold, and the remaining goals are 10 percent each, a rational executive would focus on the financial metrics, as they account for most available compensation.

Newer compensation plans recognize this complexity and use metrics in various ways other than as arithmetic portions of a total. For instance, achieving a specific workforce metric may trigger the financial goals to kick in, so the executive needs to accomplish it before recognizing the benefits of the financial performance.

Alternately, workforce goals may be multipliers of the compensation for meeting other goals (recognizing that a multiplier can be more than or less than 1).

"WIIFM." What's in it for me? How will this change affect me? Boards need to understand that viewpoint, as individuals and groups will tend to act in their own self-interest to the detriment of the organization unless it is systematically understood and addressed as part of a comprehensive change management strategy.[307] While compensation is not the only factor affecting organizational culture, it is fundamental.

For example, in 2023, Jon Lukomnik, one of the authors, was asked to talk with PGGM, the Dutch pension asset manager. PGGM was in the midst of a challenging strategy evolution. It was changing how it managed its Euro 250 billion portfolio from the traditional risk and return focus (two dimensions) to what it calls "3D," adding the impact that its investments had. The most salient audience question came from a portfolio manager. "I know how my bonus is calculated under 2D. How will it be calculated under 3D?" he asked. Clearly, compensation can either accelerate the adoption of a new strategy or create unintentional opposition.

Culture may be even more important than compensation design in determining the success or failure of a particular strategy. The phrase "culture eats strategy for breakfast" (attributed to management consultant and writer Peter Drucker, although its exact origin is disputed) underscores that the shared values, beliefs, and behaviors within a company impact strategic initiatives. In essence, while strategy provides direction and goals for an organization, culture ultimately determines whether those goals are achievable. Many mergers and acquisitions fail due to a clash of cultures, as do corporate change initiatives.[308]

Daniel Peris states,

Actually, culture eats strategy slowly. By the time the outcome is known, the brand-name strategy consultants and/or investment bankers behind the big M&A deal have moved on to the next victim. It's too late to claw back their payments, and it's very expensive to clean up the resulting mess. In a dynamic sector, first, build a flexible culture that can zig and zag. If you don't have that, don't expect necessary strategy shifts to come easily.[309]

10 Are we on or off track, and what are the strategic implications?

Lesson Worth Learning: Are expectations being met or exceeded? What are the policy implications? Should the organization stay, adjust, or change course?

We will discuss the oversight powers and roles of the board and its committees in more depth in the chapter: "Oversee the Execution of Direction within Policy." However, the board should exercise its power to oversee using the metrics developed as part of the strategic planning process. Based on actual performance compared to expectations, there should be a feedback loop back to Setting Direction and Policy to determine whether to stay on the current course, adjust, or even change course.

Conclusion

This chapter discussed the adaptive board's role in setting the strategic direction and policy expectations. Metrics, milestones, and compensation should now be clear and aligned. The board should be involved at key points because strategic thinking has to be evergreen. The next step is to present the recommended plan to the board. The plan should be constantly reviewed and refreshed as part of the powers "Approve then Delegate" and "Oversee Execution." The recommended strategy and progress should be discussed with the board regularly (Figure 4.7).

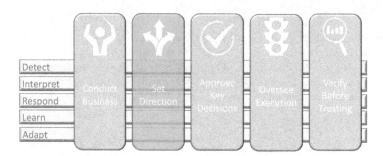

Figure 4.7: Set Direction and Policy.

By the conclusion of the current iteration of the strategic thinking and planning process, the committee or board (working in close collaboration with the executive) should have:
– Agreed upon the planning horizon.
– Checked alignment on the vision, mission, and values.

- Identified critical issues to be addressed for the organization's successful adaptation.
- Identified and evaluated the range of its real strategic options.
- Evaluated their relative pros and cons, rewards, and risks based on the organization's risk appetite (including the risks of inaction).
- Identified and prioritized the resources required.
- Identified the vital signs to measure the progress of the plan.
- Assessed the alignment of the organization's compensation and culture with the strategy.

In the next chapter, we discuss the board's power to "Approve and then Delegate" the necessary authority and resources. What are the key decisions the board must approve? What criteria should be used? What is the process of due diligence? What will be delegated?

I don't approve of anything that I don't thoroughly comprehend.
Fyodor Dostoevsky, Russian Novelist

Chapter 5
Approve key decisions, then prudently delegate

Approve Key Decisions, then Prudently Delegate:
Critical Questions and Lessons Worth Learning

Critical Questions	Lessons Worth Learning
Detect	
1. Has the board clearly identified the key decisions requiring board approval?	– Identify key decisions that require final approval by the board and those that don't. This is an active, ongoing process. There is no "set it and forget it" list.
2. Does the board have a disciplined decision process?	– Legally, prudence is judged by the process, not the results. A good process is the best way to get good results. Was there a robust process? Was it followed?
	– Disciplined processes don't work if they're ignored.
	– Calendar recurring approvals.
	– Spend the time.
	– Document due diligence.
	– Constructively challenge the recommendation.
	– Document the approval.
Interpret/Respond	
3. Does the board require that appropriate due diligence be performed before a request for board approval?	– Adaptive boards demand appropriate due diligence from executive management before considering a request for approval.
4. Have appropriate accountability, authority, and resources been prudently delegated?	– Accountability, authority, and resources must be aligned for the approval process to work correctly.
Learn and Adapt	
5. How can the board's approval process be improved?	– Adaptive boards use post-implementation reviews to refine their approval processes and increase their success rate.

Introduction

Start at the end. Unlike in Setting Direction and Policy, the board is typically involved at the end of a due diligence process when exercising its power to approve. It is being asked to approve some recommended action or policy based on due diligence conducted by a committee, executive, or someone else.

https://doi.org/10.1515/9783111344027-005

But why get approval for that recommendation and not other policies or actions? What are the key decisions retained by the board and why? What decisions are delegated to the executive? What will the decision-making and due diligence process be? Adherence to a defined process is the principal measure of prudence, but what should the approval process be?

"Noses in, fingers out." Those four words of advice to board members, attributed to John M. Nash, founding president of the National Association of Corporate Directors, succinctly suggest that the role of a board is to watch closely but not interfere with management as it goes about the day-to-day job of running the organization. It's good advice and appropriate most of the time. But it can also be simplistic. After all, if all boards ever do is watch, what happens when a board doesn't like what it sees?

Consider the following. Imagine a boat or ship with its captain, officers, and crew. It could be a sailboat, an ocean-going transport, an oil tanker, or a fishing boat. Where is the board on that boat? Is it on the bridge? In the engine room? At the helm? Manning the radar?

It's a trick question. The board is not on the boat. The board represents the boat's owners. They can visit, but they are not part of the crew. The board hires the captain, who selects the officers, who, in turn, select and manage the crew.

The analogy is apt for corporations. Indeed, the first joint stock companies and their boards were formed to represent the interests of the owners of ships traveling across the Atlantic Ocean from the old world to the new.[310]

In family-run businesses or startups where executives are also board members and principal shareholders, maintaining a balance in roles as directors is crucial. They must differentiate between personal ownership interests and fiduciary responsibilities to the company. Decisions should prioritize the company's long-term health and stakeholder interests over personal gains.

Why delegate? Boards delegate to executives because they can't – and shouldn't – do the work themselves. We all have seen situations where boards micromanage. This is a recipe for disaster and value destruction. Boards of directors are generally ill-suited to perform management tasks for several reasons:

1. **Board members are part-timers.** Directors usually meet periodically (e.g., quarterly) and are not involved in the organization's daily operations. Their limited time commitment means they do not have the continuous engagement required for effective management, even if they have management expertise. That's important to remember since corporate and not-for-profit boards often feature current or former CEOs whose instincts make it tough for them to keep their fingers out.

2. **Delays in decision-making**. Management tasks often require quick decision-making and responsiveness to daily challenges. Due to their structure and pe-

riodic meeting schedule, boards are not designed for rapid, day-to-day decision-making.

3. **Govern, not manage.** The primary role of a board of directors is to govern, not manage. As stated throughout this book, this involves five basic powers: conducting the business of the board and its committees, setting strategic direction, approving key decisions, overseeing the execution of direction within policy, and verifying the reliability of advice and information they receive and the reports they issue. The board should not get involved in day-to-day management unless a problem or opportunity has policy implications. Obviously, the board should be available to advise and support management. But not manage.

4. **Lack of industry and organization-specific expertise**. Board members often come from varied professional backgrounds and may not have specific expertise in the industry or operational knowledge of the organization. This diversity benefits strategic oversight but can disadvantage detailed management tasks.[311]

5. **Independent**. Boards are intended to function independently from management to provide unbiased oversight. If they were involved in management, their ability to objectively evaluate the executive team's performance and make impartial decisions would be compromised.

6. **Strategic vs. operational focus.** The board should focus on long-term strategy, risk management, and ensuring the organization adheres to its vision, mission, and values. On the other hand, management should focus on recommending and executing strategies and handling operational details, which requires a different skill set and perspective to execute. That's why they are called executives.

Delegation is the norm. When boards try to manage (rather than govern), they create confusion about who is in charge, which can delay decision-making, create factions, and paralyze an organization. When boards overreach, they can create power battles with executives and confusion in the ranks.

Except for the rare situations where a board wants to sideline management due to a crisis or conflict, organizations work best when boards give clear instructions to management and the necessary authority and resources to achieve the delegation. Boards should pave the way and then get out of the way.

So, if delegation is the norm, why does virtually every board retain the final approval rights over some subset of decisions? That sounds contrary to the "noses-in-fingers-out" doctrine. Why not let management or a committee decide without board approval once an issue has been delegated to them?

The board retains responsibility. While boards can delegate authority and resources, they cannot delegate responsibility, which is also why some directors find it hard to let go of management prerogatives. Therefore, boards need mechanisms to ensure that critical enterprise functions meet expectations and are managed within approved policy. This allows directors to let go but still retain oversight. Most organizations have multiple such mechanisms, and the power to "Approve" is among the most powerful of them.

The power to "Approve" allows the board to delegate to another party (usually executive management or a board committee) the authority to recommend but to reserve for itself the final authority to decide on that recommendation. This ensures that the proposed course of action is within board policy.

"Approve Key Decisions" occupies the space on the spectrum between "Set Direction and Policy" and "Oversee Execution." With "Set," the board is actively involved throughout the process. At the other end of the spectrum is "Oversee," where there is no presumption of board involvement. With "Oversee," no board action is required if results are within tolerances (i.e., within policy). Indeed, the board may only need to acknowledge that it received the information (discussed further in Oversee).

With "Approve," the board makes a decision at the end of a due diligence process. It should also have approved – or at least been comfortable with – the process and the due diligence criteria in advance of the recommendation being made (Figure 5.1).

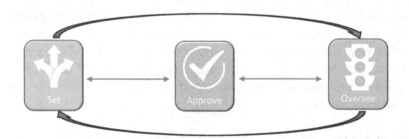

Set	Approve	Oversee
• Set determines an organization's strategy and policy. • Strategy provides a range of options in extreme uncertainty. • Policy determines the amount and type of risk a board is willing to accept and the expectations of performance and the related tolerances.	• Approve distinguishes those decisions that require board approval from those that can be fully delegated to management and only overseen by the board. • Recommendations for board approval are based upon agreed criteria and a process of due diligence.	• The executive is accountable for execution of board approved direction within policy. • The board oversees actual performance compared to expected performance (policy). • Performance within expected ranges requires no board action. • Performance outside of expected ranges is evaluated to see if there are policy implications.

Figure 5.1: Set, Approve, Oversee.

In addition to delegating to executives, boards can also delegate to committees (or, occasionally, outside entities such as law firms). As discussed previously, committees can dedicate more time than the full board to research, review, develop in-depth knowledge, and constructively challenge recommendations. The board can review committee reports and benefit from their more in-depth research. The board can then vote to approve (or not) the committee's recommendations.

Powers reserved. By reserving final approval, the board not only fulfills the need to make sure policy is being followed but also sends two important signals. First, it highlights issues the board believes are important enough to warrant it making the final decision. This clarifies the board's view between material decisions relating to policy and the operational details that are better left to management. This tells management – and the whole organization – what is unilaterally within management's purview and what lines management should not cross without prior board approval. This way, executive authority – and its limits – are clearly delineated.

In the spotlight. The second impact is subtle and often forgotten but powerful. By reserving approval, the board creates a "Hawthorne effect" around those decisions. A hundred years ago, in 1924, at the Western Electric Hawthorne manufacturing plant in Cicero, Il., social scientists tried an experiment to understand the impact of different light levels on workers' productivity.[312] Eventually, researchers began to understand that, irrespective of the number of lumens, productivity increased when the workers perceived that they were being observed. In other words, people act differently when they know they are being observed.

Through the years, researchers have suggested various causes of the Hawthorne effect, from the fact that people simply respond to increased attention to what psychologists call the "demand effect," that is, trying to please the observers.[313] Though some have said the impact of the Hawthorne effect is overstated,[314] it has proven to be both persistent and positive, even if not quite of the magnitude first thought.

When a board reserves final approval to itself, executives understand that their proposed plan of action will be subject to scrutiny. The knowledge that the board will debate and vote on a recommendation is usually enough to ensure that the recommendation is based on a robust process, substantive research, and an analysis that will satisfy the board.

Certainly, some recommendations subject to approval are nearly always pro forma (e.g., requiring a board resolution to authorize signatories). It's noteworthy that those approvals are often required by regulation. Clearly, the regulators want to signal to both management and the board that these seemingly administrative tasks are important; they constitute an authorization to use organizational assets.

Critical questions the board should always ask before approving key decisions and delegating

This chapter asks five critical questions and provides answers based on lessons worth learning from the successes and failures of others in exercising the power to approve and then prudently delegate:

1. Has the board clearly identified the key decisions requiring board approval?
2. Does the board have a disciplined decision process?
3. Does the board require an appropriate level of due diligence to be performed before a request for board approval?
4. Have appropriate authority and resources been prudently delegated?
5. Is there a systematic way to improve the board's approval process and track record of success?

1 Has the board clearly identified the key decisions requiring board approval?

> In any moment of decision, the best thing you can do is the right thing,
> the next best thing is the wrong thing, and
> the worst thing you can do is nothing.
> *Theodore Roosevelt, 26th[h] U.S. President*

Lesson Worth Learning: Identify the key decisions that require final approval by the board and those that don't. This is an active, ongoing process. There is no "set it and forget it" list

The board's and committees' responsibilities and delegations to executives are typically described in the organization's bylaws, charters, and governance policies. Those documents codify standing delegations and their limitations.

However, other delegations are ad hoc. For instance, many board delegations include blanket statements saying that the delegate is given all necessary authority to carry out a board's policy decision (up to a limit). By contrast, other delegations explicitly ask the delegate to propose a course of action that the board must ratify at some future date before that action is implemented, thereby asserting the board's prerogative to "approve."

Make it clear. The board should explicitly state the type of delegation it is making and, if the issue must be returned to the board for approval, a time frame. Typically, for board committee recommendations, the board retains final decision authority. Sometimes, regulation requires action by the entire board rather than management or a committee, in which case approvals fulfill the requirement.

State corporation laws typically outline powers reserved to the board alone: amending the corporate charter (also known as certificate of corporation) or by-laws; adopting an agreement of merger or consolidation; recommending to the stockholders the sale, lease, or exchange of all or substantially all the corporation's assets; recommending or vetoing a dissolution of the corporation; declaring dividends; or issuing stock.[315]

But most boards make decisions beyond these six areas. There is no universal guidance or definitive all-inclusive list of the matters that ought to be decided through the board's approval power (as opposed to those to be wholly delegated or wholly retained, such as the decisions under "Conduct Business").

The lack of a "clear" line is why effectively defining and then communicating which decisions are subject to the board's "Approval" power is paramount. A clear distinction between those actions that require board approval versus those that have been delegated wholly to management smooths the path to a constructive board/management relationship.

By contrast, opacity and confusion almost always lead to charges of board micromanagement or executive management running amok. We've seen that play out too often. That said, boards typically reserve final approval power for two types of decisions: 1) Legal and 2) Material.

Legal. Board approvals as defined by law or regulation. For instance, many jurisdictions require the board to designate the organization's officers. It's almost universally required that the board approve the annual financial statements, even though the finance staff, CFO, the audit committee, and the external auditor usually know them better than the non-audit-committee members. Still, in most jurisdictions, the board must vote to release them and is responsible for them.

Decisions that legally require board approval may also depend on the nature and purpose of the organization and the jurisdiction. For example, in the United States, the law requires mutual fund boards to approve the hiring, firing, and compensation of the fund's chief compliance officer (CCO), even if that person works day-to-day for the sponsoring asset management organization.[316]

While the issues subject to approval will vary with each organization's facts and circumstances, some of the decisions that legally require board approval often include:[x]

– Fundamental changes to the nature of the organization, such as material mergers, acquisitions, or divestitures.
– Material changes to the organization's financial situation, such as issuing new debt or equity and buying them back. This could also include the pur-

---

x Some of these may also require approval of the shareholders or of a subset of the board, such as all independent or non-conflicted directors.

chase, sale, or lease of major or long-term assets, issuance of dividends, and special distributions to stockholders.

- Appointing directors and officers. If an organization does not properly vote to approve directors or officers, it can cause legal complications for future actions taken by those directors and officers.
- Hiring, terminating, and compensating the independent auditor. In addition, there may be special requirements for the board's independent members to approve.
- Establishing, amending, or discontinuing employee pension/benefit, profit-sharing, and insurance plans.
- Issuing board reports, including the annual financial statements.
- Setting the dates for the annual general or extraordinary meetings.
- Changing the legal domicile of the entity.
- Entering into important agreements such as financing agreements, intellectual property and licensing agreements, and large leases.
- Instituting or settling litigation.

Material. These are policy decisions requiring board approval but are not specifically identified by law or regulation. Again, the specifics will vary with each organization's facts, circumstances, and governance philosophy. Some common policies requiring board approval include:

- the strategic plan
- hiring, terminating, and compensating the CEO and chief audit executive
- adopting a budget

The board needs to decide what is "material" rather than "day-to-day" or operational.[317] Boards often ask legal counsel to help determine the difference between the material and the day-to-day. Certainly, substantive and material recommendations such as the strategic plan, a merger, a significant commitment of capital, a new business line, or entering a new market should receive increased scrutiny and constructive challenge, and probably approval by the board. Consider the above as a starting point; other issues might be considered material by a particular organization.

What's material for your organization? Many boards go beyond the legally mandated list of decisions and retain approval power for a broader set of decisions to ensure accountability. This may include any issue area of special interest to the board, such as signaling its importance to the organization or external stakeholders.

Some decisions are retained to ensure the organization stays within its quantitative and qualitative risk appetite, which is why many boards set dollar thresholds for invoking the "approve" power. A decision that involves a dollar exposure below that threshold can be implemented without board approval (though board notification may be required).

Of course, dollars alone do not determine an organization's risk profile; organizations often require approval before executive management can invest materially in a new product, service, acquisition, or geography.

Such a policy serves two purposes. First, management must consider and educate the board on the new types of risks the new strategy will encounter. Second, it forces the board to expressly accept or reject the new strategy and concurrent change to the organization's risk profile. Ideally, that also includes understanding the risks of and to the new strategy and adjusting the organization's risk appetite.

Another reason for a board approval policy is to prevent conflicts and misalignments.

For instance, Aetna Corp. was publicly a strong supporter of the Affordable Care Act. However, the insurer faced a public backlash in 2012 when it emerged that it had made contributions totaling $7.5 million to two trade groups. These groups, in turn, used part of that money to disparage and try to derail the health care program.[318]

That attracted a shareholder proposal at the company's annual meeting to require the board to be involved in setting policy for and reporting on political spending. The shareholders' supporting statement to that proposal specifically cited the risk of misalignment. They noted, "We believe that it is inappropriate for the Board to delegate these important matters to management."[319]

Shareholders reinforced the message that fundamental issues should remain at the board level. Nonetheless, some boards delegate these issues to management and then merely oversee political spending, for example, by requiring the board to approve an annual report detailing political spending and alignment – requirements that Aetna had met but were deemed insufficient.

What does your board do? There should be a delegation of authority policy that clearly delineates the types of decisions delegated to the executive and those retained by the board. The main components of competently delegating authority include those shown in Table 5.1.

2 Does the board have a disciplined decision process?

Adaptive boards have disciplined decision-making processes. These include a calendar of decisions to be approved, ensuring appropriate due diligence before the board acts on a request for approval, and engaging with management through constructive challenge.

Table 5.1: Delegation of Authority.

Task Assignment	Clearly define and assign specific tasks or responsibilities to the delegate.
Granting of Authority	Provide the delegate with the necessary authority to make decisions and take actions required to complete the assigned tasks.
Accountability	Hold the delegate accountable for the outcomes and performance of the assigned tasks. The delegator remains ultimately responsible for the delegated tasks.
Communication	Ensure clear and open communication about expectations, boundaries, and progress between the delegator and the delegate.
Resources and Support	Provide the necessary resources, tools, and support required for the delegate to perform the delegated tasks effectively.
Monitoring and Feedback	Establish mechanisms for monitoring progress and providing feedback to ensure that the tasks are being carried out as expected and to address any issues that arise.

Lesson Worth Learning: Legally, prudence is judged by the process, not the results. A good process is the best way to get good results. Was there a robust process? Was it followed?

> Prudence is not the same thing as caution. Caution is a helpful strategy when you're crossing a minefield; it's a disaster when you're in a gold rush.
> *John Ortberg, American Author and Speaker*

Process is paramount. An overarching principle of prudence and fiduciary duty is that it is process-oriented rather than result-oriented. The determination of prudence is about how the decision was made but rarely dictates a specific result. That said, a good process is among the best ways to drive good results.

Prudence is evaluated based on the facts and circumstances at the time a decision is made, not with the benefit of perfect hindsight. For example, investment decisions are judged on the rationale for making them at the time, not on the eventual investment results. Circumstances also matter. That same decision may or may not be prudent within an overall portfolio but not as a stand-alone investment.

Some of the most common causes of lawsuits against corporate directors for breach of fiduciary duty include, for example:[320]

1. securities fraud claims, including fraud and deceit
2. inaccurate reporting of financial data
3. poor corporate governance
4. deficient accounting
5. insider trading
6. misstatements or omissions of material facts

7. violations of Section 10(b) of the Securities Exchange Act and Rule 10b-5
8. violations of Sections 11 and 12 of the Securities Act related to public offerings
9. missed earnings guidance
10. misleading statements about future performance
11. regulatory issues
12. merger-integration issues
13. environmental issues
14. cryptocurrency-related allegations

The most frequent trigger for these lawsuits is typically a significant drop in a company's stock price following the disclosure of negative information. Plaintiffs often allege that the company and its executives made false or misleading statements that artificially inflated the stock price prior to the drop.

While directors may be protected to some extent by indemnification provisions, insurance, or legal defenses, those defensive tactics do nothing to drive value creation. Directors acting diligently, ethically, and in accordance with their fiduciary duties do so not just to minimize the risk of litigation but to instill a culture, fulfill their obligations nobly, and ultimately drive organizational success.

Directors must exercise care and diligence and stay reasonably informed about the business to make informed decisions. While they can rely on professional opinions, they must seek further guidance when necessary. A good heart with an empty head is a fiduciary violation.

Recognizing the inherent discretion and judgment involved in business decisions, courts may uphold decisions made by officers and directors if they acted in good faith, had a reasonable basis for their decision, and had a legitimate business purpose. This rule grants directors and officers some protection against liability.

It is in the organization's best interests that the board act prudently and, in the event of litigation, be able to demonstrate it. Documentation of the board's processes is essential for demonstrating prudence. Policies and practices must be thoughtful and use careful forward-looking analysis. Well-informed expert advice should be obtained when needed. Here are a few lessons worth learning to help create that process.

Lesson Worth Learning: Calendar recurring approvals

Approving budgets and financial statements, electing board officers, and many other decisions occur annually. Committee work plans often state which tasks should be accomplished in what quarter. At some organizations, multi-year events are repeated. All those should be calendared a year in advance. Building a forward calendar of required decisions can help to ensure a "no surprises" approach.

Advance calendaring also improves efficiency and facilitates the coordination of board education sessions and/or information sessions with the decisions to which that education applies. Remember to include the output from each committee's work plans as inputs into the board's annual calendar, with appropriate notes on what committee work requires full board approval.

Lesson Worth Learning: Disciplined Processes Don't Work if They're Ignored

To understand why a disciplined decision process for approving a particular issue is a hallmark of adaptive boards, consider what can happen when that disciplined process doesn't exist.

Recall that in "Conduct Business," Enron's board waived ethics rules, allowing its CFO to have an economic interest counter to the company in the special purpose vehicles. This ultimately helped to bankrupt the seventh-largest corporation in the United States.

But the obvious absurdity of that decision – at least in hindsight – begs the question: Why didn't the approval process at the board prevent these decisions? The answer: What process? It was minimal, at best, and even worse, the board ignored what little process there was. Here is the U.S. Senate report about the Enron board meeting when LJM1, the first of the private equity vehicles, was approved:

> Despite these highly unusual features, the Board ratified the code of conduct waiver and approved the LJM1 proposal with little study or debate. For example, contrary to the Board's usual practice, the LJM1 proposal was never reviewed by the Finance Committee before it was submitted to the full Board for consideration. It was presented to the Board itself for the first time in written materials faxed to Board members 3 days before the special meeting.
>
> During the meeting itself, the Board's discussion of the proposal appears to have been minimal. The Board minutes show that the special meeting considered a number of matters in addition to the LJM1 proposal, including resolutions authorizing a major stock split, an increase in the shares in the company's stock compensation plan, the purchase of a new corporate jet, and an investment in a Middle Eastern power plant. Mr. Lay also discussed a reorganization underway at Enron. Yet the entire meeting lasted 1 hour.[321]

The board flunked the process. Normally, such a proposal should have had a deep dive committee review. That didn't happen. Normal practice is for all materials to be delivered to board members at least a week before.[322] That didn't happen. And it's fair to infer that with a stock split, purchase of a corporate jet, investment in a new power plant, and a major corporate reorganization also on the agenda for a meeting that only lasted an hour, there wasn't much constructive challenge if there was any discussion at all.

The inevitable result? An ad hoc and rushed approval vote that led to the company's failure.

Lesson Worth Learning: Spend the time

As the U.S. Senate's Enron report suggested, a disciplined decision-making process is impossible without time allotted to it. That's why, in "Conduct," we suggested putting action items first, not last, on the agenda. Remember to allow adequate time for constructive questioning.

Lesson Worth Learning: Document due diligence

Even before an item is brought to the board for approval, the process and rationale for making the recommendation should be documented. That record, either in full or in summary, should be available to board members who want more details on that item. It answers the question: "What was management thinking?"

Due diligence has been used since at least the mid-15th century in the literal sense of "requisite effort." Centuries later, the phrase has developed a legal meaning: "the care that a reasonable person takes to avoid harm to other persons or their property."[323] More recently, *due diligence* has extended its reach into more wide-ranging business *contexts, signifying the research a company performs before engaging in a financial (or other significant) transaction.* We use it here to refer to management's work in developing a recommendation for the board.

Lesson Worth Learning: Constructively challenge the recommendation

This is especially true if there is any doubt or lingering question about the decision. By satisfying itself with the competence of management's due diligence and analysis, the board lays the groundwork for acting (or not acting) based on the information and assurances received. Absent such satisfaction, the board would be in the untenable position of either acting on information it did not trust or, perhaps worse, attempting to collect the information by itself.

Lessons Worth Learning: Document the approval

After a decision is reached, a written record of approvals helps prevent misunderstandings, captures any caveats or conditions attached to the approval, and provides a record for the board in case of a legal challenge. Board meeting minutes should document approvals, which should be approved by the board at a subsequent meeting and then filed appropriately.

Approvals between board meetings, such as those by written consent, should also be memorialized in accordance with the organization's bylaws and regulations. If such approvals are then ratified at the next board meeting, those ratifications should also be memorialized.

3 Does the board ensure that appropriate due diligence has been performed before a request for board approval?

Lesson Worth Learning: Adaptive boards require appropriate due diligence from committees and executive management before considering a request for approval

> Diligence is the mother of good fortune.
> *Benjamin Disraeli, former Prime Minister of the United Kingdom*

Presumably, the absence of diligence is the mother of misfortune. That is a lesson far too many boards have learned, from Hewlett-Packard's inflated purchase of Autonomy to Coca-Cola's disastrous "New Coke" experience.

Where's the risk? In 2016, Bayer AG, a German multinational pharmaceutical and life sciences company, acquired Monsanto, an American agrochemical and agricultural biotechnology corporation, for $63 billion.[324] The acquisition aimed to create a global leader in agriculture and enhance Bayer's crop science portfolio.

But Bayer's acquisition of Monsanto is a tale of due diligence failures (Table 5.2). The underestimation of legal and regulatory risks associated with Monsanto's Roundup weed-killing formula has led to significant financial liabilities, extensive

Table 5.2: Bayer's Acquisition of Monsanto – Failures in Due Diligence.

Underestimating Legal Risks	One of the most significant failures in Bayer's due diligence was underestimating the legal risks associated with Monsanto's flagship product, Roundup, a glyphosate-based herbicide. Despite ongoing lawsuits and controversies surrounding the product, Bayer did not fully anticipate the extent and potential financial impact of future litigation.
Insufficient Scrutiny of Regulatory Risks	Bayer did not adequately assess the regulatory environment and the growing scrutiny over glyphosate's safety. Various studies and reports had raised concerns about its carcinogenic potential, but Bayer seemingly overlooked or underestimated the potential regulatory challenges and public backlash.
Financial Liabilities	Potential financial liabilities stemming from litigation related to Roundup were not fully accounted for. Bayer faced thousands of lawsuits alleging that Roundup caused cancer, specifically non-Hodgkin lymphoma. The cost of settlements and legal fees has significantly impacted Bayer's financial health.[325]

litigation, and damage to Bayer's reputation. This case underscores the importance of thorough due diligence, particularly regarding potential legal and regulatory issues in high-stakes mergers and acquisitions.

Bayer inherited a substantial number of lawsuits from Monsanto, with plaintiffs claiming that exposure to Roundup caused their cancer. By 2023, Bayer had agreed to pay more than $10 billion to settle Roundup-related legal claims.[326] The controversy surrounding Roundup has also damaged Bayer's reputation.

Regulatory agencies worldwide have increased scrutiny of glyphosate, with some countries implementing bans and restrictions.[327] This regulatory pressure has created additional challenges for Bayer in maintaining market access and compliance. The negative publicity and public perception issues have affected Bayer's brand and consumer trust in its other products.

So, if those are examples of failed due diligence processes, what does a successful, disciplined decision process look like? Several overarching principles can help design a robust process for your organization, though, as with everything else, the exact process will depend on your organization.

Take a step back. For an approval to be calendared, someone must put it on the agenda (with the chair's agreement). So, what does the requestor – the person who put the recommendation on the agenda – owe the board and the organization?

As famed 19th-century jurist Thomas Cooley wrote, the obligation of that requestor to get the recommendation correct is broad but not unlimited. Any person "who offers services to another and is employed assumes the duty to exercise in the employment such skill as he/(she) possesses with reasonable care and diligence."[328]

This is why boards can reasonably rely upon management's representations a century and a half after Cooley. Management owes the board skill, care, and diligence before recommending an approval. But it would also be imprudent of the board to rely solely on assurances. (See "Verify before Trusting.")

In practice, what skill, care, and diligence look like varies according to the nature of the specific recommendation. For instance, the designation of a corporate officer is important, but it's also relatively straightforward. In general, boards are told who the person is, why they are being made a corporate officer, and what that corporate office is empowered to do.

If it's an outside hire, a due diligence process often entails a search firm, background checks, interviews, and reference checks. A written or verbal summary of those diligence checks should be provided to the board. If the board knows a trusted insider who has worked with the organization for years, little of that may be provided, although, at some organizations, an updated background check may be.

Of course, more complicated approval requires more robust due diligence from management.

Here's an example. In this case, a board is being asked to issue bonds (for whatever reason), thereby leveraging the company. Some of the things that should be in the management memo are the following:

Identified risks. This includes both the risk of the action being requested and the risks to its execution. In this case, a board being asked to issue bonds should understand the inherent risks of that strategy: the need to pay debt service, the responsibility to repay or refinance the principal in the future, and the indenture agreement's clauses that restrict the organization's flexibility.

Then there are the risks to the decision's execution: There is no guarantee that the organization can borrow at the indicative rate or the suggested amount. And, of course, the reasons for issuing debt, from financing growth to purchasing an asset to financing a share buyback, have their own risks.

Critical information should be verified. In the bond issuance example, the board should receive assurances that the investment bank is prepared to underwrite the issuance, that the CFO believes the debt service will not be overly burdensome, etc.

Compliance checks. In this case, will the borrowing trigger any covenants in pre-existing bonds? Is the borrowing being done in compliance with securities regulations? Are the disclosure requirements fulfilled?

The impact on stakeholders should be considered. Will equity shareholders like or loathe the borrowing? The entity's bank(s)? Existing debt holders?

In other decisions, perhaps employees, suppliers, or customers will be affected, and how they will react should be considered. If in doubt, a simple but underutilized tool is to ask the other stakeholders how they would react to a proposed course of action.

Do you have what it will take? Do you have the expertise and resources to implement the recommendation? If not, what will it take to improve your chances of success? In this example, even with competent finance and legal staff, you may want to engage third-party expertise, like an investment banker and/or securities counsel.

What are the operational requirements? Do you need an indenture trustee? New bank accounts? An investor relations function?

Has management done its job? Gathering that information is management's responsibility, not a committee's or the board's. However, where management's due diligence process ends, the board's and the committee's process begins. The board's responsibility is to make sure that management has fulfilled its responsibilities.

Toward that end, management should provide the board with a record of its due diligence process and a recommendation summary. A simple memorandum will suffice for most approvals. Still, the level of documentation can range from a single sentence for routine issues to scores, if not hundreds, of pages, including letters of comfort and a deep dive by the audit committee for things like approving annual financial statements.

This systematic approach ensures that the executive, committee, or other recommender thoroughly examines all relevant aspects and that the board has the necessary information and insight to make an informed decision.

Critical Issue Options Summary. As described in the chapter Set Policy and Direction, for complex and important approvals, management may provide a Critical Issue Option Summary (CIOS). Among the common elements of a CIOS are the following:
1. Executive summary
2. Background and statement of issues, contributing factors (significance and controllability)
3. Discussion of alternatives and options considered
4. Discussion of pros and cons of alternative options considered
5. Discussion of risks of each alternative, including the risk of inaction
6. Business case with costs and benefits
7. Recommendation for approval
8. The process of due diligence
9. Dissenting opinions expressed by stakeholders
10. Recommended questions to be asked by the board for this topic
11. Other

Finally, the board should exercise the appropriate level of constructive challenge and document the entire process in the minutes.

4 Have appropriate accountability, authority, and resources been prudently delegated?

Lesson Worth Learning: Accountability, authority, and resources must be aligned for the approval and delegation process to work correctly. This includes compensation

Act with care for the future. The board delegates authority and resources to the CEO to execute the agreed plan (with certain key exceptions). Prudent delegation is the careful and judicious assignment of tasks or responsibilities to others. It involves ensuring that the delegated tasks are appropriate for the individual's skills and abilities while maintaining oversight to ensure they are completed effectively.

Keith Johnson, formerly head of Institutional Investor Legal Services at Reinhart Law, states:

> Given the complexity and time-consuming nature of management functions, prudent delegation of certain functions is required. Directors need assistance from experienced staff and outside experts. Demands on directors' time mandate that boards delegate certain functions. But delegation requires careful attention, too.
>
> Practically, administrative and operational duties should be delegated through the CEO to staff and external service providers. However, when delegating, directors must carefully select, instruct, evaluate, and monitor them. This requires maintaining and following clear policies and processes.[329]

Good faith in the relationship between a delegator and a delegate is pivotal. It refers to the mutual trust, honesty, and transparency expected from both parties. The delegator who assigns tasks must trust the delegate to handle those tasks effectively and ethically. This involves providing clear instructions, necessary resources, and appropriate authority.

On the other hand, the delegate is expected to act in the delegator's best interest, execute duties diligently, and communicate openly about progress and challenges. Good faith enhances collaboration, ensures that delegated tasks are carried out responsibly, and builds a stronger, more effective working relationship.

Assign needed authority and resources. Prudent delegation defines the standards and ensures that the functions overseen by the board are staffed by skilled people and resourced appropriately. A very important part of prudent delegation is ensuring there are sufficient resources to carry out the agreed-upon direction.

There is a common trope on reality television: A person wants something that obviously can't exist. For example, a real estate reality show may feature a person who says they want to rent a four-bedroom modern house in Paris next to the Seine with a view of Notre-Dame cathedral. The catch? They only want to spend $800 a month. There's even a name for this: "Budget disconnect."

Watching at home, we might smugly feel superior to the oblivious television protagonist. After all, we know better than to expect champagne on a beer budget. We know how to align resources and tasks. We would never set ourselves up for failure and ridicule like that.

Unfortunately, we do. Some delegators approve a recommendation and assign responsibility but withhold the needed resources or authority to make it happen. As the following examples in Tables 5.3 and 5.4 illustrate, this is a recipe for failure in both the public sector and for public companies.

Best intentions. The misalignment of authority, accountability, and resources can occur anywhere. It doesn't have to be malicious or a power play. It can happen

Table 5.3: Failure to Adequately Resource – Public Sector.

Organization	Situation	Assigned Responsibility	Lack of Resources
Public Sector			
New York City Housing Authority (NYCHA) – Lead Paint Abatement	NYCHA's board approved a recommendation to address lead paint hazards in public housing units.[330]	The management team	Despite the approval, NYCHA struggled with insufficient funding and staffing to conduct the necessary lead paint inspections and remediation, resulting in prolonged exposure risks for residents and ongoing legal and regulatory challenges.[331]
NASA – Space Shuttle Program	Following the Challenger disaster, NASA's board and leadership approved various safety recommendations.[332]	NASA's engineering and safety teams	Despite the recommendations, there were reports of inadequate funding and resources to fully address all safety concerns, which contributed to the subsequent Columbia disaster. The lack of sufficient resources for comprehensive safety improvements was a critical issue.[333]
State of Michigan – Flint Water Crisis[334]	After the Flint water crisis was identified, various recommendations were made to address the public health emergency.[335]	Multiple state agencies	Initial efforts were hampered by insufficient funding, slow allocation of resources, and bureaucratic delays, which exacerbated the crisis and delayed the provision of safe drinking water to Flint residents.
City of New Orleans – Post-Katrina Rebuilding Efforts	Following Hurricane Katrina, the city's board approved recommendations for rebuilding infrastructure and improving disaster preparedness.[336]	Various city departments	Despite these approvals, the recovery was hindered by inadequate funding, slow federal aid distribution, and insufficient staffing, leading to prolonged recovery times and ongoing vulnerabilities.[337]

Table 5.4: Failure to Adequately Resource – Public Companies.

Organization	Situation	Assigned Responsibility	Lack of Resources
Public Companies			
Royal Bank of Scotland (RBS) – IT System Upgrade	RBS approved a recommendation to upgrade its outdated IT systems to improve banking services and security.[338]	The IT department	The IT system upgrade was marred by underfunding, leading to significant technical failures, including a major outage in 2012 that affected millions of customers.[339] The lack of sufficient resources and investment in the IT infrastructure was a key factor in the failure.[340]
Target Corporation – Canadian Market Expansion	Target's board approved the expansion into the Canadian market.[341]	Management	The project was under-resourced, with insufficient investment in supply chain infrastructure and inventory management systems. This led to significant operational issues, empty store shelves, and, ultimately, the failure of Target Canada, resulting in a costly exit from the market.
Yahoo! – Strategic Turnaround Plan	Yahoo!'s board approved a strategic plan to revitalize the company and compete more effectively in the digital space.[342]	The CEO and executive team	The plan was underfunded, and there were not enough resources allocated for critical areas like product development and marketing, contributing to the company's continued decline and eventual sale to Verizon.[343]

when everyone has the best of intentions. Here is yet another example where everyone had the best of intentions.

Malawi is one of Africa's smallest and poorest countries. Its economy and food supply are dependent on agriculture. There is little irrigation, so it's vulnerable to climate shocks, including droughts.[344] Recognizing this, international charities like Engineers Without Borders have tried to solve the problem by creating water distribution systems. Engineers Without Borders is precisely what it sounds like: engineers who want "to work on problems that matter(ed)," rather than "making a photocopier increase its speed from 149 pages a minute to 151 pages per minute."[345]

One project, paid for by Canada, was a gravity-fed system with 113 water distribution points to reduce Malawians' dependence on random rainstorms. However, just 18 months after it was completed, Engineers Without Borders found that 81 of the 113 taps did not work. A broader survey of Malawi that included multiple water distribution systems found that water systems ostensibly reached 80 percent of Malawi's population but that 40 percent of the taps did not work.[346]

As David Damberger of Engineers Without Borders notes, pipes break down. The issue in Malawi, however, was that no one had been given the authority to maintain the system. Even when local residents tried to fix the taps – and they had not formally been given the authority to do so – there were no resources. Affordable parts were scarce.

The result was a broken project, aid dollars wasted, and minimal impact. In other words, failure. Responsibility was at the donor nation level; authority to make sure the project worked was never assigned. Resources simply didn't seem to have been considered, and so didn't exist.

To make matters worse, when Engineers Without Borders investigated, they found another broken-down water distribution system nearby, unconnected to any water source. The United States had funded this one, had been built years earlier, and had suffered from the same fundamental flaws in misaligning responsibility, authority, and resources. Predictably, it was even more broken than the newer Canadian system.

These all illustrate the need to exercise care to avoid becoming the board of the "Best Intentions Paving Company."

5 How can we improve the board's approval process and track record of success?

Lesson Worth Learning: Adaptive boards use post-implementation reviews to continuously improve their approval processes and success rates

Adaptive boards learn from both mistakes and successes. In Malawi, in addition to the need to align responsibility and authority with resources, there is the failure to learn from past mistakes about why the system broke. This leads us to the need for post-implementation reviews (PIRs), which are effective tools for continuous improvement.

What is a post-implementation review? A PIR is a process used to evaluate the success and effectiveness of a project after its implementation. It aims to identify what went well, what didn't, and how future projects can be improved. A PIR can help organizations refine their project management practices and improve the success rate of future projects. The PIR might ask questions such as, "Did the project achieve its goals? Why or why not? What could have been done better?"

Table 5.5 shows some of the key components of a PIR.

Table 5.5: Post-Implementation Review (PIR).

Objective review	Assess whether the project met its objectives and delivered the expected benefits.
	Evaluate how the project outcomes align with the initial expectations, goals, and requirements. If there is a material difference, try to understand why.
Performance analysis	Measure the project's performance against key metrics such as time, cost, quality, scope, and impact.
	Compare actual performance with the project plan and identify variances. Try to understand why the variances exist.
Stakeholder feedback	Gather feedback from project stakeholders, including team members, users, clients, and sponsors, on outcomes and processes.
	Understand stakeholder satisfaction and any concerns or issues they may have encountered.
Process evaluation	Review the processes and methodologies used during the project.
	Identify any process improvements or best practices that can be applied to future projects.
Risk management	Evaluate how effectively risks were identified, assessed, and managed throughout the project.
	Document any unforeseen risks and if/how they were addressed.
Issue resolution	Analyze any issues or problems that arose during the project.
	Determine how effectively these issues were resolved and what can be learned to prevent similar issues in the future.
Resource utilization	Assess how resources (human, financial, and material) were utilized during the project.
	Identify any inefficiencies or areas where resource management could be improved.
Lessons learned	Document lessons learned, including both successes and challenges.
	Provide recommendations for future projects based on these lessons.
Future improvements	Highlight areas for improvement and strategies to enhance project success. Based on the PIR's findings, offer suggestions for future projects.

Boards that use PIRs to improve the approval process ask whether the due diligence process was appropriate, whether the decision rationales were communicated appropriately, whether there were any surprises for either management or the board during the constructive challenge periods, etc.

A word about that: The goal of no surprises is a good one, but too often, executives and boards think the solution is to throw resources at due diligence and then write it all up in a voluminous decision memorandum.

As discussed in "Conduct Business," that can result in a process and a memorandum that is DRIP – data rich but insight poor. The goal of a PIR is dual: to improve both effectiveness and efficiency. Sometimes, the conclusion is that for certain approvals, there can be a less intense due diligence process and a shorter memorandum for the board. In the extreme, perhaps a category of approvals can be eliminated entirely, with a new, more fulsome delegation to management. Reducing the extraneous helps focus the board on the essentials, i.e., "the vital few vs. the trivial many."

In addition to a PIR for the approval process generally, boards should consider whether they want a report at a future date on how the actions authorized by a specific approval have worked out, whether the issues encountered had been considered in the decision memorandum, whether the board had correctly anticipated and assigned the correct level of authority and resources to carry out its approval, etc.

Such reports help the board understand what works and why. Post-implementation reviews can provide invaluable context in the future. Many boards assign internal audit to provide such assessments.

Conclusion

In exercising its power to "Approve then Delegate," the adaptive board reviews, refines, and approves the recommended strategic plan. With this approval, the board grants the CEO authority (with certain key exceptions) and allocates the resources to execute the strategic plan within the policies established by the board.

For those key exceptions, the board reserves the power to make the final decision. The list of board-required approvals is explicit and specific and describes the limits of executive power. Due diligence is required when a request is made for board approval of one of these key decisions.

The board reviews the due diligence and may accept, refine, or reject the recommendation (Figure 5.2).

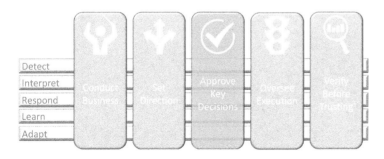

Figure 5.2: Approve Key Decisions, then Prudently Delegate.

In Chapter 6, "Oversee the Execution of Direction within Policy," we describe how the board can improve its oversight of the execution of board-approved directions within policy. Does the board have good insights into vital performance? Are the policy implications escalated on time? Is there effective feedback to "Direction and Policy Setting" based on actual performance?

Oversee

Effective oversight requires asking the right questions,
not having all the answers.
*Mary Jo White, former Chair of the U.S. Securities
and Exchange Commission*

Chapter 6
Oversee the execution of direction within policy

Oversee the Execution of Direction within Policy – Lessons Worth Learning

Critical Questions	Lessons Worth Learning
Detect	
1. **How should we exercise oversight?**	– Oversight has two contradictory meanings. One is to watch over carefully. The other is to fail to notice something. Be sure that your board and its committees are watching carefully.
2. **How can we prevent oversight failures?**	– Don't lose sight of the forest, i.e., what's vitally important, what's changing, and how fast?
3. **How do we know if vital performance is under control?**	– Focus on the "vital few." – Identify the vital signs for the vital few. – The choice of vital signs is strategic. – Require exception-based reporting (EBR).
Interpret	
4. **How do we get reliable, timely intelligence and policy insights for direction setting?**	– Set tolerance bands around acceptable performance measures. – Require root cause analysis of variations outside tolerance. – Transform the dialogue to focus on the policy implications of actual performance compared to expectations. – Gain insights by obtaining multiple sources of information. – Timely escalate exceptions to policy – Require effective escalation mechanisms for exceptions. – Require incident response protocols.
Respond	
5. **How should we respond?**	– Make recommendations re: stay, adjust, or change course.
Learn	
6. **What did we learn?**	– Assess actual performance compared to expectations – what worked well? What didn't work? Why?
Adapt	
7. **How do we adapt?**	– Should we stay, adjust, or change course? (See "Set/Approve.")

https://doi.org/10.1515/9783111344027-006

Introduction

I think that it is really important that there's federal oversight of the crypto industry.
FTX Founder Sam Bankman-Fried, later convicted of seven counts of fraud and sentenced to
25 years in prison

Be careful what you wish for. Sam Bankman-Fried wanted oversight, and he eventually got it. Within 18 months of the 2022 midterm elections, he contributed $80 million (including some through employees at FTX, his crypto exchange) to the political campaigns of both main U.S. political parties. He aimed to gain bipartisan support for regulatory frameworks that would benefit FTX and the wider crypto ecosystem.

Ironically for someone who at least said he wanted oversight, FTX operated largely without a board of directors for most of its existence. However, its U.S. entity, FTX US Derivatives, announced the establishment of a board of directors in early 2022. This board was intended to provide oversight and governance, but the broader FTX organization still lacked a comprehensive board structure, contributing to its governance failures and eventual collapse.[347]

In a court filing with the U.S. Bankruptcy Court for the District of Delaware, John Ray III, who succeeded Sam Bankman-Fried as CEO of FTX, disclosed that the company did not maintain proper books or records of customer funds and appeared to have used software to hide the misappropriation of customer money.[348] FTX's compliance was somewhere between woeful and non-existent.

Bankman-Fried is currently serving a 25-year sentence for fraud and other financial crimes related to FTX's collapse. He also forfeited $11 billion.[349] Another FTX executive, Ryan Salame, received a seven-and-a-half-year sentence. FTX went bankrupt.[350]

Bankman-Fried's misconduct was enabled by the lack of effective governance mechanisms to hold senior management accountable, compliance to ensure activities were within policy, and risk management that could say "no" to him. This oversight gap allowed Bankman-Fried and its management to engage in financially devastating and illegal activities without proper checks and balances. The poor internal controls and ineffective risk management ultimately allowed the misuse of customer funds.

Key financial information and decision-making processes were not adequately monitored or disclosed, leading to a lack of accountability. The close relationship between FTX and its sister company, Alameda Research (run by Bankman-Fried's former girlfriend), created significant conflicts of interest. This relationship was not properly managed or disclosed, leading to risky intercompany transactions contributing to FTX's financial instability.[351]

FTX operated in jurisdictions with lax regulatory frameworks, which allowed it to bypass stringent governance and compliance requirements. Thus, FTX didn't have to adhere to the same standards as firms in more strictly regulated markets. Of course, it could have adhered to higher standards, had a robust compliance process, and had a board that said no to Bankman-Fried when he gave special treatment to Alameda. But it didn't.

By not having real board oversight, FTX became the exemplar of its importance.

In this chapter, we'll discuss the board's role in overseeing the execution of direction within policy – or, in a word, *control.* How can the board know whether everything it considers vital is under control? What if it is, and what if it isn't? In other words, how to be everything that FTX's board was not.

Problems become obvious in hindsight, as at FTX, but your board has the power to avoid such embroglios in real-time by properly exercising its oversight power. Even more saliently, your board has the power to use oversight to set the stage for success by monitoring key vital signs to assure everything is "under control."

Control can be perceived positively, as in having self-mastery or leadership skills, or negatively, as in being controlling or domineering over others. In the context of a board of directors, being "under control" means several different things, including setting direction, approving key decisions, and then delegating.

First, the board needs to be reasonably assured that its directions are being executed within policy. Reasonable assurance comes from management. The board also needs to know how to verify management's statements (see "Verify before Trusting").

Second, boards are responsible for controlling the health of their organizations. Financially, boards are responsible for overseeing budgeting, financial planning, risk management, and the integrity of financial reports. Operationally, they are responsible for overseeing the organization's provision of services and/ or products that provide it with a reason to exist and do so within policy parameters.

Third, boards need to ensure compliance and culture. This means the company complies with all relevant laws and regulations to protect the organization from legal risks and its reputation and stability.

In exercising its oversight responsibilities, the board and its committees should track organizational performance's trends and policy implications against expectations. One of the most effective ways the board can exercise control is to assess whether actual performance remains within established policy ranges.

Critical questions the board should always ask about the execution of direction within policy

1. How should we exercise oversight?
2. How can we avoid failure of oversight?
3. How do we know vital performance is under control?
4. How do we get timely, reliable intelligence and insights for direction setting and oversight?

1 How should we exercise oversight?

Lesson Worth Learning: Oversight has two contradictory meanings. One is to watch over carefully, and the other is to fail to notice something. Be sure that your board and its committees are watching carefully

Oversight is how boards know whether the organization is on track toward achieving its purpose. It allows boards to cut through all the noise and contextual uncertainty to see whether performance is as expected. Oversight provides boards with early warning of when policy or execution needs to change. When done properly, oversight demonstrates the board's prudence. Boards typically delegate the primary role of overseeing performance and risk to committees within their respective mandates.

To oversee means to watch over (but not manage) and ensure things are "under control" (i.e., within policy and in compliance). Ironically, a second meaning of oversight means missing things unintentionally. As you might imagine, that causes intense concern for many directors. Some directors, fearing they may miss something important, jump to micromanaging things otherwise best left to the executive. Instead, they should refine their oversight to achieve reasonable assurance of performance within policy.

At the other end of the oversight spectrum from micromanagement is blind trust in the executive. The result is the abdication of adequate oversight. Some famous last words might have been: "They're the experts; let them do their thing. That's what we pay them for."

That's the soundtrack of willful blindness, not oversight. In addition to the overall governance failures already cited (Enron, Theranos, Volkswagen, Wells Fargo, etc.), Table 6.1 shows another very incomplete list of failed oversight. Presumably, their boards thought their organizations were under control until they weren't.

Some of these organizations didn't survive. Obviously, when an organization didn't, neither did the board. The board and executive were significantly over-

Table 6.1: Some Oversight Failures.

Organization	Failure
Lehman Brothers (2008)	Risk-management failures[352]
Siemens AG (2008)	Bribery/Lack of controls[353]
Bear Stearns (2008)	Lack of risk oversight[354]
Olympus (2011)	Misuse of funds[355]
MF Global (2011)	Lack of risk oversight[356]
FIFA (2015)	Corruption[357]
U.S. Gymnastics Association (2016)	Sexual abuse[358]
Facebook and Cambridge Analytica (2018)	Data privacy breaches[359]
Pacific Gas and Electric (PG&E) (2018)	Ineffective safety protocols[360],
Carillion (2018)	Ineffective debt management[361]
Danske Bank (2018)	Money laundering[362]
Luckin Coffee (2020)	Lack of controls[363]
Boeing 737 (2018)	Lack of safety oversight, faulty parts and installation issues[364]
Blue Bell Creameries (2019)	Food safety issues[365]
Silicon Valley Bank (SVB) 2023	Poor risk management, aggressive accounting, failure to understand deposit base[366]

hauled or completely replaced in those that did survive. Let there be no doubt: The board is held responsible in the case of failure.

The need for good governance generally, and board oversight specifically, is not limited to for-profit corporations. Let's look briefly at the oversight failure of the U.S. Gymnastics Association (USGA) in responding to the years of complaints about former physician Larry Nassar. It is a chilling story of failed oversight resulting in years of child sexual abuse.

USA gymnastics

It is any parent's worst nightmare – the person you entrust to watch over your child sexually abuses them. And hundreds of others. For years.

Now, imagine you're on the board of the organization that employs the serial predator. And that you get a warning about the situation. Then another. And another. You would act immediately, wouldn't you? After all, oversight is to make sure that actual results are within policy and are in control. Child sexual abuse – repeated over and over – certainly is no organization's idea of being under control.

So, in the real world, why did it happen? Why did no one act? Why were hundreds of girls abused, and why did USA Gymnastics (USAG), the organization responsible for the training and well-being of some of the most high-profile athletes at any Olympic games, not stop the abuse? Among the future gold medal winners who said they were abused when they were underage were Simone Biles, Aly Raisman, McKayla Maroney, Gabby Douglas, Jordyn Wieber, Kyla Ross, and Madison Kocian.[367] "(Their) biggest priority was to make sure I kept it quiet, so they'd have a good Olympics. It's disgusting," said 2016 Team USA Captain Aly Raisman.[368]

At the center of the scandal was Dr. Larry Nassar, a physician who worked for USAG, Michigan State University, and the U.S. Olympic Committee (USOC). While conducting medical exams, Nassar sexually abused hundreds of young athletes.

While the sex abuse scandal exploded in 2016, the first allegation against Nassar went back to 1992, while he was still in medical school.[369] Soon, the inevitable question was on everyone's tongue, "Where was the board?" In this case, the USAG. The answers were not pretty. USAG's focus, process, and culture contributed to, if not actually facilitating, the abuse, turning a blind eye to it.

When the scandal was finally exposed, Nassar was sentenced to 40–175 years in prison. Then, the USOC threatened the USAG with decertification, resulting in the entire board resigning under fire. Steve Penny, the USAG President and CEO, resigned and was later indicted for evidence tampering. Ultimately, the USAG had to file for bankruptcy in December 2018.[370]

So why did the board of USAG not act as it should have, and when should it have?

- Conflicted motivation: As Raisman said, they put the desire for a "good Olympics" over the welfare of their athletes. This is a classic short-term over long-term mistake. If you are on a corporate board, imagine a manufacturing plant that uses toxic materials dangerous to employees, because it's cheaper in the short run. Everyone knows it's wrong and will hurt in the long run when the conditions are exposed, but that doesn't stop some from doing it anyway.
- Completely wrong escalation policies: USAG had a policy of deliberately not escalating warning signs, which is precisely the opposite of what a healthy organization does. USAG dismissed allegations of sex abuse unless the athletes or the parents made the allegation. Others were summarily dismissed.[371] A Congressional investigation found that "USAG knowingly concealed abuse by Nassar, leading to the abuse of dozens of additional amateur athletes."[372] There is a reason we say, "Bad news has to travel fast."
- Corrupted culture: Yes, Nassar was a cancer in gymnastics. But he was a cancer that the USAG allowed to grow. In fact, the USAG was a good "host" for that particular cancer. For years, USAG took allegations of sex abuse by coaches and others and just threw them in a locked file.

For example, the 2010 coach of the year, Marvin Sharp, was reported to USAG in 2011 as a potential sex abuser. USAG only referred him to law enforcement three years later, after allegations that he was "touching a gymnast's vagina, trimming her pubic hair and taking sexually explicit pictures of her beginning when she was 12 years old." He committed suicide in jail. In another case, complaints against coach William McCabe dated back to 1998. Yet he continued to coach for almost seven more years until inappropriate e-mails he sent to an 11-year-old girl surfaced. He was sentenced to 30 years.[373]

Unfortunately, the USGA wasn't the only not-for-profit that experienced major oversight failures. The Boy Scouts of America (BSA) faced numerous allegations of sexual abuse by scout leaders over several decades, leading to a massive lawsuit and the organization's filing for bankruptcy in 2020 to address the claims.[374]

The Catholic Church has been embroiled in numerous sexual abuse scandals involving priests and minors. These scandals have surfaced globally, resulting in significant legal and financial repercussions and leading to various reforms within the Church.[375]

The United Way, a large non-profit organization, faced a scandal in the early 1990s when its national president, William Aramony, was found guilty of fraud, embezzlement, and financial mismanagement. This led to his resignation and a significant overhaul of the organization's governance and operations.[376]

The American Red Cross has faced several controversies, including mismanagement of funds and resources. After the 9/11 attacks and Hurricane Katrina, the organization was criticized for how it handled donations and aid distribution, leading to reforms and changes in leadership.[377]

The Wounded Warrior Project, which supports veterans, was embroiled in a scandal in 2016 when it was revealed that a significant portion of its donations was spent on lavish conferences and travel for its executives rather than on programs for veterans. This led to a major overhaul of its leadership and practices.[378]

Feed the Children, a charity focused on hunger relief, faced internal turmoil and legal battles when its founder, Larry Jones, was ousted amid allegations of mismanagement and misuse of funds. The organization underwent significant restructuring to recover its reputation and operational integrity.[379]

The Black Lives Matter movement has faced significant controversy and scrutiny regarding financial mismanagement and lack of transparency. Following George Floyd's death in 2020, the organization received approximately $90 million in donations. By the end of the 2021–2022 fiscal year, the foundation reported a $9 million deficit, raising questions about fund management.

In 2022, a lawsuit accused Shalomyah Bowers, an executive at the Black Lives Matter Global Network Foundation (GNF), of "siphoning" more than $10 million from donors for personal use. The lawsuit claimed that only about 33 percent of donations were given to charities, while millions were spent on consulting fees and salaries for those close to BLM's founders.[380]

No organization is immune. Where were the boards, and were they asking the right questions? Clearly not.

2 How can we prevent oversight failures?

Lesson Worth Learning: Don't lose sight of the forest, i.e., what's vitally important, what's changing, and how fast?

> Denial ain't just a river in Egypt.
> *Mark Twain, American Writer, Humorist, and Essayist*

As the U.S. Gymnastics Association example and the other oversight failures – at both for-profit and not-for-profit organizations – cited above show, there was delay, dithering, and/or denial in every case. Why? What factors caused oversight to fail? Like most failures, there were probably multiple causes.

Oversight fails because key signals and patterns were not detected or acted upon because people didn't know what to look for, didn't get timely information, had conflicting motivations, didn't act on it, didn't want conflict even if necessary, or delayed responses (Table 6.2).

Table 6.2: Some Common Causes of Oversight Failures.

Some Common Causes of Oversight Failures	
DRIP **(Data Rich but Insight Poor)**	Directors are overwhelmed by too much data and information. Hundreds of pages of data often obfuscate rather than inform. Conversely, boards can't act on information they never receive. Some boards may not receive accurate, timely, or comprehensive information from management.[381]
Bad news does not travel fast	A bad corporate culture means messengers get shot. Bad news needs to be elevated quickly and accurately so boards can act.
Lack of expertise. Or too expert. Or too deferential.	Board members may lack the necessary expertise to provide effective oversight, particularly in specialized areas like finance, technology, or regulatory compliance. Board members may think they are experts and become resistant to new ideas that contradict their beliefs. Some boards over-rely on "experts" (including management). The result is that they don't challenge those experts and blindly follow them down the wrong path.

Table 6.2 (continued)

Some Common Causes of Oversight Failures	
Conflicts of interest or lack of interest	Conflicted board members may put personal or professional interests ahead of their duty to act in the best interest of the organization. That includes friendships with management. A few board members may lack interest, defer to others, or don't come prepared.
Risk aversion or recklessness	Boards fail to adequately identify, assess, or mitigate risks, leading to unexpected problems and/or reckless decisions. Don't demand due diligence and then rely on gut feelings.
Success is a poor teacher, resulting in lack of constructive challenge	Board members assume that everything is going well and become complacent. "If it ain't broke don't fix it," "Go along to get along," and "Don't rock the boat" are philosophies that avoid critically evaluating performance or asking tough questions of one another, management and advisors
Groupthink	Boards may suffer from groupthink, where critical and diverse viewpoints and innovative solutions are overlooked. Combined with conventional wisdom, this can lead to stasis and a failure to be situationally aware.
Polarization and bad board dynamics	Interpersonal dynamics can lead to paralyzed boards that just won't act on the recommendation of one faction of the board or the other. Warnings, even if they are heard, are ignored.
Weak chair	Ineffective chairs who are unable to forge consensus result in a lack of direction, oversight, and accountability.
Dominating chair	Domineering chairs can "bend" the board to their will. They also tend to stifle constructive questioning.
Founder syndrome	Founders may resist oversight. At the same time, boards may view the founder as, literally, "foundational," resulting in a decreased desire to hold management accountable. In extreme cases, there are "flexible" ethical standards with regard to the founder.
Inadequate training, lack of continuing education	Board members may not receive adequate training on their roles, responsibilities, legal requirements, and best governance practices, and so they may not even realize they are not exercising their oversight power or are only doing so in a pro forma manner.

Table 6.2 (continued)

Some Common Causes of Oversight Failures	
Trusted but did not verify	Boards may be misled by relying on management's perspective without independently verifying information or seeking outside advice.

Are there any warning signs of these oversight failures in your organization?

A board sometimes needs to see the individual trees, but it always needs to be able to see the forest, so it should always start with the forest. That prevents getting lost in the operational details and refocuses the board on the big picture, which is its primary responsibility.

3 How do we know if vital performance is under control?

Lesson Worth Learning: Focus on the "Vital Few"

Vilfredo Pareto was an Italian polymath who concluded that 80 percent of an effect is typically caused by 20 percent of the factors. Similarly, boards should focus on what J. M. Juran, a founder of the American quality movement, called for a focus on the "vital few" factors rather than the "trivial many," thereby avoiding being overwhelmed by details that don't matter much.[382] The vital few are the performance measures that are critical to the organization and, thus, critical for the board to oversee effectively. The board should never lose sight of these.

Lesson Worth Learning: Identify the vital signs for the vital few

Vital signs are key indicators. Here are the signs typically used to assess a person's general physical health:
1. Body temperature: Normal body temperature can vary by individual, but it's typically about 98.6°F (37°C).
2. Pulse rate (heart rate): A normal resting heart rate for adults ranges from 60 to 100 beats per minute.
3. Respiration rate (breathing rate): The normal breathing rate for an adult at rest is 12 to 20 breaths per minute.
4. Blood pressure: Normal blood pressure for an adult is typically around 120/80 mmHg.
5. Oxygen saturation (SpO2): A normal level is typically between 95 percent and 100 percent, indicating how much oxygen is in the blood.

Vital signs can quickly be measured to monitor the functioning of the body's essential organs and to detect or monitor medical problems. Notice that they are generally ranges rather than a single point, reflecting natural variation. The five vital signs are quick, efficient, and effective health indicators. They may indicate the need for more testing, in which doctors can add many indicators, from blood chemistry results to magnetic resonance imaging (MRI) scans, just as boards can do "deep dives" in areas that may be problematic, confusing, or changing.

Every organization needs to know its vital signs. They indicate the state of health of essential enterprise functions. Some functions are unique to the industry, e.g., banking (credit, lending, treasury), mining (exploration, extraction, refining), forestry (silviculture, harvesting), and manufacturing (product development and design, process engineering, production planning and scheduling). Other enterprise-wide functions are common to many organizations, e.g., legal, HR, IT, finance, and accounting.

"What gets measured, gets managed" and "If you can't measure it, you can't manage it" are two favorite sayings of management gurus.[383] When a board is exercising oversight, it measures outcomes versus expectations. But be careful. Often, the metric is a "best fit" for what the board wants to measure, but it is actually not a good fit. In other words, the metric is the closest unit of measurement but not a perfect fit. That can lead to unexpected results or even gaming of the metric. The choice of "what gets measured" is key: Vital signs and tolerances should be thoughtfully defined in advance. Which metrics? is a decision that is often under-appreciated by boards.

Lesson Worth Learning: The choice of vital signs is strategic

The board should agree on the vital signs for their organization and then monitor them to check performance, risk, and compliance compared to policy. The selection of vital signs and tolerances is a strategic decision rather than an operational one because the act of measurement shapes organizational behavior, driving efforts to achieve those specific metrics. The belief that a single, perfect metric exists for every situation is incorrect and potentially dangerous. Given that metrics influence actions, it's essential to interpret them within their proper context to ensure they are understood accurately and do not lead to unintended consequences.

Choosing the right metric can align the board and the organization toward a key goal. Choosing the wrong measure can have tragic consequences. Just think of the USAG trying to have a "good" Olympics rather than protecting the athletes.

Like human vital signs, actual results rarely match expectations exactly, which is why the setting of ranges – appropriate tolerances – around expected results is critical. Variances may be over or under the performance target; the key question is: Are they within tolerances? Additionally, boards need to be aware that results that are "too good to be true" can be just that. In fact, "too good to be true" results can be early indicators of fraud and illegality.

Jon Lukomnik, one of the authors of this book, served on the WorldCom creditors committee, trying to resuscitate the telecom giant. WorldCom, a global telecom company, was the biggest fraud and bankruptcy in the history of the United States at the time. As a key telecom analyst for a competing firm told him after the fact: "We were racking our brains to understand how WorldCom hit its margins. We never thought that maybe they just made it up."[384]

The wrong choice of metrics doesn't have to result in unlawful or unethical behavior to be problematic. Nokia was once the leading mobile phone manufacturer globally. However, the company failed to maintain its dominance when smartphones began to revolutionize the market. Nokia's management focused primarily on hardware sales and market share in the feature phone segment. They measured success by the number of units sold rather than adapting to the rapidly changing technology and consumer preferences.

Focusing on the wrong measure – quantity of accounts and products sold rather than customer satisfaction – steered the company in the wrong direction.[385] Insightful readers will note that the quantity sold is a lagging indicator, and customer satisfaction is a leading indicator. At a time of rapid change, being ahead of the change will likely be a more successful strategy than being behind it. So, are your vital signs leading, lagging, or contemporaneous?

Assuming a board makes the right choices about what to measure (and that's a big assumption), there needs to be timely feedback for effective organizational learning and adaptation. Is the performance as expected or not? Is it too good to be true (e.g., WorldCom)? Is it below expectations? Are there policy implications of actual performance compared to current policy expectations? Should the organization stay the current course, adjust the course, or change the course? There needs to be feedback loops from oversight to direction, policy setting, approvals, and delegations.

Lesson Worth Learning: Require exception-based reporting (EBR)

In business, being "under control" denotes a state of acceptable stability and order. This generally means that the situation, process, or person operates within desired or expected parameters. Being "under control" implies that any potential problems or risks will be detected quickly and resolved, with outcomes that are predictably aligned with objectives.

In a statistical quality control context, a process is "in control" when it exhibits only natural variations in its output. These variations are inherent to the process itself and are usually small relative to the overall process input and output. This means that the process is stable and predictable, as determined by the process's characteristics rather than by external factors.

What's normal? The same is true for the vital signs of human health. Some variability is to be expected and is considered "normal." A temperature of 99 degrees might be considered a natural variation from 98.6. It is "in control." However, the human system would not be "in control" if your temperature spiked to 102 degrees, and then, following treatment with fever-reducing medication (an external factor) subsided to 99 degrees.

Being able to tell if someone is feverish is easy compared to the oversight needs of a board. Board challenges are more akin to being told there are a million people and you need to monitor for infectious disease outbreaks. Management can tell you how many have a fever, but how do you know if that's an acceptable number or an early warning sign of an epidemic? Is it even the right vital sign for that purpose?

In an organizational theory context, intelligence results from processing and analyzing information to make it actionable. Intelligence enables rapid comparisons to query oversight results and the related policy implications (e.g., this many with fever is or is not a normal variance, therefore, we need to or do not need to deal with an infectious disease breakout). Intelligence identifies patterns that represent opportunities or threats. An exception report provides intelligence where actual performance deviates significantly from expectations (in either direction).

The purpose of exception reports is to focus the board and management's attention on those areas that require further action. Exception reporting is a widely recognized and long-used management tool and is gaining acceptance in board rooms for business intelligence.

One popular method is the "stoplight" report, where vital signs within the approved tolerance are green, those at the margins are yellow, and those not performing as expected are red. Another option would be to highlight exceptionally good performance as blue (to highlight the good news or to serve as a warning about "too good to be true").

Any measurable function can be reported using exception reports. Indeed, these metrics and the reports can be, and preferably should be, automated. That should also allow the board to drill down, aggregate up, and move forward or backward across different time periods to gain further intelligence.

Using exception-based reporting, combined with focusing the board's attention on the "vital few" signs (positive and negative), can greatly reduce the "noise" that makes board oversight less effective.

How can this be practically applied? Think of a pyramid comprised of layers of data, information, intelligence, and insight (Figure 6.1). Each represents different stages of processing and understanding for decision-making and analysis. So, data + analysis = information; information + analysis = intelligence; and intelligence + analysis yields insight.

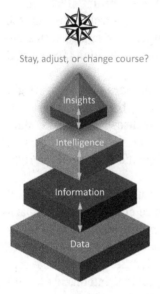

Stay, adjust, or change course?

Insights

Intelligence

Information

Data

Figure 6.1: Insights Hierarchy.

An Institutional Investment Example. Imagine you are on the board of an endowment or a pension fund. You have a fiduciary duty to oversee how billions of dollars are invested. How do you do it? Ideally, you use a pyramid approach to the things you want to oversee.

You start with data – the raw numbers and facts – and move to information aggregated from the data, then to intelligence, meaning that the information is applied within the context of your goals, and, finally, to insight, which allows you to make policy adjustments or stay the course (Figure 6.2).

Level 1: Data. Data – raw, unprocessed facts and figures without any context – form the base of the pyramid. Data can be numbers, words, measurements, observations, or even just descriptions of things. These data can be stored and transmitted but do not necessarily have any meaning on their own.

Level 2: Information. When data is processed, organized, structured, or presented in context, it becomes information. Information is understandable and can be interpreted by humans. Information is useful. Information answers basic questions such as who, what, where, when, how, and how much.

Exception reporting and oversight can begin at the information level and should feature:
- consistent, reliable monitoring and periodic reporting of metrics
- non-discretionary escalation procedures for vital signs out of tolerance
- escalation procedures for other results out of tolerance
- explanations to the board of why an exception occurred, what has changed, and what it means in terms of the response needed
- board understanding as to whether the cause of the failure is related to governance policies, people, processes, systems, or external factors (root cause analysis)
- the implications should the exception continue or worsen (How bad can it get?)

Figure 6.2 is a typical investment report given to pension funds, endowme me frames for each asset manager and breaks it down by asset class.

And, frankly, it doesn't matter whether you have assets under management of a thousand, a hundred thousand, a million, a hundred million, a billion, or 100 billion dollars – the reports are essentially the same. There can be hundreds of such tables for the largest institutional investors, particularly those with private equity programs.

The problem? It is informative but not intelligent. The report requires the reader to compare every row and column with each and every other row and column and draw any implications or conclusions themselves.

As a result, the investment staff or advisor usually walks the board through multiple tables and explains the implications at a committee or board meeting. However, these policy implications are not intuitively obvious, and the board is left to rely on the expert. This is analogous to an orchestra conductor reading the sheet music to the audience and explaining the nuances without actually playing the music. The conductor and the orchestra understand the notes, but, in many cases, the audience is left stupefied.

Level 3: Intelligence. Intelligence is the output of analyzing information to provide further context, identifying patterns (opportunities and threats), and making inferences for informed decision-making. It involves applying judgment to information, allowing the board to make sense of something in a broader context.

The state-of-the-art of creating intelligence begins with automating data collection and integration. Algorithms compare informative data against expected performance, tolerances, peer groups, and benchmarks. This enables rapid signal detection and pattern recognition to aid the identification of policy implications or execution issues. This is exactly what a new generation of artificial intelligence tools promises.

Compare Figure 6.3 (at the "information" level) showing asset class data with Figure 6.2. The same information is shown but is now communicated visually

Asset Class Data/Information

Period Ending: March 31, 2023

Total Fund
Performance Summary (Net of Fees)

	Market Value	% of Portfolio	3 Mo	1 Yr	3 Yrs	5 Yrs	10 Yrs	2022	2021	2020	2019	2018	Inception	Inception Date
Total Fund	2,528,394,368	100.0	3.8	-6.9	9.1	6.9	6.6	-12.8	18.6	12.7	17.9	-1.5	5.7	Dec-99
Policy Index			3.5	-9.0	7.9	6.2	5.7	-14.0	16.1	13.8	16.2	-0.3	5.2	
Total Fund ex Liability Beta Portfolio	2,113,199,473	83.6	4.2	-8.4	10.2	7.8	.	-14.6	22.1	14.6	20.4	-1.9	8.2	Jun-17
Alpha Portfolio Policy Index			3.7	-11.0	9.9	7.4	.	-15.5	21.0	15.4	18.8	-0.4	8.0	
Total Fund ex Parametric	2,513,284,073	99.4	3.8	-6.8	8.8	6.7	.	-12.4	18.2	12.4	17.3	-1.2	6.7	Jan-15
Policy Index			3.5	-9.0	7.9	6.2	.	-14.0	16.1	13.8	16.2	-0.3	6.1	
Total Public Domestic Equity	277,384,880	11.0												
PIMCO StocksPLUS	277,384,880	11.0	11.6	-30.8	12.5	10.5	.	-46.3	33.6	52.1	50.0	-10.4	11.3	Nov-13
PIMCO Custom Index			10.0	-36.5	8.1	8.0	.	-50.4	34.0	48.8	50.9	-11.3	9.6	
Russell 3000			7.2	-8.6	18.5	10.5	.	-19.2	25.7	20.9	31.0	-5.2	10.7	
Total Public Int'l Equity	270,163,807	10.7												
Dodge & Cox Int'l Stock (DODFX)	132,842,726	5.3	6.1	-0.4	17.3	2.9	.	-6.8	11.0	2.1	22.8	-18.0	2.6	Jun-14
MSCI AC World ex USA Value			5.3	-3.3	14.5	1.9	.	-8.0	11.1	-0.2	16.5	-13.4	2.2	
MSCI EAFE			8.6	-0.9	13.5	4.0	.	-14.0	11.8	8.3	22.7	-13.4	3.9	
WCM International Growth	137,321,080	5.4	10.4	-5.4	13.8	8.8	.	-28.6	17.2	33.1	35.6	-7.4	10.4	May-16
MSCI AC World ex USA Growth			8.6	-6.4	9.5	3.4	.	-23.1	5.1	22.2	27.3	-14.4	6.3	
Total Fixed Income	158,893,129	6.3												
Met West Core Plus Fixed Income	70,847,472	2.8	3.7										1.4	Dec-22
Bmbg. U.S. Aggregate Index			3.0										0.7	
SSgA Long U.S. Treasury Index	88,045,657	3.5	6.6	-16.0	-11.3			-29.6	-4.7	17.7	14.8		0.5	Nov-18
Bloomberg LT Treasury			6.2	-16.0	-11.3			-29.3	-4.6	17.7	14.8		0.5	
Total Real Estate 1 Qtr Lagged	255,160,459	10.1												
StepStone Group Real Estate 1 Qtr Lagged	255,160,459	10.1	-1.8	9.9	13.5	11.4	.	21.3	22.3	2.4	8.4	8.3	10.2	Sep-16
NCREIF-ODCE 1 Qtr Lagged			-5.0	7.5	9.9	8.7	.	22.1	14.6	1.4	5.6	8.7	8.7	
Total Commodities	82,604,300	3.3												
Invesco Balanced Risk Commodity	82,604,300	3.3	-1.7	-6.5	22.8	.	.	8.9	19.7	7.6	5.5	.	8.1	Dec-18
Bloomberg Commodity Index TR USD			-5.4	-12.5	20.8	.	.	16.1	27.1	-3.1	7.7	.	7.3	
Total Infrastructure	78,797,787	3.1												
IFM Global Infrastructure (US) LP	78,797,787	3.1	2.6	9.6	11.8	10.7	10.3	8.2	17.4	3.1	14.6	17.3	10.5	May-10
NCREIF-ODCE			-3.2	-3.1	8.4	7.5	9.5	7.5	22.2	1.2	5.3	8.3	10.6	
Total Private Equity 1 Qtr Lagged	320,439,703	12.7												
Hamilton Lane Private Equity 1 Qtr Lagged	320,439,703	12.7	1.5	-1.4	17.6	15.0	15.3	4.5	49.8	4.4	10.0	17.8	16.6	Oct-08
Russell 2000 1 Qtr Lagged			2.7	-11.6	17.5	4.7	8.0	-20.4	14.8	20.0	25.5	-11.0	10.2	

Typical Client Report

Figure 6.2: Asset Class Data/Information.

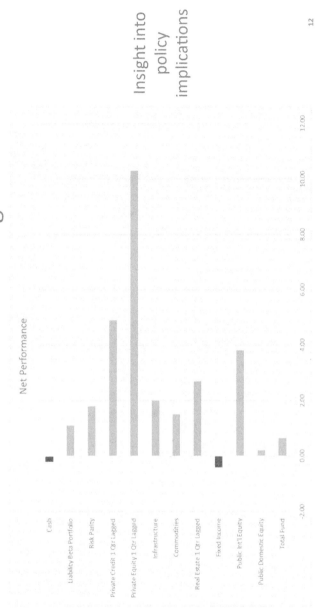

Figure 6.3: Asset Class Performance Intelligence.

with reference to actual performance compared to expectations. Figure 6.3 converts the data into a graphic that provides a single-page heads-up display. This enables the board to see at a glance whether actual investment performance is meeting policy expectations. Trends can also be shown to spotlight potential performance issues or successes.

Level 4: Insight. The aggregation of data, information, and intelligence should result in insights into the organization's policy implications and/or execution ability. This is the feedback loop from oversight to strategy and policy setting. Do the results of oversight suggest the board should have the organization stay the course, adjust course, or change course based on its current policy?

Insights are the deep, accurate understanding of relationships, patterns, or trends derived from intelligence. While intelligence explains "what" is happening, insights delve into "why" or "how" it is happening, often leading to breakthroughs, deeper understanding, or strategic changes. Insights provide value by revealing direct actions that can be taken or new, more effective ways of doing things based on a deep understanding of the intelligence. Insights use the patterns of the past to create future action.

From data to information to intelligence to insight. Each of the four levels is important in devising an oversight program for a board. Without data, there can be no information, intelligence, or insight. Absent insight, the organization is limited to understanding the past and the present and has a limited view of its future. Each of the four stages builds upon the previous one, adding more context, analysis, and value, moving from simple raw data to a deep understanding that can facilitate informed decision-making.

Figure 6.4 shows a summary page for that same investment board. Acceptable performance (within expected tolerance/volatility bounds) is shown in green, marginal performance is shown in yellow, and, if there had been any, out-of-tolerance performance would be in red.

All the underlying data and information are available. Still, the aggregated view enables the board and executives to quickly gain insight and understand the policy implications of actual performance compared to policy. It aggregates the data and allows the board to easily see the big picture over different periods. And it's dynamic; board members and executives can drill down to more detailed reports – all the way down to the data level – if they choose.

Figure 6.4: Investment Dashboard.

Lesson Worth Learning: Require visualization for insight of large volumes of data

Information is a source of learning. But unless it is organized, processed, and available to the right people in a format for decision making, it is a burden, not a benefit.
William Pollard – former Executive Director of Oak Ridge Institute of Nuclear Studies

The fact that the insight hierarchy builds from data to information to intelligence to insight begs the question: What's the best form of presentation to turn volumes of random data into actionable insight? As the old saying goes, a picture is worth a thousand words (and an equal number of tables of numbers). Visualization enables insight.

Data visualization can identify correlations, trends, and patterns that might not be obvious in tabular data. This can be crucial for statistical analysis, forecasting, and decision-making processes. By placing data and information appropriately within the "Insight Hierarchy," data visualization aids intelligence and insights.

Visualizations can communicate relationships and complex data more effectively than narratives or tables, making them powerful tools for storytelling in business or research contexts. Charts and graphs can often be more easily understood by a diverse audience (such as a board), making the underlying data more universally accessible. Color coding, such as in a stop light chart, can also help to highlight exceptions. Graphs and charts can also be interactive, allowing users to explore and manipulate data dynamically.

While tables are excellent for providing detailed, precise numerical values (usually at the data or information levels), visualizations help understand the broader context, make abstract data more concrete, and facilitate communication and analysis.

4 How do we get reliable, timely, intelligence, and policy insights for direction setting?

Expect The Best. Prepare For the Worst. Capitalize On What Comes.
Zig Ziglar, Author and Motivational Speaker[386]

Significant variances in performance compared to expectations are both blessings and warnings. For adaptive boards, variances scream out a series of questions: What, if anything, has changed? Was the difference due to performance, or were our initial expectations wrong? Should we react or watch and wait? Is the change a blip? If it's a changed condition, is it likely to accelerate or decline? In other words, effective boards try to understand if the variance was a fluke or if the board needs to adapt its policy to account for the unexpected result.

Lesson Worth Learning: Require root cause analysis of exceptions

It is common for a board to require an analysis of the root causes of unwanted or unexpected variances and clarify management's responsibility for further mitigation or other action. Boards sometimes also require a root cause analysis when the result is much better than expected. Such a reaction can catch the "too good to be true is too good to be true" situations, like WorldCom. But, even in cases where too good to be true is actually true and positive, doing a root cause analysis can help a board understand if the great results are replicable, where additional resources ought to be applied, etc.

Whether the variation is negative or positive, when vital signs are selected correctly and show significant unexpected variations from the expected performance, there are often policy implications. In such cases, executive management should escalate to the board the exception, its possible causes, and any recommended policy actions.

Lesson Worth Learning: Transform the dialogue to focus on the policy implications of actual performance compared to expectations

Is everything critical under control? In the end, oversight exists to ensure operations are "under control," i.e., performance is as expected. When an unexpected result indicates things aren't within policy limits, i.e., not in control, the board needs to focus on what, if any, the policy implications are.

Management should provide the board with:
- a direct link to current policy for easy reference
- an explanation of the policy implications
- a recommendation of whether to stay, adjust, or change course, with rationales

The board then needs to determine whether it agrees. As discussed in "Set Direction," one way to respond to an unexpected variance is to consider the options available, ordered from the least the board can do (which is usually stay the course) to tweaking the strategy (minor adjustments) to the most (change course). Having such a structured conversation following a significant unexpected result is the critical link between Oversee and Set.

Directors should use constructive challenge to query those explanations and recommendations. Once the board reaches a consensus on what, if any, policy changes should be made, that decision should be documented. Even if no changes are made, it's good policy for the minutes to reflect that the board considered the exception and discussed whether a policy response was needed.

Lesson Worth Learning: Gain insights by obtaining multiple sources of information

Effective oversight leads to direction and policy insight. Exception reporting helps a board focus on the exceptions rather than "normal" performance. owever however the board needs to ensure that the reports of quote normal performance are reliable The board needs to ensure that reports of "normal" performance are verified. We discuss this in the following chapter: "Verify before Trusting."

Avoid groupthink. Boards of directors can avoid groupthink and improve the reliability of intelligence and insights on critical policy issues by getting information from a combination of sources:
– expert consultations
– professional research firms
– think tanks and academic institutions
– government relations and lobbying teams
– internal analytics teams
– strategic use of technology
– networking and industry groups
– regular training and updates
– open-source intelligence

Engaging with industry experts, policy analysts, and consultants in relevant fields can provide valuable insights. Hiring research firms can help gather and analyze data, trends, and developments that impact the industry and policy environment. These firms often have access to resources and networks that individual organizations may not.

Collaborations with think tanks and academic institutions can offer rigorous analysis and research-based insights into policy trends, implications, and strategic responses. These professionals can provide insights into legislative changes and regulatory updates, helping the board understand the political landscape and anticipate policy shifts. Some boards incorporate such external expert presentations into formal education and/or strategic planning sessions; others prefer to invite such experts to board dinners for more informal conversations. Some do both.

Advanced analytics, artificial intelligence, and big data can help synthesize vast amounts of information to forecast trends and policy impacts. Leveraging internal resources to analyze market trends, regulatory changes, and other external factors can tailor insights to the organization's specific strategic needs. Combining that specific knowledge with broader specialist knowledge, such as that available from think tanks, academic institutions, and domain-expert consultants, can spark epiphanies of understanding for board members.

Participating in industry associations, policy roundtables, and networking events can provide crucial insights and foresight on policy matters. Ensuring board members regularly receive training and updates on critical policy issues can maintain their awareness and preparedness to make informed decisions.

Use open-source intelligence (OSINT). OSINT is the process of collecting and analyzing information from publicly available sources to gain intelligence and insight. Open sources include public internet and social media data, traditional mass media, specialized journals, conference proceedings, and more.[387]

The information gleaned from these sources is so valuable for understanding a wide range of subjects, from market trends to security threats, that approximately 80–90 percent of intelligence used by the Central Intelligence Agency (CIA) comes from open sources, according to estimates.[388] This high reliance on OSINT is due to the vast amount of information accessible through these means and the advancements in technology that allow for efficient collection and analysis of such data.

All organizations can make better use of OSINT in several ways:
- structured analysis
- technology integration
- skill development
- cross-functional teams
- continuous monitoring

Boards should suggest management develop a structured framework for collecting, processing, and analyzing open-source information if it hasn't already done so. If it has, boards should understand the program's capabilities and limitations. The OSINT program's three-fold framework involves 1) defining clear objectives, 2) identifying relevant data sources, and 3) employing analytical methods to extract actionable insights.

Lesson Worth Learning: Timely escalate exceptions to policy

If a process is in control, it implies that no interventions are needed. Any points or patterns that fall outside these limits suggest that special causes are affecting the process, indicating that it is "out of control" and may require corrective actions. This concept is commonly visualized and monitored using control charts, which help identify trends, shifts, or any signs of performance that deviate from what's expected under normal operating conditions. Control charts immediately make signs of "abnormality" very apparent.

Figure 6.5 shows upper and lower control limits on performance and how improving controls can reduce unwanted variability. (NB: There inevitably comes a time when the cost of control improvements exceeds the improvement, i.e., the law of diminishing returns.)

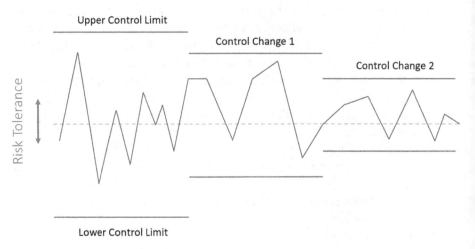

Figure 6.5: Tightening Process Control Limits.

The board's policy expectations define risk tolerance and accountabilities. They are the brakes. What range of variability is to be expected? Is it normal? What is cause for concern or immediate action? What is the plan (Figure 6.6)?

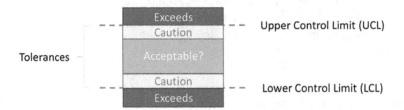

Figure 6.6: Expected vs. Actual Performance Tolerances.

The board needs to approve policy tolerances (limits) for vital performance dimensions. This is part of direction and policy setting discussed in "Set Direction," but it is when exercising the board's "Oversee Execution" power that "the rubber hits the road." The board's policies establish an acceptable range of performance variability, i.e., its risk tolerance. The board then needs to require that vital performance be tracked and unwanted or unexpected variations be reported timely (Figure 6.7).

This is the time to assess actual performance compared to the board's expectations and determine whether the results are acceptable (according to policy) or

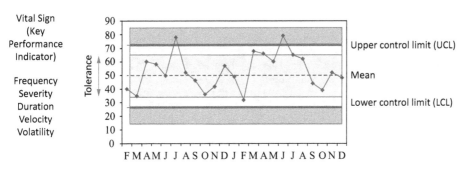

Figure 6.7: Vital Signs and Control Limits.

whether further action is required. When performance begins to approach or breach established thresholds, the board needs to be informed and advised of the policy implications.

The board then needs to decide whether to alter policy or take other action. This should be direct input to Set Direction and Policy. Table 6.3 outlines the conditions necessary for there to be an effective response when actual results deviate beyond the board's risk tolerance.

Lesson Worth Learning: Require effective escalation mechanisms for exceptions

Table 6.3: Board Escalation Success Elements.

Be accessible	Make board members accessible to senior management for urgent matters. Practically, that means sharing private phone numbers, e-mails, etc.
Have access	Provide unfettered board accessibility to relevant data and the ability to make ad hoc inquiries into the data to disaggregate and aggregate it. There should be an agreed-upon process for this, to provide the needed data in a way that doesn't overtax the executive through responding to ad hoc requests.
Define critical risk limits	Designate, in advance, specific triggers or thresholds that necessitate escalation.
Require an escalation protocol	Just as there should be specific triggers for escalation, organizations benefit from having a pre-defined escalation protocol. That formal pathway should detail how information moves from employees to management and then to the board. The protocol should also include which officials (i.e., CEO, CFO, executive director, head of internal audit, chief compliance officer) have the authority to escalate matters directly to the board.

Table 6.3 (continued)

Review and refine the escalation protocols	As with all board policies, regularly reviewing the escalation process ensures it is working effectively. Feedback sessions with stakeholders can help to refine the process.
Require training	Regularly train staff and management on the escalation process to ensure they understand when and how to escalate issues. This also requires promoting a culture that encourages speaking up without fear of retaliation.
Require routine reporting of exceptions	Implement regular reporting mechanisms so that management can update the board on potential issues. This can be through regular meetings, written reports, or an exception-based (EBR) dashboard that tracks key metrics and risks.
Leverage technology	Leverage technology to monitor and report issues in real time. Automated systems can help in detecting anomalies and triggering alerts that can be escalated appropriately.
Be prepared	Have a crisis management plan in place for potential catastrophic events.

Lesson Worth Learning: Require incident response protocols

Table 6.4: Escalation Process Example: Data Breach Incident using Adaptive Governance Process (AGP).

Detect	Automated monitoring systems detect anomalies (signals) in data access or breaches and send immediate alerts to the IT security team.
Interpret	The IT security team conducts a preliminary assessment to confirm or reject the breach and determine its severity based on the amount of data compromised, the nature of the data, and the potential impact on the company.
Respond	The chief information security officer (CISO) is notified of the incident. If the breach meets predefined criteria (e.g., it affects a certain number of users or involves sensitive information), the CISO must escalate the issue to the chief executive officer (CEO) and the legal team. Activate the response team responsible for managing the incident. The response team often includes members from IT, legal, compliance, public relations, and other relevant departments. The team membership is determined before the breach. Escalate to the board. If the breach is deemed severe (e.g., potential for significant financial loss or personal data or operations compromised, or major reputational damage), the CEO and CISO promptly inform the board of directors. This is usually done through an urgent, specially convened meeting or a secure communication channel established for critical updates. Alternately, some situations require notice to the chair of the audit committee, or to the full audit committee. The board reviews the information provided, assesses the implications of the breach, and provides strategic guidance on the response. This might include legal actions, public relations strategies, and measures to prevent future incidents. Execute board decision. The response team implements the decisions and strategies approved by the board. The board is continuously updated throughout the resolution process.

Table 6.4 (continued)

Learn	All steps and decisions are documented thoroughly. Post-resolution feedback from all stakeholders, including board members, is gathered to learn and improve the escalation process.
Adapt	Once the immediate crisis is managed, a detailed post-incident review is conducted. This review is presented to the board, highlighting what occurred, how it was handled, the effectiveness of the response, and recommendations for future prevention.

The structured escalation process (Table 6.4) using the AGP ensures that critical issues are managed efficiently and reach the board quickly for timely decision-making. It reflects a proactive approach to governance and risk management. The documentation and post-incident review steps seek to improve the underlying state that caused or allowed the crisis.

When incidents occur, the board should require management to conduct a root cause analysis (RCA) and suggest solutions or improvements to prevent such incidents in the future as part of the post-incident review. For external factors beyond the organization's control, the board should require plans to improve resilience, focused on areas such as business continuity, disaster recovery, and cyber security.

"Always a better way" Toyota Corporation. The devastating earthquake and tsunami in Japan in 2011 affected many global companies. The Tohoku region features a heavy concentration of auto part suppliers, and production, particularly for Japanese carmakers, basically ground to a halt. Toyota reported that it stopped or slowed the production of 150,000 cars.

As a result, the Japanese carmaker undertook significant steps to enhance its resilience to natural disasters and other unforeseen events, including:
– supply chain diversification
– inventory management
– business continuity planning (BCP)
– regular drills and employee training
– technology utilization
– financial resilience
– stakeholder communication

Toyota began multi-sourcing parts rather than relying on a single supplier since single suppliers are also single sources of failure. It also started keeping slightly more inventory on hand than "just in time" manufacturing concepts would suggest to minimize disruption from delayed parts deliveries.

Recognizing that its business continuity plans (BCPs) were only as strong as the weakest link, Toyota revised its own and worked with all its suppliers – including small ones – to ensure that they also had robust BCPs.

The automaker also doubled down on technological mitigations. Toyota was an early user of AI and predictive analytics to foresee supply chain disruptions.

Finally, Toyota updated its communications practices, keeping all stakeholders – employees, franchisees, regulators, and customers – informed. Through these strategies, Toyota's board has minimized the risks associated with uncontrollable adversities and ensured that its operations are resilient and capable of quick recovery, demonstrating a proactive and comprehensive approach to disaster resilience.[389]

Respond, Learn, and Adapt. The Toyota example demonstrates how organizations can apply the Adaptive Governance Process. It illustrates the feedback loops that need to exist between Setting Direction, Approving Key Decisions, and Overseeing Execution.

Once the policy implications of performance and risk are understood, boards should ask:
- **How should we respond?** Elicit recommendations on staying the course, making adjustments, or changing direction entirely.
- **What did we learn?** Evaluate actual performance against expectations – identify what worked well and what didn't.
- **How do we adapt?** Decide whether to stay, adjust, or pivot based on the lessons learned and strategic needs.

Conclusion

This chapter describes the challenges the board faces in overseeing performance and risk. We ask and answer four critical questions every board should ask about oversight and describe the lessons worth learning from others' successes and failures. We suggest several oversight tools, from exception-based reporting and data visualization to escalation policies, to help boards understand whether vital functions are performing as expected and that performance and risk are within policy unless otherwise notified (Figure 6.8).

The next chapter discusses the board's power to "Verify before Trusting." In "Oversee," the board relies on reasonable assurances from management regarding performance. Verification bolsters this reasonable assurance by obtaining independent reassurance. Why should the board verify before it trusts? Who can the board trust? What is reasonable? Why obtain independent reassurance? Are our systems of internal control effective?

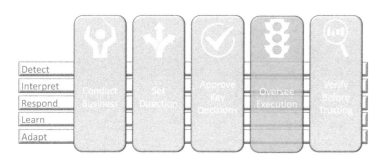

Detect
Interpret
Respond
Learn
Adapt

Conduct Business | Set Direction | Approve Key Decisions | Oversee Execution | Verify Before Trusting

Figure 6.8: Oversee the Execution of Direction within Policy.

Concepts are vindicated by the constant accrual of data and
independent verification of data.
No prize, not even a Nobel Prize, can make something
true that is not true.
Stanley B. Prusiner, Nobel Laureate, Physiology or Medicine, 1997

Chapter 7
Verify before trusting

1. What is our role in obtaining reasonable assurance?

- Reasonable assurance is a high standard of assurance, but it is not absolute.
- The board can reasonably rely on assurances from the executive and the opinions of independent third parties.

2. Why and how should we verify before trusting?

- Those most familiar with controls are best able to circumvent them.
- The greatest source of risk is what you think you have under control when you really don't.

3. Why and how can we obtain independent reassurance that information, advice, and reports are reliable?

- Professional skepticism enables constructive challenge.
- Being independent of management means an individual or entity is outside management's chain of command.
- The board can delegate authority and resources, but it cannot delegate its overall responsibility. A board typically exercises its power to verify through the Audit/Risk Committee (as well as other committees).
- The board should establish an effective system of checks and balances.
- Avoid single points of failure.

4. How can we be reassured that the system of internal control is effective?

- Calculated risks must be taken. No one is perfect, and no organization is immune.
- The 1st Line is primarily accountable for overall performance, risk, and compliance within the policy parameters established by the board.
- The 2nd Line has primary accountability for advising and supporting the 1st Line executive officers, staff, and the board.
- The 1st and 2nd Lines are in the direct line of the chain of command from the chief executive.
- Internal Audit (the 3rd Line) is independent of management and is primarily accountable for providing independent internal verification and advice to the board, typically through the Audit Committee.
- IA is not a compliance function.
- The 4th Line of independent auditors and advisors provides External Verification and Advice. It must be managed by the board.
- External auditors play a vital role in verifying various aspects of an organization's performance.
- Boards of directors retain various types of independent experts to help them make well-informed decisions and comply with legal and regulatory requirements. Boards should retain whatever external advice they need. When retained directly by the board, these third parties are independent of management.

https://doi.org/10.1515/9783111344027-007

Introduction

> Approximately 89% of major frauds are committed by individuals in high-ranking and
> trusted positions within organizations, particularly by CEOs and CFOs.
> *Fraudulent Financial Reporting: 1998–2007*[390]

Trust, like reputation, is gained in inches per year and lost in feet per second.
Trust is essential to relationships, societies, and institutions. It is the great lubricant
in interpersonal relationships. Imagining a world without trust creates a hellscape
where every interaction must be made explicit in fine detail, negotiated, agreed
upon, formalized, contracted, and, if necessary, litigated. The frictional transaction
costs of everyday life – and business – would be prohibitive.

But trust is ephemeral. It creates vulnerability. It can be easily lost or damaged,
resulting in suspicion and conflict. Unreliable information or advice can lead to poor
decisions and a sudden loss of reputation and value. And it destroys trust, throwing
a wrench, rather than lubricant, into the corporate governance mechanism.

Trust can also be affected by context as misunderstandings multiply. Today,
our society is politically polarized. We seem to be plagued by constant scandals,
unethical behavior, media misinformation, "fake news," deep fakes on social
media, and refusals of those constantly partaking of that fake news to accept fact.
This is both the result of and a cause of a lack of trust.

The late U.S. Senator Daniel Patrick Moynihan said, "You are entitled to your
own opinions; you are not entitled to your own facts."[391] Unfortunately, his wisdom has been lost on many. Trust comes from repeated verifications. Not the
other way around.

**Economic disparities, technological change, demographic shifts, and geo-
political conflicts are accelerating.** As the Edelman trust barometer explains, "Rapid innovation offers the promise of a new era of prosperity, but
instead risks exacerbating trust issues, leading to further societal instability
and political polarization."[392]

Everything we have advocated in this book so far – using constructive challenges, reaching consensus, and forging adaptive solutions – helps develop trust.
Trust also comes from repeated verification of the reliability and timeliness of
information, advice, and reports.

Critical questions the board should always ask about verification

1. What is our role in obtaining reasonable assurance?
2. Why and how should we verify before trusting?
3. Why and how should we require independent verification and reassurance?
4. How can we be reassured that the system of internal control is effective?

1 What is our role in obtaining reasonable assurance?

Lesson Worth Learning: Reasonable assurance is a high standard of assurance, but it is not absolute

> Reasonable assurance is a high level of assurance. But it is not absolute assurance.
> It is obtained when the auditor has sufficient appropriate audit evidence to reduce audit
> risk (i.e., the risk that the auditor expresses an inappropriate opinion when the financial
> statements are materially misstated) to an acceptably low level.
> *Public Company Accounting Oversight Board (PCAOB)*

Reasonable reliance refers to the degree to which a person or entity can depend on another party's information, advice, or actions in making decisions. It assumes that the party providing the information is competent, unconflicted, and acting in good faith. Reasonable reliance applies when a board of directors relies on the reports, advice, and information provided by executives, advisors, or other professionals.

While reasonable assurance involves trusting that the information or advice is accurate, it is not naïve trust. Some conditions engender that trust. The party providing the information or advice must be competent and qualified, with no intention of misleading. There should be no conflict of interest that would provide a reason for biased information or advice. Reasonable reliance must be in good faith, meaning there should be no reason to doubt the accuracy or integrity of the information or advice. Boards are not allowed to turn a blind eye when something seems awry, as did so many in the list of verification failures (see Table 7.1).

By contrast, absolute assurance implies complete certainty without a scintilla of doubt. It does not allow for any errors, omissions, or uncertainties. Absolute assurance requires the elimination of all possible risks. Unfortunately, absolute assurance is generally impractical and often impossible due to the inherent limitations of information and processes.

Absolute assurance is usually prohibitively costly, as resources would have to be committed to achieve it. Absolute assurance would mean guaranteeing that financial statements are completely accurate with no possibility of error, a standard that is not feasible in practice. Even under a reasonable assurance standard, the Public Organization Accounting Oversight Board reported that in 2023, public company audits – even those of the "big four" accounting firms with the most global resources – had a 26 percent deficiency rate.[393][xi]

---

xi The PCAOB notes that deficiency rate applies to a non-random group of audits selected for inspection and so should not be assumed to apply to the universe of public company audits. It also notes that the deficiency rate applies to a variety of issues, many of which may not require restatements of the financial statements.

Relying on reasonable assurance allows the board to make informed decisions without expecting unrealistic guarantees. Reasonable assurance evaluates sufficient and appropriate evidence but acknowledges the presence of risks and uncertainties. It balances the cost of providing assurance with the benefits derived from it, recognizing that additional assurance efforts may not be economically justified given the "law of diminishing returns."

Lesson Worth Learning: The board can reasonably rely on assurances from the executive and the opinions of independent third parties

The board may reasonably rely on the information and reports provided by the organization's executives and on the advice and information provided by independent external auditors and advisors, such as lawyers, accountants, and consultants. As noted, this assumes a level of competency and expertise and no incentives or desires to mislead on behalf of the information providers.

Executives should be able to provide the board with a reasonable assurance and confidence that:
- Financial statements are free of material misstatement and prepared in accordance with applicable accounting standards.
- Internal controls are effective in preventing and detecting fraud and errors.
- Disclosure controls ensure an appropriate level of review before information is made public.
- The organization complies with relevant laws, regulations, and policies.
- They have no conflicts.
- Risks are being identified, assessed, and managed appropriately.

Boards also have obligations when relying on information provided by others. They should perform an adequate level of due diligence to verify reliability. At that point, trust should run two ways. Executives should be able to reasonably rely on the board for strategic guidance and oversight and to not play "gotcha." Executives should also expect the board to make informed and prudent decisions based on the information and recommendations provided by the executives and advisors.

Similarly, third-party advisors, such as auditors and legal counsel, rely on the information and context provided by the board and executives to give accurate and relevant advice. They expect that the information given to them is complete and truthful.

Boards must verify before trusting. Reasonable reliance builds trust and efficiency in corporate governance by ensuring that decisions are based on reliable and expert information, thus enabling the board to fulfill its fiduciary duties effectively. Reasonable assurance is necessary for a working relationship, but the potential for abuse means that it is not sufficient.

2 Why and how can we verify before trusting?

Who are you going to believe, me or your own eyes?
Julius Henry "Groucho" Marx, American Comedian

The CPA Leadership Institute identifies why independent verification is essential:[394]

- CEOs and CFOs are involved in almost 90 percent of all major accounting frauds.
- CEOs participate in accounting fraud for personal gain (by maximizing equity incentives).
- CFOs typically get involved because they succumb to pressure from CEOs.
- CEO accounting fraud is often driven by narcissism combined with a high degree of power.
- Despite the audit committee's oversight role, CEOs and CFOs continue to drive the audit firm selection process, which can compromise auditor independence.

If this is true for fraud, then board members need to at least consider that it might be true for other forms of misrepresentation, like "gaming" the numbers or skewing an analysis to produce desired results.

For all those reasons, it would be imprudent to trust before verifying.

Auditors call this mindset "professional skepticism." That is why one of the board's most significant powers is the power to verify the reliability of the information and advice received and the reports that the board must issue to others. Consistent verification builds and maintains trust.

Effective verification helps prevent fraud, mismanagement, and unethical behavior, thus safeguarding the interests of all stakeholders in every industry sector. The idea of verification is not to end trust between management and the board but to create an environment and context where trust flourishes as verifications consistently prove the board's and management's trustworthiness.

Lesson Worth Learning: Those most familiar with controls are best able to circumvent them

Several years ago, Rick Funston, one of the authors, asked a conference of about 150 internal auditors to break into groups and develop hypothetical methods to defraud their organizations in ways that would avoid detection, given their knowledge of internal controls. In less than 30 minutes, each group was able to develop a circumvention.

Who is Jérôme Kerviel? Jérôme Kerviel is a former French derivatives and stock trader who worked for Société Générale, one of Europe's largest banks. In January 2008, Société Générale discovered that he had engaged in unauthorized trading, leading to a loss of $7.1 billion.[395]

Kerviel had started his career at Société Générale in the middle office, where he gained a thorough understanding of the bank's risk management and control procedures. Later, as a trader, he created fake hedging transactions, fictitious counterparties, and false trades to mask the total risk exposure and make it appear as though his trades were balanced and within risk limits. He produced fake documents and emails, as well as backdated transactions, to fit within the expected patterns and circumvent detection by the compliance and risk management departments.

After Société Générale finally discovered Kerviel's activities, Kerviel was arrested and charged with breach of trust, forgery, and unauthorized use of the bank's computers. In describing the fraud, Société Générale said Kerviel's "in-depth knowledge of the control procedures" enabled him to manipulate the system effectively to avoid detection and to override automatic alerts and inquiries from the risk management team.[396] In 2010, he was convicted and sentenced to five years in prison, with two years suspended.[397] He was also ordered to repay the €4.9 billion, a symbolic gesture highlighting the magnitude of the loss.[398]

Unfortunately, Kerviel isn't the only miscreant who knows his way around controls. In each of the examples shown in Table 7.1, trusted senior executives used their knowledge to circumvent controls. As always, the board of directors was held responsible for organizational failures, especially those involving the failure to verify. Clearly, no industry is immune.

Table 7.1: Example Verification Failures.

WorldCom (2002)	WorldCom was a roll-up of many telecommunications companies. The accounting systems were never truly merged, and the board failed to effectively oversee corporate finances.[399] This allowed the executives to commit what was the largest accounting fraud in American history at the time.[400] This verification failure ultimately culminated in bankruptcy.
Tyco International (2002)	Tyco's CEO and CFO siphoned off hundreds of millions of dollars through unapproved loans and fraudulent stock sales, as well as excessive spending on non-business expenses.[401] The board allowed these financial misdeeds to go unchecked, resulting in significant legal penalties and bankruptcy.[402]
Peregrine Systems (2002)	This enterprise software organization filed for bankruptcy following the discovery of financial irregularities and fraud amounting to hundreds of millions of dollars.[403] The board's failures in auditing and financial verification allowed these discrepancies to go unnoticed for years.[404]

Table 7.1 (continued)

HealthSouth (2003)	The CEO and other executives falsely inflated the organization's earnings.[405] The board's failure to detect and prevent financial misstatements resulted in substantial legal consequences and financial losses.[406]
Le-Nature's (2006)	The $685 million fraud at a $30 million in revenue small beverage company could be the exemplar of why people ask, "Where was the board?" Despite numerous warnings – the CFO saying during an audit that he doubted the numbers were correct, a sudden firing of the outside auditor, documented weaknesses in the control environment, a lack of checks and balances, nepotism, and the CEO controlling the financial reporting system – the fraud was allowed to continue.[407]
Lehman Brothers (2008)	The board of Lehman Brothers failed to properly assess the risks associated with its investments in subprime mortgages and complex financial instruments.[408] The lack of due diligence and risk management[409] led to the firm's bankruptcy, triggering the 2008–2009 Global Financial Crisis.[410]
Satyam Computer Services (2009)	Satyam's board failed to verify the organization's financial reporting and internal controls.[411] The organization's founder admitted to inflating revenues and profits for years, leading to a major corporate scandal.[412]
Olympus (2011)	Olympus Corporation engaged in a decade-long scheme directed by the chairman of the board to hide investment losses through improper accounting. The other board members failed in oversight and verification, even when CEO Michael Woodford questioned the accounting. At that point, the board deliberately turned a blind eye and dismissed Woodford. When the irregularities were finally exposed, the company lost 75 percent of its value, shuttered 40 percent of its manufacturing capacity, and board members were personally sued.[413]
Barclays LIBOR (2012)	The London Inter-bank Offered Rate (LIBOR) scandal involved numerous banks, including Barclays, where traders manipulated interest rates to profit from trades or to make the bank appear more stable during the financial crisis.[414] The board's failure to ensure compliance with regulations and its own procedures led to massive fines and a loss of trust in the banking sector.[415] In the end, the entire financial sector moved away from LIBOR to the less manipulable "Secured Overnight Financing Rate."[416]
Tesco (2014)	Tesco overstated its profits by £263 million due to improper revenue recognition and aggressive accounting practices.[417] The board failed to verify the financial reports and internal controls, leading to a significant loss of shareholder value.[418]
Valeant Pharmaceuticals (2015)	The board did not thoroughly vet/understand the risks of Valeant's aggressive acquisition strategy and questionable business practices.[419] This was both a failure of "Set," as the board did not understand the risk profile of the business strategy,[420] and of "Verify," as the lack of verification of the assumptions underlying the sustainability of its business model led to significant financial losses and legal scrutiny.[421]

Table 7.1 (continued)

Volkswagen emissions (2015)	The Volkswagen emissions scandal revealed that the organization had installed software to cheat on emissions tests. Independent verification of regulatory compliance and internal controls could have prevented the widespread fallout, damage to the organization's reputation, and a $4.3 billion fine.[422]
Toshiba (2015)	Toshiba's unrealistic profit targets incentivized management to systematically misreport profits. The board's failure to verify the adequacy of financial control practices facilitated the scandal.
Pacific Gas and Electric (PG&E) (2019)	PG&E's board failed to verify the organization's safety practices and infrastructure maintenance.[423] This oversight contributed to devastating wildfires in California and ultimately led to PG&E's bankruptcy.[424]
Wirecard (2020)	This German payment processor filed for insolvency after revealing that €1.9 billion in cash balances on the organization's books could not be verified. The incident exposed severe lapses in board verification, particularly concerning the auditing processes and financial controls within the organization.[425]
FTX (2022)	This failed crypto-exchange didn't have a board until 2022, and even then, the board didn't oversee, much less verify.

The above litany of failures is daunting. All were breaches of trust, reliability, and, in many cases, law. And they were all caused by board failures to verify. They are a tiny subset of the universe we could have listed. We include them to make clear what happens when executives or boards are not trustworthy and when verification doesn't happen.

Thankfully, they remain the exception. Exceptions do not mean that the board may not rely on representations by management as part of reasonable assurance. However, they do highlight that verification is necessary as part of that reliance.

"Trust but verify" is a phrase widely attributed to former U.S. President Ronald Reagan, who frequently used it during his negotiations with the Soviet Union on arms control in the 1980s. It is a translation of the Russian proverb "Доверяй, но проверяй" (Doveryay, no proveryay), which Reagan thought might resonate well in the context of U.S.–Soviet relations.

However, for boards, it's verify before trusting (not vice versa, as most people think). You would not, for example, buy a company or a material asset without understanding its value before, not after, closing the transaction. You wouldn't hire someone who said, "Trust me, I'll give you my resume later."

Trustworthiness needs to be earned and then maintained. What follows are methods – both structural and procedural – to do just that, beginning with the most important lesson.

Saying "trust me" raises red flags. A recent study revealed that the more often a company uses "trust" words is correlated with negative trust outcomes.[426] Compared to those who didn't use words like "ethical," "integrity," and "responsibility," companies that used these words experienced decreased interest in the company's stock, higher audit costs, were 15 percent more likely to receive a comment letter from the Securities and Exchange Commission and had worse corporate responsibility assessments. When it comes to trust, walking the walk is much better than just talking the talk.

Zero Trust Model and continuous verification. The concept of Zero Trust is a cyber-security precept. A core principle of Zero Trust is "never trust, always verify." This assumes that no entity, whether inside or outside the network, should be trusted by default. Every access request must be thoroughly vetted. The goal is to minimize the risk of unauthorized access by ensuring that only authenticated and authorized users can access resources.

As with fraud, boards should be aware that a significant portion of cyberattacks originate from within an organization. About 43 percent of all data loss is due to insider threats, whether they are intentional malicious actions or unintentional errors by employees.[427]

Continuous verification is critical in Zero Trust. Instead of granting broad access after a one-time verification, Zero Trust requires continuous verification of identity, devices, access privileges, and behavior to detect and respond to suspicious activities. You may not like having to enter passcodes that are texted to your phone for two-factor authentication, but we all do so because we understand that verifying identity before allowing access prevents fraud.

Boards can meaningfully apply the same principle of continuous verification to all vital aspects of reporting. Unfortunately, as we have seen in multiple industries across multiple decades, trust without continuous verification is imprudent. This is why boards should continuously "verify before trusting."

Lesson Worth Learning: The greatest source of risk is what you think you have under control when you don't

> It ain't what you don't know that gets you into trouble,
> it's what you know for sure that just ain't so.
> *Mark Twain, American Writer, Humorist, and Essayist*

You don't get any warning and aren't prepared. Meaning that you had better be sure about what you are counting on – because if you are wrong, it can really hurt. It's how many boards of directors get blindsided.

That's what happens when "green isn't really green" on the stoplight exception report – in other words, when management suggests performance is normal and within expectations. But it's not.

While good faith and reasonable assurance are necessary, they are not sufficient. Knowing management has robust checks and balances in place helps the board have confidence in the information and advice they receive and the reports they issue.

But, and it is a big but, because the board greatly depends on the reliability of the information and advice it receives from management and third parties, it also needs to verify the reliability of the information and advice independently.

Internal and external audit and other third parties can independently verify:
–   the reliability of financial information and reports
–   legal, regulatory, and policy compliance
–   the reliability of advice received
–   performance expectations are being met, and risks are being managed
–   resource allocation is as expected
–   the system of internal control is effective

Verification is the process of independently establishing the truth, accuracy, or validity of something. It reassures the board that the information it uses for decision-making is accurate, adequately complete, and reliable and that the people or systems providing the information are trustworthy. This can involve cross-checking data, consulting primary sources, or using third-party reviews or audits to confirm the information.

By verifying before trusting information and advice, the board can protect the organization from potential risks, make informed decisions, and effectively fulfill its fiduciary duties (Table 7.2). This approach builds a culture of accountability, transparency, and ethical governance, which is essential for any organization's long-term success and sustainability.

Table 7.2: Why Verify?.

Why Verify?	
Fiduciary Duty	**Legal responsibility:** Board members have a fiduciary duty to act in the best interests of the organization and its shareholders. Verifying information helps them fulfill this legal obligation.
	Due diligence: Verifying information and advice creates a due diligence process that can protect the board from legal liability and reinforce its commitment to fulfilling its fiduciary responsibilities.

Table 7.2 (continued)

Risk Management	**Mitigating risks:** Verifying information and advice helps identify and mitigate potential risks that could harm the organization, including financial misstatements, compliance violations, and strategic missteps.
	Preventing fraud: Verifying information and advice can help the board detect and prevent fraudulent activities.
Informed Decision-Making	**Accurate information:** Verification ensures that the board's decisions are based on factual and trustworthy data.
	Avoiding bias: Verifying advice and information helps the board avoid relying on a single point of view or on incomplete information.
Accountability and Transparency	**Building trust:** Verification processes enhance accountability and transparency within the organization, building trust among shareholders, employees, and other stakeholders.
	Ethical standards: Ensuring the accuracy and reliability of information and advice promotes a culture of integrity within the organization.
Performance Monitoring	**Evaluating executives:** Verifying performance data enables the board to accurately assess the performance of executives and management compared to their goals.
	Resource allocation: Accurate information on resource allocation and internal controls ensures that resources are used efficiently and effectively to support the organization's objectives, as directed by the board.
Compliance	**Regulatory requirements:** Verifying compliance with legal, regulatory, contractual, and policy requirements helps to avoid penalties, fines, reputational damage, and, in extreme cases, criminal prosecution.
Long-Term Sustainability	**Strategic alignment:** Verification ensures that the board's strategic decisions align with the organization's long-term goals and sustainability and its resource allocation decisions.
	Stakeholder confidence: Verifying information and advice helps maintain the confidence of investors, customers, and other stakeholders.

3 Why and how can we obtain independent reassurance that information, advice, and reports are reliable?

Lesson Worth Learning: Professional skepticism enables constructive challenge

The board and its committees should adopt a professionally skeptical attitude, defined as having a questioning mind and critically assessing evidence.[428]

Professional skepticism enables constructive challenge. Constructive challenge doesn't work if board members naively accept all responses to their questions. That is constructive challenge in form only; however, professional skepticism – critically assessing the answers and the evidence – creates the substance.

Remember that the entire process should be exercised without emotion, rancor, or adversarial behavior. The aim is to ensure a thorough understanding of the reliability of information for direction-setting, approval, and oversight. As we note throughout, while authority can be delegated, the responsibility for oversight and verification cannot. This means the board must retain the responsibility to thoughtfully question delegates and auditors, highlighting the importance of effective questioning and constructive challenge.

The role of the Audit/Risk Committee. There is a reason that Cindy Fornelli, the former executive director of the Center for Audit Quality, says the audit committee has become like the utility drawer in your kitchen, where you put everything important that doesn't have another more logical place to put it. Yes, the audit committee oversees financial reporting, risk management, and compliance processes. However, the increasing complexity of today's world has also seen the audit committee take on issues like cyber-security, data privacy, and changing regulatory requirements. All that scope creep may be appropriate, but refocusing on the core obligations of an audit committee can help a board use its power to verify effectively and efficiently (Table 7.3).

Table 7.3: Audit Committee Roles.

Role	Tasks
Oversee Internal Audit	Establish and maintain a robust internal audit function.
	Oversee the internal audit function, including its independence, scope, resourcing, and findings. This includes hiring, firing, evaluating, and compensating the head of internal audit.
	Review and approve internal audit plans and reports.
Oversee Financial Reporting	Review financial statements to ensure that they are accurate and complete and that they comply with accounting standards.
	Determine appropriate accounting policies.
	Monitor the effectiveness of internal control systems over financial reporting.
	Require the effectiveness of disclosure controls so that corporate reports to stakeholders are as accurate as possible.

Table 7.3 (continued)

Role	Tasks
	Oversee the external auditor's work, including their independence, performance, and findings.
	Select external auditors to independently review and verify the financial statements and the system of internal control.
	Understand and approve key external and internal audit planning metrics such as scope and materiality.
Promote an effective control environment	Require regular assessments of the control environment to assure that employees at all levels understand the importance of accuracy and integrity in reporting.
	Require confidential reporting channels be established for employees to report unethical or illegal activities without fear of retaliation.
	Require that all whistleblower reports be reviewed promptly and appropriately investigated, and that the program be periodically quality checked.
	Reinforce commitment to ethical and control standards with finance staff during audit committee meetings.
Require effective internal control	Require regular assessments of the effectiveness of the organization's internal control systems, including through internal audits and control self-assessments.
	Require segregation of duties and strong internal controls to prevent fraud and errors.
	If appropriate, engage third-party firms to conduct independent assessments of internal controls, compliance programs, and risk management practices.
Oversee risk remains within established tolerances	Be situationally aware; require the identification of key risks facing the organization, including financial, operational, and compliance risks.
	Require risk assessments of the potential impact and velocity of identified risks and preparedness.
	Review management's strategies to mitigate risks.
Oversee compliance and ethics	Oversee the organization's compliance with relevant laws, regulations, and internal policies.
	Verify legal, policy, and contractual compliance.
	Require a comprehensive compliance program that includes regular training, monitoring, and reporting on legal and regulatory requirements.
	Require a senior executive (typically the chief compliance officer) beresponsible for monitoring compliance and reporting directly to theboard or relevant board committee.

Table 7.3 (continued)

Role	Tasks
	Establish and oversee structures and processes that allow bad news to travel quickly, such as whistleblower hotlines and anonymous ethics violation reporting.
	Regularly review regulatory filings to ensure they are accurate and submitted in a timely manner. Compare the information in the filings with management reports to the board and note any discrepancies.
	Promote and enforce a culture of ethical behavior and integrity.
Oversee related party transactions (RPTs)	Require a list of related parties and verify its accuracy.
	Review and approve transactions between the company and related parties to ensure they are conducted at arm's length and in the best interest of the company. Oversee the disclosure of such RPTs.
Ensure adequate resourcing	Understand and advocate for the needed resources for the various compliance, internal controls, internal audit, etc., functions to ensure accurate information is being used inside the organization and reported to outside stakeholders.

Lesson Worth Learning: Being independent of management requires that an individual or entity be outside of management's chain of command

Management provides reasonable assurance. However, verification requires independent reassurance, and no one in the management chain of command is independent. Independence ensures that there is no undue influence, conflicts of interest, or bias that might compromise the individual or entity's ability to provide impartial advice, oversight, or decision-making. Or even the appearance of such a conflict.

Independent parties generally include:[xii]

– the internal auditor
– external auditors and other third-party advisors retained directly by the board, such as actuaries, cyber security, legal counsel, and governance consultants

To maintain the required level of separation and objectivity, the board (typically through its committees) is responsible for hiring, firing, evaluating, and compensating the head of internal audit, as well as the external auditors and advisors.

---

xii We do not include the corporate secretary in the list of independent assurance providers because in most organizations the corporate secretary does not report directly to the board. In the few that do – a practice we encourage – the corporate secretary would also be considered independent.

Lesson Worth Learning: The board can delegate authority and resources, but it cannot delegate its overall responsibility. A board typically exercises its power to verify through the Audit/Risk Committee (as well as other committees)

To leverage the board's time and expertise, boards form committees such as nominating, audit/risk, and compensation to research, oversee, and verify performance and risk in all critical areas.

As noted earlier, every committee should conduct its business in an orderly and disciplined manner. That means they should verify the reliability of information and advice given within their charter and the reliability of reports provided by the board to others (such as sustainability reporting or quarterly performance updates). So, the audit committee tries to verify the financials; the compensation committee verifies the performance metrics, calculations, the compensation report, etc.

Committees also oversee the use of advice from external qualified experts. The committees are responsible, in the first instance, for performing due diligence on those experts, with a particular focus on their independence, credentials, reputation, and the relevance of their expertise to your specific organization. It's also important that the committee understands where the experts get their facts; are they from management, or are the facts gathered independently?

Audit Committee responsibilities include ensuring the accuracy of financial statements, engaging external auditors, approving audit plans and fees, requiring effective internal control systems, overseeing disclosure controls, and supervising internal audits.

In recent years, audit committees have expanded their responsibilities to include operational risk (including cyber-security) and compliance oversight. However, it is essential to avoid overloading the committee with tasks to ensure they can effectively carry out their oversight and verification functions. Regular executive sessions with senior finance staff, external auditors, internal auditors, and compliance and risk management heads are considered a leading process for audit committees. They contribute to reasonable assurance.

How engaged the audit committee is during those meetings is key. For instance, every external auditor will ask whether or not the audit committee is aware of any fraud or malfeasance. The vast majority of audit committee members just say no, and the external auditor moves on to the next question.

One PwC partner, however, noted that there was a much more robust discussion with a particular audit committee chair when they were asked, "If someone were going to commit fraud at that particular organization, how would he/she do it?" That led to a discussion of controls around those specific processes.[429]

Lesson Worth Learning: The board should require an effective system of checks and balances

Show me the incentives, and I will show you the outcome.[430]
Charlie Munger, Vice-Chairman, Berkshire Hathaway

Compliance reports are essential for board oversight. They encompass functions as varied as fraud hotlines, regulatory inquiries/findings, and cyber-security incident reporting. In regulated industries, boards are responsible for ensuring effective control environments and can face legal action if regulators identify shortcomings.

While setting the right "tone at the top" is essential, it is insufficient. Boards must establish a comprehensive system of checks and balances with clear roles, responsibilities, accountabilities, and lines of relationships for governance, control, and oversight.

Those checks and balances convey the right tone and help implement it. Compensation also needs to be considered; the best compliance program in the world will struggle if the organization's incentives are misaligned.

Many boards (often through the audit committees) routinely receive compliance reports and assess violations to determine whether they are isolated incidents, indicate the need for improvements in the compliance program, or result from perverse incentives.

These boards and committees also frequently collaborate with external and internal auditors, compliance officers, and legal executives to discuss topics such as training, resource allocation, regulatory change, and potential incentives or performance metrics that might inadvertently encourage employees to breach compliance rules. Failure to address these issues can lead to significant damage to the organization, as demonstrated by cases like the Wells Fargo cross-selling scandal.

Table 7.4 lists what the board should do to assure that internal controls are effective.

Table 7.4: Checks and Balances.

Establish clear policies and procedures	Require management to have comprehensive policies and procedures in place. These should cover all aspects of the organization's operations and provide clear guidance on internal control measures.
Ensure someone specific "owns" each aspect of the compliance program	Ensuring that a specific individual owns each aspect of the compliance program creates accountability, letting management and the board know exactly whom to contact if there is an issue.

Table 7.4 (continued)

Require regular monitoring and testing	Require a robust framework for ongoing assessment and that any identified weaknesses are promptly addressed. In some regulated industries, the chief compliance officer must certify annually that the compliance program is properly designed to meet its goals. In integrated audits, external auditors must test whether internal controls over financial reporting are appropriately designed to meet their objectives.
Promote ethical conduct	Promote ethical behavior by endorsing a code of conduct and ensuring that it is communicated and enforced throughout the organization.
Provide training and education	Require that employees at all levels are adequately trained in internal control procedures and understand their roles in maintaining an effective control environment.
Leverage technology	Require the adoption of technological solutions for monitoring, reporting, and managing internal controls and risks.

Lesson Worth Learning: Avoid single points of failure

The concept of checks and balances involves establishing mechanisms that prevent any one individual or group from having excessive control. The audit committee plays a pivotal role in implementing and maintaining these mechanisms within the organization. As shown in Table 7.5, there are actions the audit committee can take to create a robust system of checks and balances.

Table 7.5: Avoiding Single-Point Failures.

Segregation of duties	Require clear segregation of duties within the organization. This prevents conflicts of interest and reduces the risk of errors and fraud by ensuring that no single individual has control over all aspects of any critical process.
Dual authorization	Require that processes requiring approval from multiple parties are in place, thereby providing an additional layer of oversight. This is the norm in many areas, particularly regarding control of corporate assets, such as requiring two different authorized persons (who don't report to each other) to move money from a corporate account.
Independent review	Require regular independent reviews of key processes and controls. These reviews can provide an objective assessment of the control environment and highlight areas for improvement.

Jeff Bezos' Telephone Call. Sometimes, what you intuit is incompatible with what management tells you. That's what happened to Executive Board Chair and CEO Jeff Bezos shortly after he founded Amazon. As he tells the story,

> We had metrics that showed that our customers were waiting less than 60 seconds when they called a 1–800 number to get phone customer service. But we had a lot of complaints that it was longer than that. When the data and the anecdotes disagree, the anecdotes are usually right
>
> "It's usually not that the data is being miscollected, but that you're not measuring the right thing. If you have a bunch of customers complaining about something at the same time, and your metrics say they shouldn't be complaining, you should doubt the metrics." So, at a meeting with the person who kept insisting that the 60-second metric was accurate, Bezos picked up the phone and dialed customer service. "We just waited in silence for more than ten minutes, I think. Oh, wow. I mean, it was a long time. And so, it dramatically made the point that something was wrong with the data . . ."[431]
>
> We weren't measuring the right thing. And the (call in the middle of the meeting) set off a whole chain of events where we started measuring it correctly. That's an uncomfortable thing to do, but you have to seek truth, even when it's uncomfortable.[432]

Not everyone is Jeff Bezos. But the need to gain reasonable assurance about the information you are given as a board member is universal. Table 7.6 shows some example questions the board and/or audit committee should always ask of operating management.

Table 7.6: Example Questions the Audit Committee Should Ask of Management.

Performance	Example Questions the Audit Committee Should Ask of Management
Financial Performance and Reporting	What are the key financial metrics and performance indicators, and how are we tracking against our budget and forecasts?
	Can you explain any significant variances between the actual results and the budget or prior periods?
	Are there any emerging financial risks or issues that we should be aware of?
Compliance and Risk Management	What measures are in place to ensure compliance with regulatory requirements and company policies?
	What compliance violations have occurred? Do any indicate a systemic risk or a weak specific control or are they all "one-offs"? Has there been a root cause analysis to see why we have these violations?
	How are we managing the key risks identified in our risk register, and have there been any significant changes to these risks?
	What internal controls are in place to prevent fraud and ensure the integrity of financial reporting?

Table 7.6 (continued)

Performance	Example Questions the Audit Committee Should Ask of Management
Strategy and Execution	How are we progressing with the implementation of our strategic initiatives?
	What are the major challenges and opportunities we foresee in the next quarter/year? Longer term?
	How are we monitoring and measuring the success of our strategic plans?
Operations and Performance	What are the current operational challenges, and how are we addressing them?
	Can you provide an update on our major projects and initiatives, including timelines and budgets? What are the variances?
	How are we ensuring operational efficiency and cost control?
Internal Audit and Controls	How are we determining our internal audit plan?
	What were the findings from the most recent internal audits, and how are we addressing any issues identified?
	Are there any areas where you feel additional internal audit focus is needed?
	How are we ensuring that our internal controls are robust and effective?
Corporate Governance	Are there any governance issues or concerns that the board/audit committee should be aware of?
	How are we ensuring that our governance practices align with industry best practices and regulatory expectations?
Human Resources and Culture	What are the key talent and workforce challenges we face, and how are we addressing them?
	How are we fostering a culture of compliance, ethics, and accountability within the organization?
	What initiatives are in place to ensure employee engagement and retention?
Technology and Cyber-security	How are we leveraging technology to improve our operations and competitive position?
	What are our key cyber-security risks, and how are we mitigating them?
	What personal data do we maintain and how are we protecting it?
	Which are our key cyber-security vendors, what do they do, and where do we think we can improve?
	Are there any recent incidents or breaches, and what have we learned from them?

4 How can we be reassured that the system of internal control is effective?

Lesson Worth Learning: Calculated risks must be taken. No one is perfect, and no organization is immune

The Institute of Internal Auditors (IIA) introduced the "Three Lines of Defense" model in 2013 to categorize the various functions in an organization. The original model was updated in 2020 to reflect value creation roles as well as value defense, referred to simply as the Three Lines Model.[433] We have continued to evolve this model because we have seen confusion about the roles of the various lines, including the role of independent external auditors and advisors that were not included in the original model.

The Four Lines Model (Figure 7.1) is a governance framework to clarify and improve comprehensive performance and risk management within an organization. Each of the four lines plays a distinct role in creating, delivering, and protecting value.

The 4 Lines of Value Creation and Defence

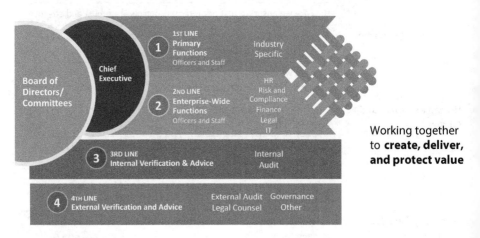

Figure 7.1: The Four Lines Model.

The model begins with the board of directors and its committees. The board is responsible for the organization's overall performance. The board recruits, selects, evaluates, compensates, and plans for the succession of the chief executive officer (CEO). The board delegates authority and resources to the CEO, subject to the powers reserved for the board. It cannot delegate its responsibility.

The role of the CEO. The CEO is accountable to the board to:

1. Research, advise on policy options, and seek board direction and policy determination.
2. Direct and control operations and execute the agreed-upon direction within policy.
3. Manage overall performance, risk, and compliance within policy.
4. Record, report, and escalate exceptions with policy implications.
5. Engage and consult stakeholders.
6. Reasonably assure the board that performance and risk are as expected unless otherwise notified.

The CEO is essentially the chief everything officer, who is the single point of accountability and interaction between the board, the organization's officers and staff, and external stakeholders.

There is a direct reporting relationship between the executive officers and staff and the chief executive. Some may have a dotted-line relationship to the board and its committees: Although these officers and staff may have frequent contact with the board, they are within the chief executive's chain of command.

Having a single point of overall accountability and coordinated access to officers and staff has important benefits for the board. It gives the board a chance to seek answers to critical questions and assess the organization's bench strength.

In terms of verification, we note that these interactions can help provide reasonable assurance that information is accurate but cannot provide independent reassurance because the chief executive selects, evaluates, and leads the officers and staff of the first and second lines. Therefore, the CEO remains the primary point of contact between the board and the officers to set priorities, coordinate work, and follow up to make sure that there are timely responses.

The role of the 1st line primary business functions. The first line is comprised of the officers and staff who perform industry-specific functions, for example, bankers at a bank, miners at a mine, and engineers at an aerospace or defense company. These primary functions are largely unique to the specific industry.

Lesson Worth Learning: The first line is primarily accountable for overall performance, risk, and compliance within the policy parameters established by the board

This includes:
−   Deliver expected performance within policy.
−   Advise and support the board.
−   Advise, monitor, record, and timely report operational performance, risk, and compliance.

-   Escalate significant exceptions and incidents with policy implications according to escalation procedures.
-   Reasonably assure operations, risk, and compliance are as expected, and controls are effective unless otherwise notified.

The role of the second line enterprise-wide functions. The second-line functions are typically common to all medium and large organizations and include, for example, human resources, legal, information technology, risk, compliance, and finance and accounting. From the board perspective, a key, but too often unnoted second line function is the corporate secretary.

Corporate secretaries typically are, or report through, the general counsel, so they are not independent, even though their function is to support the board. (Very few organizations have the corporate secretary directly report to the board, which would move them to the third line, along with internal audit. It's a thought worth considering, given the corporate secretary's responsibilities.) Good corporate secretaries are worth their weight in gold, both for facilitating board meetings and for providing unvarnished information and insight to the board.

Lesson Worth Learning: The second line has primary accountability for advising and supporting first-line executive officers, staff, and the board

-   Support the first line within policy.
-   Provide enterprise frameworks and tools for effective operational performance, risk, and compliance.
-   Identify, investigate, and escalate significant exceptions with policy implications and options.
-   Reasonably assure risk and compliance are as expected and controls are effective unless otherwise notified.
-   Together, the first and second lines are mutually accountable to:
-   Propose and/or set tolerances.
-   Design and implement risk and compliance infrastructure and controls.
-   Test, investigate, report, and remediate operational risk and compliance performance.
-   Constructively engage and consult with colleagues and other stakeholders.

Lesson Worth Learning: The first and second lines are in the direct line of the chain of command from the chief executive

We've discussed the direct line in the chain of command, from the chief executive to the first and second lines. Now, let's talk about two separate lines: the third and fourth lines, composed of the independent relationships that are not in management's chain of command.

The role of the third line is internal audit (IA). The Institute of Internal Auditors defines internal auditing as

> an independent, objective assurance and consulting activity designed to add value and improve an organization's operations. It helps an organization accomplish its objectives by bringing a systematic, disciplined approach to evaluate and improve the effectiveness of risk management, control, and governance processes.[434]

Internal audit provides its independent opinion and advice to the board. IA communicates with the chief executive but does not report to the chief executive (except for administrative functions, such as scheduling vacation and payroll issues) This ensures an independent relationship between the internal auditor and the board outside of management's chain of command. Internal audit can be insourced and/or outsourced to an independent third-party provider. Either way, IA plays a key role in verifying, thereby allowing boards to have reasonable assurance about management's assertions.

Lesson Worth Learning: Internal Audit (the third line) is independent of management and provides independent verification and advice to the board, typically through the Audit Committee

Internal Audit has the primary accountability to:
- Provide the board with independent verification and advice about the reliability of management's reports.
- Provide reasonable assurances about whether the organization is adhering to policy.
- Opine as to whether controls are effective and efficient.
- Offer independent advice to management and the board as needed.

Lessons Worth Learning: IA is not a compliance function

We have too often seen organizations misuse internal audit, focusing it on compliance rather than risk-based audits of processes, procedures, and controls. Sometimes, the misuse follows a pattern:
1) Internal Audit discovers a compliance failure.
2) The board asks IA to propose a fix, which it does.
3) The board asks IA to implement the fix, beginning the wrong-headed transformation from IA to compliance.

Assigning IA resources to compliance compromises the integrity of the IA function (since compliance reports to management) and makes it more difficult for IA to determine if control systems are adequate to perform their tasks. Compliance is a first- and second-line responsibility.[435] There is no such thing as an independent "quasi 2.5 line"; once IA's independence is compromised, its value is diminished materially.

Table 7.7 shows some sample questions audit firm BDO suggests the audit committee should always ask of Internal Audit.[436] We have modified a few of them.

Table 7.7: Example Questions the Audit Committee should ask of Internal Audit.

1.	What was the extent of your work on the most recent financial audit?
2.	Were there any changes to the scope of work performed from the scope envisioned when it was planned?
3.	If you assisted the external auditor, was there adequate coordination? Did management impose any limitations on you?
4.	Were any significant problems encountered?
5.	Are you aware of any actual or possible illegal or questionable activity or payments?
6.	Are you aware of any conflicts of interest between officers or employees and the organization?
7.	Are you aware of any significant deficiencies or material weaknesses in internal control that management or the external auditors did not identify?
8.	Are you aware of any related party transactions not disclosed in the financial statements?
9.	What are the department's goals and objectives for this year?
10.	What will be the scope of your activities this year?
11.	How will you monitor the organization's code of conduct?
12.	Do you feel your staffing is adequate?
13.	What is your evaluation of the external auditors' services for the past year?
14.	Are the organization's systems functioning with maximum efficiency at a reasonable cost?
15.	What is your assessment of the capabilities of management?
16.	Are there any other items that should be discussed with the audit committee?

The role of the fourth line – Independent external auditors and advisors. While the fourth line was left out of the IA three-line model, our work with boards has consistently found that independent experts, including external auditors, external legal counsel, industry specialists, governance consultants, etc., have a salutary impact on independent reassurance.

To do so, the independent experts need to be competent and to have a direct reporting relationship with the board, usually through relevant committees. Although they cooperate and liaise with management, they serve as the board's independent auditors and advisors. That means that boards should not only hire and evaluate them but also manage their engagement(s).

Lesson Worth Learning: The fourth line of value creation and defense provides external verification and advice. It must be managed by the board

> The key job of the audit committee is simply to get the auditors to divulge what they know . . .
> to do this the committee must make sure that the auditors worry more about misleading
> its members than about offending management . . . When auditors are put on the spot, they
> will do their duty. If they are not put on the spot . . . well, we have seen the results of that.
> *Warren Buffett, Chairman and CEO of Berkshire Hathaway*[437]

Of course, administrative issues run through management, but the fundamental scope of the engagement, the discussion of findings, and the evaluation of the experts belong to the board. This ensures that the independent experts understand that their primary accountability is to the board, not management, lest Warren Buffet's warning become prophesy.

When the board does not directly manage the independent fourth-line experts, boards may feel that management has "captured" the experts, whether or not that is the actual case. That serves no one's purpose, as it results in frustrated external experts whose opinions and insights are ignored, management that feels its best efforts to help are being impugned, and a board that thinks management is trying to manipulate it. That is expensive, a drain on both the board's and management's time and focus and damaging to the organization.

Lesson Worth Learning: External auditors play a vital role in verifying various aspects of an organization's performance

Directors are legally accountable for financial statements, but external auditors issue an opinion on whether the financial statements are free of material misstatements and presented in accordance with relevant accounting standards. Independence is the most crucial factor in making an auditor's opinion worthwhile, even outweighing other factors like professional standards, training, and expertise. Auditors must maintain independence from management and report only to the board.

While verifying financial statements is their primary responsibility, external auditors can also perform other verification functions and even some internal audit functions, but they should avoid consulting functions. They are legally obligated to "read and consider" other disclosed information by the organization. However, they generally won't formally test or opine on it unless contracted for an "agreed-upon procedures" review.

Table 7.8 lists some example questions Deloitte suggests the audit committee should always ask of External Audit:[438] We have modified some of them and added a question or two. Also, remember external auditors offer reasonable, not absolute, reassurance.[439]

Table 7.8: Example Questions the Audit Committee should ask of the External Auditor.

1.	Does the independent auditor have sufficient knowledge and experience to address the risks and types of transactions managed by the organization, and are the auditor's specialists engaged where applicable?
2.	Does the independent auditor communicate to the audit committee in a clear, succinct, and timely manner? Is communication focused and prioritized on the right areas?
3.	Is the committee engaging in an ongoing dialogue, both formal and informal, with the independent auditor to discuss topics beyond required communications?
4.	Does dialogue include, for example, perspectives on management and tone at the top, business trends, and the regulatory environment in financial reporting and standard setting? In instances where the company's needs are evolving, is the audit team also evolving with appropriate talent to serve the company?
5.	When the auditor scoped the audit, what were the key risk areas it wanted to focus on? Did any of them change during the audit? What were the findings?
6.	How does the independent auditor evaluate the reasonableness of significant estimates made by management? How does the auditor challenge these estimates?
7.	What top three areas did the independent auditor spend the most time discussing with management during the reporting period?
8.	Was management cooperative and forthcoming with requested information and documentation in these areas?
9.	What technology does the independent auditor use (data analytics, AI, remote sensing, etc.) to improve the effectiveness and efficiency of its audits?
10.	How does an independent auditor deliver value and insights to management and the committee beyond the audit?

Table 7.8 (continued)

11.	Does the committee meet separately with the independent auditor outside the presence of management? With individual members of management? With the internal auditor?
12.	What does the independent auditor think of management's capabilities and processes? Is the finance function staffed correctly?
13.	Does the finance function have appropriate technology to enable it to fulfill its responsibilities?
14.	Did the auditor find any issues with the system of internal control or the disclosure controls?
15.	(To be asked of a continuing external auditor) Between last year and this year, were there any notable changes in policies, procedures, controls, or the external situation specifically relevant to our organization?
16.	Is there anything else the committee should know?

Lesson Worth Learning: Boards of directors retain various independent experts to help them make well-informed decisions and comply with legal and regulatory requirements. The board should retain whatever external advice it feels it may need. When retained directly by the board, these third parties are independent of management

Even expert boards need and use specialized, independent advisors to help the board fulfill its fiduciary duty of care. It's appropriate and necessary to rely on management for reasonable assurance. However, in many cases, it isn't practical to develop an internal staff that has all the deep expertise a contemporary organization may need, e.g., cyber-security, geo-political risk, or other specialized fields.

It can also be prudent to get an independent "second opinion" to avoid groupthink, minimize "blind spots," and as a form of risk mitigation and verification. Independent advisors to the board provide a fresh perspective on complex issues, offer insights into leading practices among peers, and help the board make better-informed decisions. External expert advisors should also be able to constructively challenge the board and management and identify alternatives that haven't been considered or different pros and cons.

Finally, subject matter experts stay abreast of their fields and so can help boards with situational awareness. As a result, external advisors are a key source of continuing education for the board. They bring specific expertise, and boards typically incorporate them into their director education. This is a leading practice and should be considered during the advisor selection process (Table 7.9).

Table 7.9: Example Independent Advisors[xiii].

Type of Advisor	Example Roles
Legal	– Corporate lawyers: Specialize in corporate law, mergers and acquisitions, regulatory changes, and other legal matters, including topics specifically relevant to the organization (non-profit law, environmental law, admiralty law, etc.).
	– Compliance experts: Ensure the organization adheres to relevant laws, regulations, and internal policies.
Financial	– Accountants/Auditors: Provide insights on financial statements, audits, and tax issues.
	– Investment advisors: Offer guidance on investment strategies and financial planning.
Risk Management	– Risk analysts: Assess and mitigate potential risks to the organization.
	– Insurance advisors: Provide advice on appropriate insurance coverage and risk transfer strategies.
Industry	– Consultants with industry-specific knowledge: Offer insights into market trends, competition, and industry best practices.
Human Resources	– HR consultants: Assist with talent management, compensation, and organizational development.
	– Executive search firms: Help with the recruitment of senior executives and board members.
Technology	– IT consultants: Provide advice on technology strategy, cyber-security, and digital transformation.
	– Data privacy experts: Ensure compliance with data protection regulations and best practices.
Environmental and Social Governance (ESG)	– Sustainability consultants: Advise on environmental impact, sustainability practices, and reporting.
	– Corporate social responsibility (CSR) advisors: Guide the organization's social responsibility initiatives and community engagement.

---

xiii Some of the types of independent advisors may also be valuable to management. However, when hired by management, they are considered first or second line, and so are not independent and cannot provide independent reassurance to the board.

Table 7.9 (continued)

Type of Advisor	Example Roles
Strategy	– Management consultants: Offer strategic advice on business growth, market entry, and competitive positioning.
Communications and Public Relations	– PR firms: Manage public relations, crisis communication, and corporate reputation.
	– Brand consultants: Assist with branding, marketing, and stakeholder engagement strategies.
	– Social media: Design and/or implement social media strategies.
Governance	– Offer advice on board structure and composition and help clarify powers reserved, roles and responsibilities, review and/or help develop governance policies and frameworks, support board self-evaluation and performance, provide training and development, support risk management and compliance, support strategic planning, and support compliance and documentation of governance practices.

Conclusion

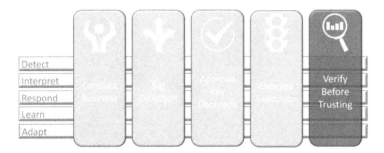

Figure 7.2: The Adaptive Board: Verifies before Trusting.

As this chapter demonstrates, obtaining independent verification before trusting is prudent and creates a positive cycle of accountability and trust. Figure 7.2 Independent verification is obtained through internal audit and the board's external auditors and advisers. They are independent because they are not part of management's chain of command.

So, while management can provide reasonable assurance, IA and independent experts can provide independent reassurance, demonstrating the board's prudence and professional skepticism. They can also provide situational awareness, board education, and improved efficiency. But it is the independent verification that the board cannot obtain elsewhere that proves the board's commitment to prudency.

The board's other powers may seem more important – "Conduct Business" is at the heart of everything the board does, "Set Direction and Policy" is intellectually stimulating and the subject everyone loves to talk about, and "Approve Key Decisions" and "Oversee Execution" form the bulk of most board agendas and take most of the focus, meeting after meeting. But "Verify" forms the foundation for the other reserved powers to function effectively.

Repeated verification builds trust and provides a solid basis of accepted data and analysis for the board to exercise its independent judgment. "Verify before trusting" is a preventive measure and virtuous cycle for productive intra-board and board/management dynamics.

The five powers, together with the adaptive governance process, strengthen the corporate governance fabric of any organization. They tie each power together.

Toto, I have a feeling we're not in Kansas anymore.
Dorothy – The Wizard of Oz

Chapter 8
Conclusion

Governing in the 21st century is vastly more challenging than it used to be.
Shift happens fast. Today's boards are expected to address an exceptionally broad
range of issues, from work-from-home policies to cyber-security, technological
shock waves, climate change, politics (domestic and global), shifting regulations,
demographics, pandemics, and artificial intelligence. And that range just keeps
getting broader: The pace of change, in terms of scale, speed, and interaction, is
accelerating exponentially.

Meanwhile, organizations' lifespans are shrinking as boards grapple with the
need to keep up with and overcome these challenges. To succeed in this dynamic
environment, the rate of internal change must match or exceed the rate of external change. This begins with the board's ability to adapt and make decisions collectively, a key factor in navigating the challenges of the 21st century.

No one joins a board to fail. There are many reasons why people choose to become board members, from professional growth to networking opportunities, fulfilling a sense of civic duty and a desire to give back, financial compensation, reputation
and prestige, intellectual challenge, and the opportunity to mentor. Unfortunately,
when things go wrong, as they increasingly do, the board often gets the blame. Rarely
do they get credit when things go well. Yet today's world would not function without
board members tirelessly working to govern their organizations.

Where was the board? This is perhaps one of the most feared questions of directors. Failures, from Credit Suisse, Hertz, Thomas Cook, Silicon Valley Bank to We-
Work, still happen. So, too, do scandals, from the U.S. Gymnastics Association
turning a blind eye to sexual abuse to the Theranos and FTX frauds. How did the
board conduct itself? How did it set direction and policy? Approve key decisions?
Did it delegate prudently? Oversee performance and risk? Verify the reliability of
information and advice?

The pace of change has outstripped conventional collective decision-making.
The absence of a comprehensive framework for board governance – until now –
is a significant challenge. Many of the tools directors currently rely on are relics
of previous centuries. For example, many not-for-profit and some for-profit organizations still conduct meetings according to *Robert's Rules of Order*, a guide
published in 1876, the same year Alexander Graham Bell invented the telephone.

Agendas don't get the strategic attention they deserve. The most consequen-
tial items are still typically scheduled last when time is short, and directors are
tired. Voluminous board books (although now digital and in a portal) still dominate the boardroom, drowning directors in data but lacking insight.

https://doi.org/10.1515/9783111344027-008

The result is that part-time directors are expected to work even harder and spend more and more of their limited time. Like switchboards and rotary dials, there is a limit to what such raw effort can do. This underscores the urgent need for a modern, comprehensive framework to enable better and faster decision-making in the 21st century (Figure 8.1).

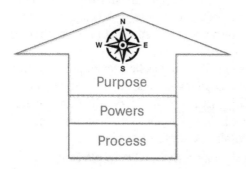

Figure 8.1: Adaptive Governance.

Purpose. The purpose of the organization is to ceaselessly create, deliver, capture, and protect value (however the board defines it) despite uncertainty and adversity. An essential purpose of governance is to enable faster adaptation while making the highest and best use of resources. Adaptive governance is about making better decisions faster and making the highest and best use of everyone's time.

The five powers. The board's responsibilities of loyalty and care are well known, but much less attention has been paid to governance and the powers the board exercises to fulfill its duties and decision-making processes. That has been our focus. What are the board's essential powers? What are its decision-making processes? Are they applied with discipline? How can they contribute to resilience and adaptability? That's why we wrote this book.

At the heart of this book are five chapters describing the five essential powers reserved for a board to govern, and that enable adaptation:
- Conduct the Business of the Board
- Set Direction and Policy
- Approve Key Decisions, then Prudently Delegate
- Oversee the Execution of Direction within Policy
- Verify before Trusting

Boards fulfill their fiduciary duties through the exercise of these five powers. By strategically restructuring agendas, employing constructive challenges, enhancing situational awareness, setting innovative directions, and providing insightful reporting and oversight, we have aimed to equip directors with a coherent governance framework. This includes utilizing analytical tools such as data visualization, critical issues and opinion summaries, and failure modes and effects analyses, along with numerous other specific suggestions, to better address the challenges of the 21st century.

A disciplined process to use the powers to adapt. Deliberate adaptation demands continuous learning and a disciplined approach to decision-making. We have described how these tools can be used in a five-step cycle of adaptive discipline:
– Detect signals and patterns
– Interpret (threats or opportunities)
– Respond
– Learn
– Adapt

Interweaving the five powers with the five adaptive governance processes creates the warp and weft of a 5x5 adaptive governance framework (AGF) and a more resilient and agile organizational fabric (Figure 8.2).

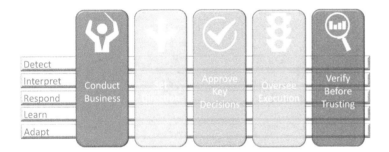

Figure 8.2: 5x5 Adaptive Governance Framework (AGF).

One size fits one. Of course, nothing in the real world is as neatly self-contained as our 5x5 AGF. Moreover, as we have noted throughout, "one size fits one." The bespoke journey begins with the organization's overarching purpose and the environment's inevitable uncertainty, which presents both opportunities and adversity.

Continuous adaptation. While we believe our 5x5 framework is a useful visual construct for today's issues and using today's tools, its real strength is that it, too, is adaptive. Inevitably, different directors and boards will learn and adapt over time until the framework evolves to their specific situation. We see that not as a flaw in the framework but as proof of its value.

Adapt or fail! The choice is yours. There is a better way. Effective boards evolve and adapt. Hopefully, this book will provide directors and executives with a framework and tools to do just that.

List of figures

https://doi.org/10.1515/9783111344027-009

List of tables

https://doi.org/10.1515/9783111344027-010

Appendices

A. The 5x5 adaptive governance framework example

Table A.1 provides a one-page overview of this book using the 5x5 adaptive governance framework.

https://doi.org/10.1515/9783111344027-011

Table A.1: Illustration of Application of the 5x5 Adaptive Governance Framework.[xiv]

Adaptive Governance Process	Purpose — Powers of the Board				
	Conduct	**Set**	**Approve**	**Oversee**	**Verify**
Detect	– A high-performing ethical culture – Commitment to consensus building and making the highest and best use of everyone's time and talents	– "Vital few" success factors – Life or death assumptions – Vital signs – Thresholds – Requisite conditions – Continuously scan for symmetric and asymmetric signals	– Request board approval if above executive thresholds – Due diligence complete	– Vital signs are within thresholds "in control" – If not, escalate exceptions (Exception-based reporting)	– Independent reviews and audits are obtained – Information and advice received are reliable – Reports issued are reliable
Interpret	– Committee assignments and board members' expertise align with the	– Strategic Implications	– Meets criteria for approval?	– Threat/Opportunity? – Policy Implications?	– No material differences are identified
Respond	– organization's specific issues and challenges – Robust director succession	– Strategic options	– Approve – Refine – Reject	– Recommend stay, adjust, change course	– Improvements are recommended
Learn	– Effective selection, evaluation, compensation, and succession planning for	– Desired effects? – See Oversee	– Post-implementation review (PIR) – Improve due diligence	– Desired effects? – Monitor whether changes bring vital signs within controls	– Follow-up review/ audits of open items are conducted
Adapt	– chief executive officer	– Stay, adjust, change course	– Recommend stay, adjust, change	– Recommend stay, adjust, change	– Recommend stay, adjust, change

xiv For illustration. No illustration could encompass every situation, but this one includes some of the more common process steps a board will encounter as it uses an adaptive governance process across all five of its powers. It is not intended to be all encompassing.

B. Self-assessment

How well does your board govern? Would you agree or disagree with the following statements:

0 = Don't know
1 = Strongly disagree
2 = Disagree
3 = Agree
4 = Strongly agree

Table B.1: Board Self-Assessment.

Powers of the Board	Self-Assessment
Conducting the Business of the Board and its Committees	
1. We have a high-performing organizational culture that promotes ethical behavior, transparency, and accountability.	
2. Our board dynamics enable consensus building and make the highest and best use of everyone's time.	
3. Our committee assignments and board members' expertise effectively address the organization's specific issues and challenges.	
4. We plan board and committee succession effectively.	
5. We effectively select, evaluate, compensate, and plan for the succession of the chief executive officer.	
Setting Direction and Policy	
1. Our board is clear about its role in setting strategy vis-à-vis the executive.	
2. Our strategic plan is truly strategic.	
3. Our organization (people, policies) is aligned with the strategy.	
4. We have identified critical issues – opportunities and risks.	
5. All realistic strategic options have been evaluated.	
6. Our strategic direction is clear to the board and stakeholders.	
7. Our strategic goals and metrics have been agreed upon.	
8. We know whether we on or off track, and the strategic implications.	
Approving Key Decisions and then Prudently Delegating Authority	
1. Our board clearly identified the key decisions requiring board approval.	
2. Our board has a disciplined decision process.	

Table B.1 (continued)

Powers of the Board	Self-Assessment
Conducting the Business of the Board and its Committees	
3. Our board requires an appropriate level of due diligence on proposed initiatives for requests for board approval.	
4. Appropriate authority and resources have been prudently delegated to the CEO.	
5. The board approval process works effectively and efficiently.	
Overseeing the execution of direction within policy.	
1. Our board exercises effective oversight.	
2. We are effective in preventing oversight failures.	
3. We know when vital performance is under control.	
4. We get timely, reliable intelligence and insights for direction setting and oversight.	
5. We know when to stay the course, adjust course, or change course.	
Verifying the reliability of information and advice before trusting.	
1. Our board obtains reasonable assurance.	
2. Our board verifies before trusting.	
3. Our board requires independent verification and reassurance.	
4. Our board obtains reassurance that the internal control system is effective.	
Adaptive Governance Process	
We are effective in timely detecting signals and patterns.	
We have good intelligence capabilities to interpret signals and patterns and identify the policy implications.	
We are prepared with a range of realistic response options.	
We are effective in learning from our performance.	
We are able to rapidly adapt to changing circumstances.	

Endnotes

Preface

1 2021 Corporate Longevity Forecast | Innosight
2 M. S. Beasley, J. V. Carcello, D. R. Hermanson, & T. L. Neal (2010). *Fraudulent Financial Reporting: 1998–2007*. Committee of Sponsoring Organizations of the Treadway Commission (COSO).

Chapter 1: Adapt or Fail!

3 Leon C. Megginson (1963). "Lessons from Europe for American Business." *Southwestern Social Science Quarterly*, 44(1), 3–13.
4 Richard Bookstaber (2007). *A Demon of Our Own Design: Markets, Hedge Funds and the Perils of Financial Innovation*. Wiley & Sons.
5 https://www.nationalgeographic.com/science/article/mass-extinction#:~:text=More%20than%2099%20percent%20of,extinction%20is%20far%20from%20constant
6 https://www.nationalgeographic.com/science/article/mass-extinction#:~:text=More%20than%2099%20percent%20of,extinction%20is%20far%20from%20constant
7 Allison Prang (2019). "WeWork Raises Additional Capital from Softbank," *The Wall Street Journal*, January 8.
8 Catherine Thorbecke (2023). "WeWork Files for Bankruptcy," CNN, November 7.
9 John Kay and Mervyn King (2020). *Radical Uncertainty: Decision Making Beyond the Numbers*. WW Norton & Company.
10 Frank H. Knight (1921). *Risk, Uncertainty and Profit*. Houghton Mifflin Company.
11 https://www.coso.org/
12 E. C. Poulton (1977). "Quantitative Subjective Assessments are Almost Always Biased, Sometimes Completely Misleading." *The British Journal of Psychology*. https://doi.org/10.1111/j.2044-8295.1977.tb01607.x
13 Nassim Taleb (2007). *The Black Swan: The Impact of the Highly Improbable*. Random House.
14 Martin Reeves, Yuval Shmul and David Zuluaga Martinez, *How Resilient Businesses Created Advantage in Adversity During COVID-19 – BCG Henderson Institute*, November 4, 2021
15 https://horasis.org/building-back-us-business-with-resilience-and-imagination/
16 https://www.mckinsey.com/capabilities/people-and-organizational-performance/our-insights/raising-the-resilience-of-your-organization
17 S. Duchek (2020). "Organizational Resilience: A Capability-based Conceptualization." *Business Research* 13, 215–246. https://doi.org/10.1007/s40685-019-0085-7
18 https://hbr.org/2022/03/make-resilience-your-companys-strategic-advantage
19 Richard Bookstaber (2007). *A Demon of Our Own Design: Markets, Hedge Funds and the Perils of Financial Innovation*. Wiley & Sons, p. 232.
20 https://www.cmcmarkets.com/en/opto/why-are-stocks-seeing-shrinking-lifespans
21 https://www.cmcmarkets.com/en/opto/why-are-stocks-seeing-shrinking-lifespans
22 https://www.statista.com/statistics/1259275/average-company-lifespan/ "Increasing Churn Rate in the S&P 500: What's the Lifespan Of Your Stock?" https://seekingalpha.com/article/2651195-increasing-churn-rate-in-the-s-and-p-500-whats-the-lifespan-of-your-stock Note: As stated by the Seeking Alpha ar-

https://doi.org/10.1515/9783111344027-012

ticle, "While some companies are removed due to acquisitions, many are removed because they no longer qualify because of market capitalization declines."

23 https://www.imperial.ac.uk/business-school/blogs/executive-education/why-companies-die/

24 https://www.macrumors.com/2017/02/15/blackberry-hits-zero-market-share/#:~:text=BlackBerry's%20market%20share%20among%20all,in%202009%2C%20according%20to%20Gartner

25 https://www.google.com/search?q=airbnb+stock&rlz=1C1RXQR_enUS1047US1047&oq=ai&gs_lcrp=EgZjaHJvbWUqCAgAEEUYOBg7MggIABBFGDgYOzIICAEQRRgnGDsyBggCEEUYQDIMCAMQRRg5GLEDGIAEMhMIBBAuGIMBGBMcBGLEDGNEDGIAEMgYIBRBFGDwyBggGEEUYPTIGCAcQRRg90gEIMjkxOWowajeoAgCwAgA&sourceid=chrome&ie=UTF-8

26 https://companiesmarketcap.com/hilton-hotels/marketcap/

27 https://www.wsj.com/articles/peloton-chairman-john-foley-to-exit-in-management-shake-up-11663014900

28 https://www.google.com/search?q=peloton+stock&rlz=1C1RXQR_enUS1047US1047&oq=pe&gs_lcrp=EgZjaHJvbWUqEQgAEEUYJxg7GJ0CGIAEGIoFMhEIABBFGGCcYOxidAhiABBiKBTIGCAEQRRg5MgwIAhAjGCcYgAQYigUyEggDEC4YQxjHARjRAxiABBiKBTIMCAQQABhDGIAEGIoFMgYIBRBFGDwyBggGEEUYPDIGCAcQRRg80gEIMTU3NGowajeoAgCwAgA&sourceid=chrome&ie=UTF-8#cso=chart-annotations-carousel:221.77777099609375

29 https://www.globalcyclingnetwork.com/general/news/peloton-shares-plummet-in-value-as-company-struggles-to-stop-the-bleeding

30 https://www.bloomberg.com/news/articles/2024-01-11/hertz-to-sell-20-000-evs-in-shift-back-to-gas-powered-cars

31 https://www.airlines.org/dataset/u-s-bankruptcies-and-services-cessations/

32 https://www.skmurphy.com/blog/2012/08/26/five-quotes-from-branch-rickey-for-entrepreneurs/

33 https://www.wsj.com/business/nvidia-stock-jensen-huang-sega-irimajiri-chips-ai-906247db

34 Gina Keating (2012). *Netflixed*. Penguin Books, p. 9.

35 Investor Howard Marks on Luck, Risks and the Job that Got Away – Knowledge at Wharton (upenn.edu)

36 How Blackjack Saved FedEx From Bankruptcy (thinkfreight.io)

37 https://hbr.org/2021/06/dont-underestimate-the-power-of-luck-when-it-comes-to-success-in-business

38 https://en.wikipedia.org/wiki/Alvin_Toffler, https://en.wikipedia.org/wiki/John_Naisbitt

39 https://www.mckinsey.com/featured-insights/leadership/changing-change-management

40 https://www.gartner.com/smarterwithgartner/7-key-foundations-for-modern-data-and-analytics-governance

41 Donald Sull (1999). "Why Good Companies Go Bad," *Harvard Business Review*, July–August.

42 Clayton M. Christensen (1997). *The Innovator's Dilemma: When New Technologies Cause Great Firms to Fail*. 1st edn. Harvard Business Review Press.

43 Clayton M. Christensen (1997). *The Innovator's Dilemma: When New Technologies Cause Great Firms to Fail*. 1st edn. Harvard Business School Press.

44 https://quotefancy.com/quote/901674/Robert-T-Kiyosaki-Success-is-a-poor-teacher-We-learn-the-most-about-ourselves-when-we

45 Jack Welch. Former CEO and Chairman of General Electric.

46 Cited in Robert A. G. Monks and Nell Minow (2007). *Corporate Governance*. 4th edn. Blackwell Publishing, p. 266.

Chapter 2: A practical framework for adaptive governance

47 Peter Loftus (2023). "The 'King Kong' of Weight-Loss Drugs is Coming." April 3. https://www.wsj.com/articles/ozempic-mounjaro-weight-loss-drug-wegovy-eli-lilly-66f2906

48 Peter Loftus (2023). "The 'King Kong' of Weight-Loss Drugs is Coming." April 3. https://www.wsj.com/articles/ozempic-mounjaro-weight-loss-drug-wegovy-eli-lilly-66f2906

49 Eli Lilly (LLY) – Market capitalization (companiesmarketcap.com)

50 Lilly Reports Strong Fourth-Quarter 2023 Financial Results and Provides 2024 Guidance | Eli Lilly and Company

51 https://www.google.com/search?q=market+cap+lilly&rlz=1C1RXQR_enUS1047US1047&oq=market+cap+Lilly&gs_lcrp=EgZjaHJvbWUqBwgAEAAYgAQyBwgAEAAYgAQyCggBEAAYDxgWGB4yDQgCEAAYhgMYgA-QYigWoAgCwAgA&sourceid=chrome&ie=UTF-8#cso=chart-annotations-carousel:449.77777099609375

52 Lilly's Weight-Loss Drug Is a Huge Hit. Its CEO Wants to Replace It ASAP. – WSJ

53 Milton Friedman (1970). "A Friedman Doctrine: The Social Responsibility of Business is to Increase its Profits." *The New York Times*, September 13.

54 https://www.highmeadowsinstitute.org/time-rethink-corporate-governance/

55 https://drpop.org/banking-on-slavery/

56 Starbucks Announces Intention to Establish a New Environmental, Partner and Community Impact Board Committee

57 Starbucks (SBUX) earnings Q2 2024 (cnbc.com)

58 Starbucks' 'fall from grace': Howard Schultz says what company needs to fix US operations | Fox Business

59 Activist investor Elliott builds sizeable stake in Starbucks, say sources | Reuters

60 Inside Starbucks's Surprising CEO Firing and Hiring – WSJ

61 CITIZENS UNITED v. FEDERAL ELECTION COMM'N (cornell.edu)

62 How the Supreme Court's blockbuster 'Chevron' ruling puts countless regulations in jeopardy | CNN Politics

63 3 surprising consequences of the Supreme Court's immunity decision – POLITICO

64 Don't blink: The science of a 100-mph fastball | Mariners Preview 2017 (seattletimes.com)

65 https://www.amazon.com/Confessions-Augustina-Memoirs-Sinner-Saved-ebook/dp/B0D8CJ5XH4/ref=zg_bsnr_g_10332442011_d_sccl_4/137-4666039-3272821?psc=1

66 Strategy Under Uncertainty (hbr.org)

67 https://agribusiness.purdue.edu/decision-discipline/

68 https://www.forbes.com/sites/carminegallo/2011/05/16/steve-jobs-get-rid-of-the-crappy-stuff/?sh=2b7356997145

69 Walter Isaacson (2001). *Steve Jobs*. Simon & Schuster, p. 363.

70 https://www.forbes.com/sites/forbesleadershipforum/2013/06/13/the-crucial-edge-that-makes-a-board-exceptional/?sh=314f7e537a86

71 Cited in Jon Lukomnik and James H. Hawley, "Moving Beyond Modern Portfolio Theory: Investing That Matters," Routledge Press, 2021.

72 https://newspaceeconomy.ca/2023/10/28/spacex-starship-iterative-design-methodology/#:~:text=Instead%20of%20extensive%20planning%20and,data%20to%20improve%20subsequent%20designs.

73 https://www.mindk.com/blog/iterative-development/

74 https://dcroi.org/publications

75 Frederick Funston and Stephen Wagner (2010). *Surviving and Thriving in Uncertainty: Creating the Risk Intelligent Enterprise.* Wiley & Sons, p. 209.

76 Bill Gates (1995) *The Road Ahead.* Viking Press.

77 https://crm.org/articles/xerox-parc-and-the-origins-of-gui

78 Deborah C. Stephens, Gary Heil, and Tom Parker (1997). *One Size Fits One: Building Relationships One Customer and One Employee at a Time*. Van Nostrand Reinhold. ISBN 9780442020637 (ISBN10: 0442020635) 1997

79 https://www.gsam.com/content/gsam/us/en/advisors/resources/investment-ideas/gsam-model-po

80 https://www.nacdonline.org/education-and-events/elearning-courses-on-demand-courses/virtual-director-professionalism/

Chapter 3: Conduct the business of the board

81 Ben Horowitz, Kevin Kenerly(2019). *What You Do Is Who You Are: How to Create Your Business Culture*. Harper.

82 https://www.fastcompany.com/3046630/7-business-leaders-share-how-they-solved-the-biggest-moral-dilemmas-of-their

83 https://www.theguardian.com/careers/2016/feb/11/is-googles-model-of-the-creative-workplace-the-future-of-the-office

84 Phoebe Wall Howard (2024). "New Trend Survey Shows Workers Willing to Take 20% Pay Cut for Better Work/Life Balance," *Detroit Free Press*, January 11.

85 Interview with Esther Colwill by F. Funston, November 7, 2007.

86 https://hbr.org/2017/09/what-motivates-employees-more-rewards-or-punishments

87 Kenneth Arrow (1974). *The Limits of Organization*.W.W. Norton & Company.

88 Personal communication with the author Frederick Funston

89 https://www.wsj.com/articles/the-airline-safety-revolution-11618585543 by Andy Pasztor, updated April 16, 2021 12:08 pm ET

90 https://www.wsj.com/business/airlines/plane-safety-airlines-boeing-never-been-safer-adbe2453?st=3r4en7r63vf5w62&reflink=articleemail share_

91 https://www.newsweek.com/boeing-plea-deal-department-justice-1929969

92 LRN (2007). *LRN Ethics Study: Employee Engagement: A Report on How Ethics Affects Corporate Ability to Attract, Recruit and Retain Employees*.

93 Peter Behr and David Hilzenrath (2002). "Top Executives Blamed in Enron's Fall," *Washington Post*, February 3. See also *The Role of the Board of Directors In Enron's Collapse: Report Prepared by the Permanent Subcommittee on Investigations of the Committee on Governmental Affairs* (United States Senate, July 8, 2002).

94 Sarah Berger (2019). "Top Reason CEOs Were Ousted in 2018 was Because of Scandal," CNBC, May 15.

95 LRN Benchmark of Ethical Culture, LRD Advisory Services, October 2021.

96 https://www.patagonia.com/core-values/

97 https://www.greatplacetowork.com/certified-company/1000745

98 https://www.patagonia.com/why-recycled/

99 https://www.theguardian.com/fashion/2019/apr/03/patagonia-fleece-vest-tech-bro-uniform

100 https://www.futureofbusinessandtech.com/employee-wellbeing/inside-patagonias-corporate-culture-that-prioritizes-flexibility-and-work-life-balance/

101 https://wornwear.patagonia.com/

102 https://www.patagonia.com/one-percent-for-the-planet.html

103 https://www.patagonia.com/stories/100-percent-today-1-percent-every-day/story-31099.html

104 https://www.patagonia.com/our-footprint/

105 https://www.patagonia.com/our-footprint/working-with-factories.html

106 https://www.inc.com/jason-aten/with-1-sentence-patagonia-just-gave-a-masterclass-on-how-to-treat-your-people.html

107 https://www.patagonia.com/hidden-cost-of-clothes/

108 https://www.fdic.gov/resources/resolutions/resolution-authority/resplans/plans/wellsfargo-idi-2312.pdf

109 U. S. Department of Justice press release (2020). "Wells Fargo Agrees to Pay $3 Billion to Resolve Criminal and Civil Investigations into Sales Practices Involving the Opening of Millions of Accounts without Customer Authorization," February 21.

110 U. S. Department of Justice press release (2020). "Wells Fargo Agrees to Pay $3 Billion to Resolve Criminal and Civil Investigations into Sales Practices Involving the Opening of Millions of Accounts without Customer Authorization," February 21.

111 https://www.justice.gov/opa/press-release/file/1251346/dl

112 https://companiesmarketcap.com/wells-fargo/marketcap/

113 https://money.cnn.com/2017/04/24/investing/wells-fargo-scandal-board-annual-meeting/index.html

114 https://www.cnn.com/2021/01/15/investing/wells-fargo-bank-earnings-scandal/index.html

115 https://occ.treas.gov/news-issuances/news-releases/2021/nr-occ-2021-10.html

116 https://www.bbc.com/news/business-51594117,

117 Emily Flitter (2020). "The Price of Wells Fargo's Fake Account Scandal Grows by $3 Billion," *The New York Times*, February 21.

118 Matt Egan (2016). "Wells Fargo's Reputation is Tanking, Survey Finds," CNN Business, October 24.

119 Ross Kerber (2016). "Top U.S. Bank Regulator Says Wells Fargo Case Shows Sales Risks," Reuters, September 15.

120 Stephen Davis and Jon Lukomnik, "All is not well at Wells," Compliance Week, September 27, 2016.

121 Op cit., Davis and Lukomnik.

122 Op cit. Davis and Lukomnik

123 Ann Marsh (2018) "Wells Fargo Ends Fight with a Whistleblower in Fake-Accounts Scandal," FINANCIAL PLANNING (January 20), https://www.financial-planning.com/news/wells-ends-fight-with-whistleblower-in-fake-accounts-scandal. Quoted in "Wells Fargo Fake Accounts" case study, prepared for Penn Law Regulatory Law and Policy Seminar.

124 U. S. Department of Justice press release (2020). "Wells Fargo Agrees to Pay $3 Billion to Resolve Criminal and Civil Investigations into Sales Practices Involving the Opening of Millions of Accounts without Customer Authorization," February 21.

125 op. cit., Davis and Lukomnik

126 https://www.cbsnews.com/news/the-hard-fall-of-wells-fargos-carrie-tolstedt/

127 https://corpgov.law.harvard.edu/2017/04/22/one-take-on-the-report-of-the-independent-directors-of-wells-fargo-vote-the-bums-out/

128 https://money.cnn.com/2017/04/24/investing/wells-fargo-scandal-board-annual-meeting/index.html

129 https://www.latimes.com/business/la-fi-wells-fargo-sale-pressure-20131222-story.html

130 https://money.cnn.com/2016/09/08/investing/wells-fargo-created-phony-accounts-bank-fees/index.html

131 https://www.annualreports.com/HostedData/AnnualReportArchive/w/NYSE_WFC_2013.pdf (excerpt from page 51).

132 https://woodruffsawyer.com/insights/wells-fargo-director

133 Matt Egan (2016). "Wells Fargo's Reputation is Tanking, Survey Finds," CNN Business, October 24. https://money.cnn.com/2017/04/24/investing/wells-fargo-scandal-board-annual-meeting/index.html

134 https://fortune.com/2017/06/11/wells-fargo-scandal-culture/

135 While the time that directors spend on their duties vary, the average at a large company is 245 hours a year, or about six weeks of full-time work. The number skyrockets if there is a crisis, such as a bankruptcy or take-over. https://blog.nacdonline.org/posts/board-compensation-times-distress

136 https://agribusiness.purdue.edu/why-disciplined-decision-making-is-crucial/#:~:text=Discipline%20in%20our%20decision%20making,analyze%20each%20of%20those%20alternatives.

137 Henry M Robert III (2020), *Roberts Rules of Order*, 12th edition, PublicAffairs

138 https://www.brainyquote.com/authors/blaine-lee-quotes

139 https://hbr.org/2018/03/how-to-be-a-good-board-chair .

140 Elise Walton, PhD (2011). A Working Paper published by the Millstein Center for Corporate Governance and Performance, February.

141 J. M. Juran, Frank M. Gryna, Jr. and R. S. Bingham, (1969). *Quality Control Handbook*. 3rd edn. McGraw Hill Book Company, pp. 2–16.

142 Some personality characteristics such as honesty, the ability to work respectfully in a group, and having the time and desire to fulfill a director's responsibility are baseline requirements that apply to all board members and therefore generally are not included in a skills matrix.

143 https://www.jimcollins.com/concepts/first-who-then-what.html

144 Charles Elson (2023), "Outside in with Jon Lukomnik," podcast at 24:09.

145 CalPERS Proxy Voting Guidelines, February 2023, p. 2.

146 Independent Directors Council/Investment Company Institute, 2023 Directors Practices Study, August 2023.

147 See *Report of the NACD Blue Ribbon Commission on Director Compensation* (NACD, 1995). This Commission was chaired by Robert Stobaugh and included Charles Elson, whose views on director pay have been influential.

148 "Board of Directors Compensation: Past, Present and Future." https://corpgov.law.harvard.edu/2017/03/14/board-of-directors-compensation-past-present-and-future/

149 https://hbr.org/2016/12/the-secrets-of-great-ceo-selection

150 Joyce Chen (2023). Equilar, "CEO Tenure Rates," Harvard Law School Forum on Corporate Governance, posted August 4.

151 https://chiefexecutive.net/lessons-on-succession-from-the-microsoft-ceo-search-saga/

152 https://www.cnet.com/tech/tech-industry/a-closer-look-at-the-microsoft-insiders-who-didnt-get-the-job/

153 https://www.computing.co.uk/news/2319857/microsofts-ceo-search-to-continue-into-2014-according-to-john-thompson

154 https://stockanalysis.com/stocks/msft/employees/

155 https://companiesmarketcap.com/apple/marketcap/

156 https://www.apple.com/job-creation/

157 https://www.forbes.com/sites/stuartrlevine/2024/01/05/succession-planning-takes-character-trust-and-respect/?sh=5f4f210d1880

158 Claudio Fernandez-Araoz, Gregory Nagel, and Carrie Green (2021). "The High Cost of Poor Succession Planning," *Harvard Business Review*, May–June.

159 Johnson and Johnson 2023 Proxy Statement and Additional Definitive Proxy Solicitation Materials, pp. 64–65.

160 Johnson and Johnson 2023 Proxy Statement and Additional Definitive Proxy Solicitation Materials, pp. 61.

Chapter 4: Set direction and policy

161 Christensen, Clayton M. (1997). *The Innovator's Dilemma: When New Technologies Cause Great Firms to Fail*. Harvard Business School Press.

162 https://www.visualcapitalist.com/cp/largest-companies-from-2000-to-2022/

163 Nvidia CEO Jensen Huang, 2009, @EconomicArchive.com

164 https://www.cnet.com/tech/computing/history-of-digital-cameras-from-70s-prototypes-to-iphone-and-galaxys-everyday-wonders/

165 Michael J. de la Merced, Michael (2012). Eastman Kodak Files for Bankruptcy, *The New York Times*, January 19.

166 Peter F. Drucker (2001). *The Essential Drucker*. Collins Business, p. 20.

167 https://www.oxfordreference.com/display/10.1093/acref/9780191826719.001.0001/q-oro-ed4-00012282

168 *Strategy & Leadership*, 35(5), January 2007.

169 James C. Collins and Jerry I. Porras (1994). *Built to Last: Successful Habits of Visionary Companies*. Wiliam Collins.

170 https://theweek.com/tech/inside-sam-altmans-extraordinary-firing-from-openai

171 https://sfstandard.com/2023/11/17/openai-sam-altman-firing-board-members/

172 https://blog.hubspot.com/ai/openai-ceo-fired

173 https://www.slashgear.com/1452262/sam-altman-openai-leadership-history-timeline/

174 https://www.ruleoneinvesting.com/blog/how-to-invest/warren-buffett-quotes-on-investing-success/

175 Owen D. James (2017). "Brain Science Perspectives on Investor Behavior and Decision-making Errors." *Seattle University Law Review*, 41, 349–366.

176 Andrew G. Haldane and Richard Davies (2011). "The Short Long," Speech, May.

177 https://www.wsj.com/business/airlines/boeing-calls-time-on-the-great-american-outsourcing-e5391563?st=0buojqrjpq4kz46&reflink=article_

178 https://www.theverge.com/2017/6/13/15782200/one-device-secret-history-iphone-brian-merchant-book-excerpt

179 https://www.ictinc.ca/hs-search-results?term=seventh+generation+principle&type=SITE_PAGE&type=LANDING_PAGE&type=BLOG_POST

180 https://www.marketingweek.com/short-term-targets-perverse-incentives-hurt-businesses/

181 Thomas J. Peters and Robert H. Waterman (1982). *In Search of Excellence: Lessons from America's Best-Run Companies*. Collins Business Essentials.

182 https://www.historyofinformation.com/detail.php?id=337

183 Hindsight, Foresight, And No Sight (Jun 85,Vol:36 Issue:4) (americanheritage.com)

184 https://bigthink.com/pessimists-archive/air-space-flight-impossible/

185 https://www.mlive.com/flintjournal/business/2008/07/accuracy_not_the_forte_of_auto.html

186 https://en.wikipedia.org/wiki/History_of_Microsoft

187 https://www.zdnet.com/article/surface-tension-the-long-strange-history-of-the-windows-tablet/

188 https://www.christenseninstitute.org/blog/data-is-a-poor-judge-of-opportunity/

189 https://www.linkedin.com/pulse/how-photo-giant-failed-see-digital-picture-kodak-michael-effanga/

190 https://www.linkedin.com/pulse/kodaks-invention-digital-camera-paolo-landoni/

191 https://www.indigo9digital.com/blog/blockbusterfailure

192 https://www.businessinsider.com/blockbuster-ceo-passed-up-chance-to-buy-netflix-for-50-million-2015-7

193 https://fortune.com/longform/sears-couldve-been-amazon/

194 https://www.cleo.com/blog/downfall-of-sears

195 https://www.todayifoundout.com/index.php/2013/03/excite-had-a-chance-to-buy-google-for-750k-but-turned-it-down/

196 https://www.hardtimes.co.za/why-excite-rejected-google-for-750k/

197 https://bettermarketing.pub/how-yahoo-missed-out-on-hundreds-of-billions-again-and-again-905f3bc86413

198 https://finance.yahoo.com/news/remember-yahoo-turned-down-1-132805083.html

199 https://bettermarketing.pub/how-yahoo-missed-out-on-hundreds-of-billions-again-and-again-905f3bc86413

200 https://phys.org/news/2012-04-britannica-halt-triggers-sales.html
201 https://www.csmonitor.com/Books/chapter-and-verse/2012/0314/Encyclopedia-Britannica-puts-an-end-to-print-publishing
202 https://www.theguardian.com/books/2012/mar/13/encyclopedia-britannica-halts-print-publication
203 https://appleinsider.com/articles/10/12/07/apple_co_founder_offered_first_computer_design_to_hp_5_times
204 https://www.linkedin.com/pulse/1970-xerox-parc-hotbed-innovation-groundbreaking-robert-lavigne/
205 https://spectrum.ieee.org/xerox-parc
206 https://inspireip.com/what-happened-to-digital-equipment-corporation/
207 https://digitalcommons.assumption.edu/cgi/viewcontent.cgi?article=1005&context=business-faculty
208 https://en.wikipedia.org/wiki/Influence_of_the_IBM_PC_on_the_personal_computer_market
209 https://akshatsinghbisht.com/why-nokia-failed-and-lost-its-mobile-market/
210 https://www.reddit.com/r/explainlikeimfive/comments/2olz1f/eli5_why_blackberry_went_from_a_leader_in_the/?rdt=57773
211 https://medium.failfection.com/motorolas-rise-and-fall-how-it-lost-its-relevance-4ca96156ca57
212 https://pdxscholar.library.pdx.edu/cgi/viewcontent.cgi?article=1178&context=etm_fac
213 https://www.cnbc.com/2021/10/19/how-evergrande-found-itself-on-the-wrong-side-of-chinas-regulators.html
214 https://www.npr.org/2024/01/30/1227554424/evergrande-china-real-estate-economy-property-collapse
215 https://www.jpmorganchase.com/ir/annual-report/2023/ar-ceo-letters#section-4
216 https://quoteinvestigator.com/2017/09/14/home-computer/#:~:text=Apparently%2C%20in%201977%20during%20a%20crucial%20period%20for,individual%20to%20have%20a%20computer%20in%20their%20home
217 https://www.wsj.com/business/nike-running-sneakers-competition-1d735fc8?st=g5qhm328gamwtdh&reflink=article_
218 https://thehistoryofcomputing.net/ibm-pivots-to-services-in-the-90s
219 https://techstartups.com/2023/04/14/in-1997-apple-was-on-verge-of-bankruptcy-with-a-1-billion-loss-now-the-iphone-giant-makes-1-billion-every-3-days/
220 https://stories.starbucks.com/press/2022/starbucks-founder-howard-schultz-takes-the-helm-as-starbucks-chief-executive-officer/
221 https://stories.starbucks.com/press/2008/starbucks-increases-number-of-u-s-company-operated-store-closures-as-part/
222 https://stories.starbucks.com/press/2008/u-s-store-closures-announced-july-2008/
223 https://www.wsws.org/en/articles/2002/07/xero-j01.html
224 https://www.cbc.ca/news/business/xerox-ceo-ursula-burns-on-how-she-transformed-the-company-1.2766774
225 https://www.npr.org/2012/05/23/153302563/xerox-ceo-if-you-don-t-transform-you-re-stuck
226 https://retailwire.com/discussion/best-buys-strategy-renew-blue-ignite-the-possible/
227 https://www.tjwaldorf.com/renew-blue-best-buys-turnaround/
228 https://www.cnet.com/tech/services-and-software/netflixs-lost-year-the-inside-story-of-the-price-hike-train-wreck/
229 https://www.theguardian.com/media/2011/sep/19/netflix-shares-dvd-streaming-qwikster
230 https://www.digitalamerica.org/evolution-convenience-blockbuster-netflixandchill/
231 *Adaptive Governance: Board Oversight of Disruptive Risks.* 2018 NACD Blue Ribbon Commission Report.
232 https://kpmg.com/kpmg-us/content/dam/kpmg/pdf/2024/transforming-the-enterprise-of-the-future-report.pdf
233 Joseph A. Schumpeter (1942). *Capitalism, Socialism, and Democracy.* New York: Harper & Brothers.
234 https://blog.deagostini.com/2022/11/ships-battle-trafalgar/

235 https://en.wikipedia.org/wiki/Moneyball_%28film%29

236 https://www.businessinsider.com/amazon-go

237 https://fortune.com/2022/03/03/amazon-killer-bookstores-closing-retail-book-locations/

238 https://www.wsj.com/business/airlines/southwest-airlines-cuts-revenue-outlook-shares-slide-2aa0d696?st=pn7kl2ke7hhk845&reflink=article_email_share

239 https://hbr.org/1997/11/strategy-under-uncertainty

240 https://en.wikipedia.org/wiki/Blockbuster_%28retailer%29

241 https://apnews.com/article/netflix-dvd-video-mail-blockbuster-streaming-b60e8b312ec395cd69b3522ac842a9c7

242 https://southwest50.com/our-stories/a-turning-point-the-birth-of-the-10-minute-turn/

243 L. Trigeorgis and J. J. Reuer, (2017). "Real Options Theory in Strategic Management." *Strategic Management Journal*, 38(1), 42–63.

244 https://www.axios.com/local/atlanta/2022/03/15/southwest-airlines-rising-fuel-costs-fuel-hedging

245 https://www.independent.co.uk/tech/iphone-12-release-date-delay-apple-a9647251.html

246 https://www.cnn.com/2024/05/09/business/chevrolet-killing-off-chevy-malibu-sedan/index.html#:~:text=The%20Chevrolet%20Malibu%2C%20the%20last,this%20year%2C%20the%20company%20announced

247 https://www.assemblymag.com/articles/97788-tesla-rethinks-the-assembly-line

248 https://www.ncbi.nlm.nih.gov/pmc/articles/PMC9433349/

249 A. K. Dixit and R. S. Pindyck (1994). *Investment under Uncertainty*. Princeton University Press.

250 https://www.coso.org/guidance-erm

251 Daniel Kahneman and Amos Tversky (1972). "Subjective Probability: A Judgment of Representativeness." https://www.sciencedirect.com/science/article/abs/pii/0010028572900163

252 Nassim Taleb (2007). *The Black Swan: The Impact of the Highly Improbable*. Random House.

253 John C. Maxwell (2000). *Failing Forward: Turning Mistakes into Stepping Stones for Success*. Thomas Nelson.p.4

254 https://www.automotivelogistics.media/after-the-disaster-in-japan/7408.article

255 https://newparts.com/articles/mass-air-flow-sensor-repair-cost/

256 https://en.wikipedia.org/wiki/2024_CrowdStrike_incident#:~:text=On%2019%20July%202024%2C%20American,Windows%20computers%20running%20the%20software.

257 https://abcnews.go.com/US/american-airlines-issues-global-ground-stop-flights/story?id=112092372#:~:text=A%20wave%20of%20IT%20outages,based%20computers%20ceased%20to%20work.

258 Tom Peters and Robert H. Waterman (1982). *In Search of Excellence: Lessons from America's Best-Run Companies*. Harper Publishing.

259 https://gizmodo.com/microsoft-failures-windows-vista-cortana-zune-internet-1849071697

260 https://nira.com/microsoft-history/

261 https://www.wsj.com/tech/ai/microsoft-nadella-openai-inflection-9727e77a?st=ob0r9h9kfldyg0n&reflink=article_email_share

262 https://www.wsj.com/tech/ai/microsoft-nadella-openai-inflection-9727e77a?st=ob0r9h9kfldyg0n&reflink=article_email_share

263 https://how.complexsystems.fail/

264 https://www.coso.org/critical-to-success

265 https://www.spacexstats.xyz/

266 https://www.space.com/spacex-starship-third-test-flight-faa-investigation

267 https://phys.org/news/2024-03-spacex-3rd-starship-space-lost.html.

268 https://www.nextbigfuture.com/2024/04/spacex-tower-landings-key-to-supercheap-space-access.html

269 V. F. Ridgway (1956). "Dysfunctional Consequences of Performance Measurements." *Administrative Science Quarterly*, 1(2), 240–247.

270 https://ultimateclassicrock.com/ford-pinto-history/

271 https://www.autoweek.com/news/a2099001/ford-100-defective-pinto-almost-took-fords-reputation-it/

272 https://mjalterlaw.com/the-ford-pinto-memo-the-cost-to-repair-vs-the-cost-of-paying-injured-victims/

273 https://www.shortform.com/blog/enron-collapse/

274 https://www.investopedia.com/terms/e/enron.asp

275 https://money.cnn.com/2009/01/15/news/companies/eli_lilly/

276 https://www.nbcnews.com/health/health-news/eli-lilly-settles-zyprexa-lawsuit-1-42-billion-flna1c9453543

277 https://www.smfg.co.jp/english/chronicle20/history20/section1502.html

278 https://www.economicsobservatory.com/why-did-lehman-brothers-fail

279 https://www.cnbc.com/2018/09/05/fannie-mae-freddie-mac-are-uncle-sams-cash-cows-a-decade-after-crash.html

280 https://www.bloomberg.com/view/quicktake/fannie-mae-and-freddie-mac-irbtxzdk

281 https://www.nber.org/system/files/working_papers/w21108/w21108.pdf

282 https://www.thestreet.com/personal-finance/what-happened-to-aig

283 https://www.washingtonpost.com/national/health-science/bps-cost-cuts-contributed-to-oil-spill-disaster-federal-probe-finds/2011/09/14/gIQA0x24RK_story.html

284 https://www.propublica.org/article/did-bps-cost-cutting-time-saving-decisions-set-the-stage-for-gulf-disaster

285 https://www.newsomelaw.com/practice-areas/product-liability/faq/how-many-deaths-and-injuries-were-caused-by-the-takata-airbags/

286 https://www.beasleyallen.com/defective-airbags/

287 https://www.usnews.com/news/articles/2014/06/10/what-led-to-the-veterans-affairs-scandal

288 https://psnet.ahrq.gov/issue/review-alleged-patient-deaths-patient-wait-times-and-scheduling-practices-phoenix-va-health

289 https://en.wikipedia.org/wiki/Volkswagen_emissions_scandal

290 https://www.bbc.com/news/business-34324772

291 https://money.cnn.com/2017/01/06/investing/wells-fargo-replace-sales-goals-fake-accounts/index.html

292 https://en.wikipedia.org/wiki/Wells_Fargo_cross-selling_scandal

293 https://hbr.org/2016/10/the-leadership-blind-spots-at-wells-fargo

294 https://hellosayge.com/resources/uber-the-true-cost-of-toxic-leadership/135 Collision course: Uber's terrible 2017 | Uber | The Guardian

295 Collision course: Uber's terrible 2017 | Uber | The Guardian

296 https://www.theguardian.com/technology/ng-interactive/2017/dec/27/uber-2017-scandals-investigation

297 https://www.latimes.com/business/la-fi-mattel-slump-20180131-story.html

298 https://archive.epic.org/privacy/data-breach/equifax/

299 https://en.wikipedia.org/wiki/2017_Equifax_data_breach

300 https://www.fool.com/investing/2018/11/17/why-ge-is-down-51-in-2018.aspx

301 https://www.cnn.com/2020/12/10/investing/ge-stock-investigation-sec-settlement/index.html

302 https://www.technologyreview.com/2021/10/05/1036519/facebook-whistleblower-frances-haugen-algorithms/

303 https://theconversation.com/facebooks-algorithms-fueled-massive-foreign-propaganda-campaigns-during-the-2020-election-heres-how-algorithms-can-manipulate-you-168229

304 https://growthnatives.com/blogs/analytics/metrics-targets-and-their-role/

305 Erika Andersen (2022). "Change Is Hard. Here's How to Make it Less Painful," Harvard Business Review, April 7. https://hbr.org/2022/04/change-is-hard-heres-how-to-make-it-less-painful

306 https://www.wsj.com/articles/ozempic-mounjaro-weight-loss-drug-wegovy-eli-lilly-66f2906

307 https://www.ncbi.nlm.nih.gov/pmc/articles/PMC8026241/

308 https://www.linkedin.com/pulse/fatal-role-culture-clash-mega-ma-deals-td-shepherd-co-/

309 https://www.linkedin.com/in/daniel-peris/recent-activity/all/

Chapter 5: Approve key decisions, then prudently delegate

310 For an interesting book on the topic of early boards of directors, see Deborah Midanek (2018). *The Governance Revolution: What Every Board Member Needs to Know Now!* De Gruyter. https://www.amazon.com/Governance-Revolution-Every-Board-Member/dp/1547416440

311 https://corpgov.law.harvard.edu/2022/01/05/board-oversight-key-focus-areas-for-2022/

312 J. McCambridge and Dr. J. Witton Elbourne (2014). "Systematic Review of the Hawthorne Effect: New Concepts are Needed to Study Research Participation Effects." *J Clin Epidemiol*, 67(3), 267–277. DOI: 10.1016/j.jclinepi.2013.08.015. Epub 2013 Nov 22. PMID: 24275499; PMCID: PMC3969247.

313 See, generally, https://en.wikipedia.org/wiki/Hawthorne_effect.

314 Steven D. Levitt and John A. List (2019). "Was There Really a Hawthorne Effect at the Hawthorne Plant? An Analysis of the Original Illumination Experiments." NBER working paper No 15016.

315 Chapter 1 of the Delaware Code, Title 8

316 Rule 38a-1 of the Investment Company Act of 1940.

317 https://www.cooleygo.com/decisions-need-approval-board-directors/

318 Constance E. Bagley, Bruce Freed, and Karl Sandstrom (2015). "A Board Member's Guide to Corporate Political Spending," *Harvard Business Review*, October 20.

319 https://www.sec.gov/divisions/corpfin/cf-noaction/14a-8/2015/unitarianuniversalist021115-14a8.pdf.

320 https://securities.stanford.edu/clearinghouse-research.html

321 Permanent Committee on Investigations of the Committee on Governmental Affairs of the U. S. Senate, "Role of the Board of Directors in Enron's Collapse," July 8, 2002, p. 25.

322 https://www.nacdonline.org/about/board-of-directors/governance-guidelines/

323 reasonable care Definition, Meaning & Usage | Justia Legal Dictionary

324 Bayer and Monsanto to Create a Global Leader in Agriculture (prnewswire.com)

325 Monsanto Roundup Lawsuit | June 2024 Update (lawsuit-information-center.com)

326 Years After Monsanto Deal, Bayer's Roundup Bills Keep Piling Up – The New York Times (nytimes.com)

327 Glyphosate: where is it banned or restricted? (rfi.fr)

328 Cooley on Torts, quoted in Public Company Accounting Oversight Board attestation standard 101.

329 Personal communication with the authors.

330 https://www.amny.com/housing/health-dept-nycha-cover-up-lead-paint-child-hospitalized-lawsuit/

331 NYCHA Lead Paint Lawsuits | Landmark Verdicts Against NYCHA (rheingoldlaw.com)

332 https://ocw.mit.edu/courses/16-891j-space-policy-seminar-spring- 2003/9c2cca9cb3411cea8edd7d2-b880117e9_challengerlessons.pdf

333 Space Shuttle Columbia | ThinkReliability, Case Studies

334 Management Weaknesses Delayed Response to Flint Water Crisis (epa.gov)

335 A 20-year review of Flint finances shows consequences of lack of investment | Gerald R. Ford School of Public Policy (umich.edu)

336 New Orleans, 10 Years after Katrina – Federal Reserve Bank of Atlanta (atlantafed.org)

337 DUSP NOLA Equitable Rebuilding.doc (mit.edu)

338 Royal Bank of Scotland fined for 2012 IT system failure – The Global Treasurer

339 2012 RBS Group computer system problems – Wikipedia

340 The Failure Of RBS To Successfully Perform A Software Upgrade (panorama-consulting.com)

341 In surprise move, Target exits Canada and takes $5.4 billion loss | Reuters

342 Mayer on the defensive as Yahoo! board 'explores strategic alternatives' to the latest turnaround plan (diginomica.com)
343 Why did Yahoo Fail? The Rise and Fall of a Tech Giant | Enterprise Tech News EM360 (em360-tech.com)
344 https://gfmag.com/data/economic-data/poorest-country-in-the-world/
345 https://www.ted.com/talks/david_damberger_what_happens_when_an_ngo_admits_failure/transcript
346 https://www.ted.com/talks/david_damberger_what_happens_when_an_ngo_admits_failure/transcript

Chapter 6: Oversee the execution of direction within policy

347 https://malk.com/the-downfall-of-ftx-a-case-for-good-governance/
348 https://malk.com/the-downfall-of-ftx-a-case-for-good-governance/
349 David Yaffe-Bellamy and J. Edward Moreno (2024). "Sam Bankman Fried Sentenced to 25 Years in Prison," *The New York Times*, March 28.
350 https://apnews.com/article/ftx-sam-bankman-fried-ryan-salame-crypto-f999baec34226d277bff373a8077d565
351 https://walton.uark.edu/insights/posts/culture-controls-and-corporate-governance-lessons-from-the-ftx-fiasco.php
352 https://fastercapital.com/content/Risk-Management-Lessons-from-Lehman-Brothers–Demise.html
353 https://apnews.com/article/europe-business-government-and-politics-e74d2a1e851f63a778ee1e2735e61a6b
354 https://fastercapital.com/content/Bear-Stearns–A-Case-Study-in-Risk-Management-Failure.html
355 https://www.ethicssage.com/2012/01/financial-statement-fraud-at-olympus.html
356 https://abcnews.go.com/Business/mf-global-bankruptcy-risk-management-corzine/story?id=14868344
357 https://www.britannica.com/event/2015-FIFA-corruption-scandal
358 https://www.nytimes.com/2016/08/05/sports/olympics/usa-gymnastics-sexual-abuse-coaches.html
359 https://en.wikipedia.org/wiki/Facebook%E2%80%93Cambridge_Analytica_data_scandal
360 https://www.nytimes.com/interactive/2019/03/18/business/pge-california-wildfires.html
361 https://www.linkedin.com/pulse/carillion-4-years-what-went-wrong-can-we-learn-documents-suck/
362 https://research.cbs.dk/en/publications/the-danske-bank-money-laundering-scandal-a-case-study
363 https://sevenpillarsinstitute.org/case-study-luckin-coffee-accounting-fraud/
364 https://www.npr.org/2024/01/19/1225466035/boeing-737-max-faa-door-plug-alaska-crashes-ntsb
365 https://natlawreview.com/article/not-so-sweet-failure-to-timely-recall-contaminated-ice-cream-results-major
366 https://www.investopedia.com/what-happened-to-silicon-valley-bank-7368676
367 Marisa Kwiatkowski (2021). "Larry Nassar's Abuse of Gymnasts, Including Simone Biles Went Back Decades. Why it Still Matters in Tokyo," *USA Today*, July 21.
368 Heather Udowitch (2000). "The Larry Nassar Nightmare: Athletic Organizational Failures to Address Sexual Assault Allegations and a Call for Corrective Action." *DePaul Journal of Sports Law*, 16(1), Article 6.
369 Heather Udowitch (2000). "The Larry Nassar Nightmare: Athletic Organizational Failures to Address Sexual Assault Allegations and a Call for Corrective Action." *DePaul Journal of Sports Law*, 16(1), Article 6.

370 Heather Udowitch (2000). "The Larry Nassar Nightmare: Athletic Organizational Failures to Address Sexual Assault Allegations and a Call for Corrective Action." *DePaul Journal of Sports Law*, 16(1), Article 6.

371 Marisa Kwiatkowski, Mark Alesia, and Tim Evans (2016). "A Blind Eye to Sex Abuse: How USA Gymnastics Failed to Report Cases," *Indianapolis Star*, August 4.

372 Heather Udowitch (2000). "The Larry Nassar Nightmare: Athletic Organizational Failures to Address Sexual Assault Allegations and a Call for Corrective Action." *DePaul Journal of Sports Law*, 16(1), Article 6.

373 Marisa Kwiatkowski, Mark Alesia, and Tim Evans (2016). "A Blind Eye to Sex Abuse: How USA Gymnastics Failed to Report Cases," *Indianapolis Star*, August 4.

374 https://en.wikipedia.org/wiki/Boy_Scouts_of_America_sex_abuse_cases

375 https://en.wikipedia.org/wiki/Catholic_Church_sexual_abuse_casesCatholicChurchsexualabuse cases–Wikipedia

376 https://www.nytimes.com/2011/11/14/business/william-aramony-disgraced-leader-of-united-way-dies-at-84.html

377 The American Red Cross Faces Organizational Integrity Challenges (auburn.edu)

378 https://harbert.auburn.edu/binaries/documents/center-for-ethical-organizational-cultures/cases/american-red-cross.pdf

379 https://thenonprofittimes.com/npt_articles/feed-the-children-fires-founder-larry-jones/

380 https://www.nbcnews.com/news/nbcblk/black-lives-matter-activists-accuse-executive-stealing-10-million-dono-rcna46481

381 https://ntrs.nasa.gov/api/citations/20150002939/downloads/20150002939.pdf

382 J. M. Juran, F. M. Gryna, and R. S. Bingham (1951). *Quality Control Handbook*. 3rd edn. McGraw Hill Book Company.

383 While the quote is often attributed to Peter Drucker, the Drucker Institute denies he ever said it. https://drucker.institute/thedx/measurement-myopia/

384 Private conversation per Jon Lukomnik

385 https://predictableprofits.com/where-did-nokia-go-wrong-and-six-lessons-you-can-learn-from-them/

386 *Business Fitness*, November 22, 2021.

387 https://warontherocks.com/2022/10/building-an-open-source-intelligence-buyers-club/

388 Personal communication from the CIA's Deputy Director of Analysis.

389 https://www.ineak.com/case-study-toyotas-response-to-the-2011-earthquake-and-tsunami/

Chapter 7: Verify before trusting

390 https://egrove.olemiss.edu/cgi/viewcontent.cgi?article=1534&context=aicpa_assoc

391 https://www.goodreads.com/quotes/63402-you-are-entitled-to-your-opinion-but-you-are-not

392 https://www.edelman.com/trust/2024/trust-barometer

393 https://www.wsj.com/articles/big-four-auditing-deficiencies-level-off-in-latest-inspections-962f3142?st=njn08kt7cx7fmv6&reflink=article_email_share . .

394 https://core.ac.uk/reader/231825040

395 Nicola Clark and David Jolly (2008). "Fraud Costs Bank $7.1 Billion," *The New York Times*, January 25.

396 Nicola Clark and David Jolly (2008). "Fraud Costs Bank $7.1 Billion," *The New York Times*, January 25.

397 https://www.theguardian.com/business/jerome-kerviel

398 https://www.nytimes.com/2008/01/28/business/worldbusiness/28iht-socgen.4.9558616.html?searchResultPosition=1

399 https://internationalbanker.com/history-of-financial-crises/the-worldcom-scandal-2002/TheWorld
ComScandal (2002) (internationalbanker.com)
400 https://harbert.auburn.edu/binaries/documents/center-for-ethical-organizational-cultures/cases/
worldcom.pdf
401 https://panmore.com/tyco-corporate-scandal-2002-case-analysis
402 https://www.nytimes.com/2002/09/13/business/2-top-tyco-executives-charged-with-600-million-fraud-
scheme.html
403 https://archives.fbi.gov/archives/news/pressrel/press-releases/executives-and-auditor-of-peregrine
-systems-inc.-indicted-on-securities-fraud-charges
404 https://www.nytimes.com/2002/09/23/business/peregrine-systems-makes-bankruptcy-filing.html
405 https://www.blbglaw.com/cases-investigations/healthsouth-corporation-inc
406 https://ivypanda.com/essays/healthsouth-fraud-case/
407 https://ivypanda.com/essays/le-natures-inc-case-study/
408 https://www.investopedia.com/terms/l/lehman-brothers.asp
409 https://knowledge.wharton.upenn.edu/podcast/knowledge-at-wharton-podcast/the-good-reasons-
why-lehman-failed/
410 https://www.brookings.edu/articles/history-credits-lehman-brothers-collapse-for-the-2008-
financial-crisis-heres-why-that-narrative-is-wrong/
411 https://www.linkedin.com/pulse/satyam-scam-discover-what-exactly-happened-case-manshu-garg/
412 https://www.wsj.com/articles/satyam-founder-ordered-to-pay-back-alleged-accounting-fraud-gains-
1405447107
413 https://www.ethicssage.com/2012/01/financial-statement-fraud-at-olympus.html
414 https://www.investopedia.com/terms/l/libor-scandal.asp
415 https://www.gsb.stanford.edu/faculty-research/case-studies/barclays-libor-anatomy-scandal
416 https://www.hbs.edu/faculty/Pages/item.aspx?num=43888
417 https://www.hbs.edu/faculty/Pages/item.aspx?num=56666
418 https://bmmagazine.co.uk/in-business/how-did-the-tesco-accounting-scandal-unfold/
419 https://sevenpillarsinstitute.org/valeant-pharmaceuticals-case/
420 https://www.newyorker.com/magazine/2016/04/04/inside-the-valeant-scandal
421 https://www.newyorker.com/business/currency/valeant-why-moneyball-failed-in-the-
pharmaceutical-industry
422 https://www.learnsignal.com/blog/volkswagen-emissions-scandal-overview-2/
423 https://www.nytimes.com/interactive/2019/03/18/business/pge-california-wildfires.html
424 https://www.cnn.com/2019/01/29/business/pge-bankruptcy-fires/index.html
425 https://www.ft.com/content/1e753e2b-f576-4f32-aa19-d240be26e773
426 https://www.wsj.com/finance/investing/ethics-companies-trust-
b182f2b5?st=45038ykbqpnov60&reflink=article_email_share
427 https://www.infosecurity-magazine.com/news/insider-threats-reponsible-for-43/
428 Thomas M. Cooley (1932). *A Treatise on the Law of Torts, or The Wrongs which Arise Independent
of Contract*, ed. D. Avery Haggard. 4th edn. Callaghan and Company.
429 Private conversation with Jon Lukomnik
430 https://thereformedbroker.com/2018/08/26/show-me-the-incentives-and-i-will-show-you-the-
outcome/
431 Jeff Bezos: Amazon and Blue Origin | Lex Fridman Podcast #405
432 Jeff Bezos: Amazon and Blue Origin | Lex Fridman Podcast #405
433 https://www.theiia.org/globalassets/documents/resources/the-iias-three-lines-model-an-update-of-
the-three-lines-of-defense-july-2020/three-lines-model-updated-english.pdf

434 https://www.theiia.org/en/standards/what-are-the-standards/definition-of-internal-audit/#:~:text= The%20Definition%20of%20Internal%20Auditing&text=It%20helps%20an%20organization%20accom plish,%2C%20control%2C%20and%20governance%20processes.

435 Thomas M. Cooley (1932). *A Treatise on the Law of Torts, or The Wrongs which Arise Independent of Contract*, ed. D. Avery Haggard. 4th edn. Callaghan and Company.

436 https://www.bdo.com/getmedia/5ffae93f-3641-48cd-80b2-34648c953556/NP-AC-Sample-AC-Questions-Brochure_FINAL.pdf

437 *The Essays of Warren Buffett: Lessons for Corporate America*. Released by Lawrence A. Cunningham.

438 https://www2.deloitte.com/content/dam/Deloitte/us/Documents/center-for-board-effectiveness/us-cbe-questions-for-audit-committees.pdf

439 https://pcaobus.org/oversight/standards/auditing-standards/details/AS1015

About the series editor

Alexandra Reed Lajoux is Series Editor for Walter De Gruyter, Inc. The series has an emphasis on governance, corporate leadership, and sustainability. Dr. Lajoux is chief knowledge officer emeritus (CKO) at the National Association of Corporate Directors (NACD) and founding principal of Capital Expert Services, LLC (CapEx), a global consultancy providing expert witnesses for legal cases. She coauthored *Making Money: The History and Future of Society's Most Important Technology* with Peet van Biljon (Walter de Gruyter, 2020). She has served as editor of *Directors & Boards*, *Mergers & Acquisitions*, *Export Today*, and *Director's Monthly*, and has coauthored a series of books on M&A for McGraw-Hill, including *The Art of M&A* and eight spin-off titles on strategy, valuation, financing, structuring, due diligence, integration, bank M&A, and distressed M&A. For Bloomberg/Wiley, she coauthored *Corporate Valuation for Portfolio Investment* with Robert A. G. Monks. Dr. Lajoux serves on the advisory board of Campaigns and Elections, and is a Fellow of the Caux Round Table for Moral Capitalism. She holds a B.A. from Bennington College, a Ph.D. from Princeton University, and an M.B.A. from Loyola University in Maryland. She is an associate member of the American Bar Association.

https://doi.org/10.1515/9783111344027-013

About the authors

Frederick (Rick) Funston, Rick has over fifty years of experience in both not-for-profit and for-profit sectors. His career began in crisis intervention within the public sector. He later trained hostage negotiators, medical personnel and public service workers in de-escalation techniques. He acted as a negotiator and facilitator in numerous stakeholder engagements including working with the Canadian brewing industry during the NAFTA negotiations.

This evolved into consulting roles focused on strategy and operations, organizational leadership development, performance management, program evaluation, and survey research.

Between 1998 and 2010, he was the National Practice leader for Deloitte's Governance and Risk Oversight Services. In that capacity, he served many of Deloitte's largest domestic and global clients. In 2001, Rick created the concept of risk intelligence for value creation and protection.

He is a frequent public speaker and is the principal author of *Surviving and Thriving in Uncertainty: Creating the Risk Intelligent Enterprise®*, published by John Wiley & Sons in April 2010. This book specifically targeted the governance and risk oversight needs of boards and executives in both public and private sectors.

He served on the Board of Visitors for the Oakland University School of Business Administration from 2009 to 2011 and was an Adjunct Professor for the executive MBA program. Rick left Deloitte & Touche LLP in May 2010 and formed Funston Advisory Services LLC. Between 2011 and 2012, he served as special advisor to the Risk Institute of the Max Fisher School of Business at The Ohio State University.

He is the editor and a primary contributor to *One of a Kind! A Practical Guide for 21st Century Public Pension Trustees* published in 2017. He was awarded a B.A. from York University in Ontario and an M.S.W. from Tulane University.

Rick is based in Naples, Florida.

Jon Lukomnik, long-time institutional investor, has been called one of the pioneers of modern corporate governance by Forbes.

The managing partner of Sinclair Capital LLC, a strategic consultancy to institutional investors, Jon has been the investment advisor or a trustee for more than $100 billion and has consulted to institutional investors with aggregate assets of more than $1 trillion dollars as well as public and private corporations. A Brandmeyer Fellow for Sustainable Investing and adjunct Professor of International and Public Affairs at Columbia University, Jon also is a trustee for the Van Eck mutual funds where he chairs the audit committee, and Senior Fellow at the High Meadows Institute. He serves on the Board of The Shareholder Commons and the Advisory Board of The Investment Integration Project. He previously was a member of the Deloitte Audit Quality Advisory Committee and the Standards and Emerging Issues Advisory Group of the Public Company Accounting Oversight Board.

https://doi.org/10.1515/9783111344027-014

Jon co-founded the International Corporate Governance Network (ICGN) and GovernanceMetrics International (now part of MSCI). He served for more than a decade as the executive director of the IRRC Institute and is a former Pembroke Visiting Professor of International Finance at the Judge Business School at Cambridge.

Jon has been honored three times by the National Association of Corporate Directors. Other honors include a lifetime achievement award from the ICGN, and awards from the Council of Institutional Investors, Ethisphere, Transparency Task Force, and Global Proxy Watch, among others.

Index

https://doi.org/10.1515/9783111344027-015